THE ENIGMA OF KIDSON

THE ENIGMA OF KIDSON

The Portrait of an Eton Schoolmaster

Jamie Blackett

Quiller

For Sheri, Oliver and Rosie

First published in the UK in 2017 by Quiller,
an imprint of Quiller Publishing Ltd
Reprinted 2017

British Library Cataloguing-in-Publication Data
A catalogue record for this book is available from
the British Library

ISBN 978-1-84689-250-9

Edited by Barry Johnston
Jacket designed by Arabella Ainslie
Book designed by Guy Callaby
Printed and bound in Great Britain by Clays Ltd, St Ives plc

Endpaper design taken from 'The Kidson Necktie', designed by Johnnie Boden and the author; reproduced by kind permission of Stephen Walters and Sons Ltd, Sudbury, Suffolk

Quiller
An imprint of Quiller Publishing Ltd
Wykey House, Wykey, Shrewsbury SY4 1JA
Tel: 01939 261616
Email: info@quillerbooks.com
Website: www.quillerpublishing.com

Contents

Acknowledgements

Like Lord Wavell, I feel like quoting Montaigne: 'I have gathered a posie of other men's flowers and nothing but the thread that binds them is my own.' And so I would like to thank all those who agreed to appear in this book giving their memories and often telling stories against themselves. I would particularly like to thank Sir Eric Anderson and Nat Rothschild for giving permission for their eulogies to be included and the Mortimer family for allowing their father's letters to Kidson to be published for the first time.

The book would not have been written without the support of Michael Kidson's executors, Dave Ker – whose idea it was – and David Pease, and I am grateful to them for entrusting the task to an unknown author and giving me the freedom to interpret their wishes loosely. The task would have been very much harder without the help of Jackie Tarrant-Barton, Clerk to the Old Etonian Association, whose unfailing help in putting me in touch with OEs across the globe has been invaluable. Thanks are also due to Roddy Fisher, the Eton photographic archivist, for help with the photographs. I would also like to thank Dr Paul Wingfield of Gonville and Caius College, Cambridge, genealogical researcher Charlotte Bouchier and Nigel Talbot Rice for their help with the research on the relevant chapters. And my old friend, and now PR agent, Harry Bucknall for his advice about writing a book and assistance with promoting it.

I have been fortunate to be able to ask a number of kind people to read various drafts and give me feedback, and I am very grateful to three great Eton beaks, Michael Meredith, David Evans and Andrew Gailey, and to Jane Torday, my aunt Cicely McCulloch, Char Culham, Lesley Andrews, Andrew Dalrymple, Charles Villiers and Emily Don for their help and encouragement. Johnnie Boden has also been a great supporter of the project and I would like to thank him for his enthusiasm and generosity; and also to Sir Matthew Pinsent for kindly writing the foreword.

The effort would have been wasted if Andrew Johnston of Quiller Publishing had not taken a gamble on bringing Kidson to a wider readership and I am immensely grateful to Andrew and his team at Quiller for giving it the attention to detail and quality of production that only a small independent publisher can bring; critical to this has been the work of the editor, Barry Johnston, whose skilful editing and light touch has helped to put varnish on the picture and bring Kidson's portrait into sharper focus. Thank you.

Jamie Blackett
Arbigland
March 2017

Foreword

Michael Kidson was unique. A stickler, a wit, a critic and a task master, he was at the same time a wonderful schoolmaster. His lessons were pieces of theatre, occasionally farcical, often comedic, but always a rich seam of learning if you were even half able to look. He had honed the subjects into lectures, almost literally unstoppable in full flow, but packed with intrigue, heroes and conflict. History, sex, politics, statesmanship and storytelling were all braided carefully together.

Mr Kidson was unstinting in his drive to make his boys better at what they did. He refused to countenance shoddy logic or laziness and was famously demanding on language, both written and spoken.

However, his brusque exterior was a careful act. He loved his classes and his charges. And, of course, he knew that we knew, as it were. If any doubts remain, take a minute to digest the efforts he put into so many of his pupils along the way. It also struck me just how unhappy his childhood must have been and how, in the span of his lifetime, the relationships he made at Eton made the full journey, so that in old age his boys stepped in when family could not.

What follows is a wonderful testament to a quixotic man. We should never forget that the corners of his mouth were more often than not turning up as he delivered his best acerbic lines. His adjectives might have had an edge to them, but they were never unfair.

I suppose the greatest compliment we can pay him (alongside his bursary) is to carry on his little idiosyncrasies. The world will be a richer place for an occasional 'thickhead' being castigated for his 'jejuneness'. Sadly, the ships may have sailed on the Battle of 'Trafflegar'.

We should remember him, too, making steady progress with his unmistakeable gait and impeccable dress, with an intermittently obedient spaniel nearby.

He was a giant.

Matthew Pinsent, January 2017

Education is what remains when you have forgotten everything that you were taught.

A.C. Benson, from Michael Kidson's commonplace book

Prologue

The indiscretion of biographers adds a new terror to death.

Sir George Lewis, from Kidson's commonplace book

Galloway, June 2015

'Oh, no!'

'What is it?'

'Michael Kidson – you remember, my old tutor – he's dead.'

The *Daily Telegraph* sprawled across the kitchen table, elbowing out of the way breakfast and the usual assortment of cattle passports, post-it notes and bills, and competing for my attention with my wife Sheri's need to discuss the day's agenda. I had come back in for my routine bowl of porridge and a glance at the paper after going around the farm, and there it was:

> **Kidson, Michael George MacDonald.** On Saturday 20th of June in his 86th year, peacefully. Friend and mentor to many, much loved and respected. Service of Thanksgiving, St Mary's, Lasborough, Gloucestershire, Friday 3rd of July at 2.00 p.m.

Somewhere out on the shore, the oystercatchers shrieked as someone, perhaps an otter, trespassed onto their rocks. Sadness tinged with guilt passed over me, the distance of thirty-three years shrank in an instant and I was an awkward teenager again. I hadn't seen him for years, but I had only been thinking of Michael the other day, thinking that I should try to see him on one of our infrequent trips south. Now it wasn't to be; too late.

Later, half-page obituaries of 'David Cameron's favourite master' came out in the *Telegraph* and *The Times* in the slots normally reserved for cabinet ministers and generals. Readers must have wondered why an obscure schoolmaster, who had never been a headmaster, or even a housemaster or head of department, merited such attention.

OEs took to the Twittersphere and Linkedin to salute him. Charles Moore devoted part of his column in the *Daily Telegraph* to mourn the passing of schoolmasters such as Michael. He was remembered on Radio 4's *Last Word* with tributes from Dave Ker and Johnnie Boden. His piece was sandwiched, rather incongruously, between obituaries for Cilla Black and George Cole, and I had a mental image of Michael standing in the queue at the Pearly Gates with Cilla and Arthur Daley. Cilla was shrouded against the chill winds of the stratosphere in mink, Arthur in camel hair and Michael was dressed for a day's racing in his covert coat with the brown-velvet collar. He was up to his old tricks, pretending he had never heard of either of them and getting their names wrong.

'Tell me, Cecily, are you by any chance a seamstress? I'm always on the lookout for a good seamstress.'

'Ooh, you are a laff, you are, chook.'

A few months later, Michael's executors – two former pupils of his, Dave Ker and David Pease – emailed out of the blue to see if I would be prepared to pull the many memories of Michael, and the contents of his desk, into a book as a lasting tribute from his boys.

So, here goes, like an artist commissioned by the family to paint a portrait of a much-loved and recently deceased uncle. Except that Michael had no family, instead he had the boys he once insulted, cajoled, and painstakingly nurtured into adulthood, and who became his lifelong friends.

And Michael, if you are reading this in some great library in the sky, I hope you are not too horrified that such an unlikely Boswell, a boy you once described as a fairly indolent fellow, has been entrusted with this delicate task.

Please God, don't let me split an infinitive.

CHAPTER ONE

Eton Revisited

You may have heard it said that you are here to be prepared for a life of distinction. Not a bit of it. You are here to be kept off the streets during your difficult years. So you will be made to work every hour God gives you. If you are dim, you will be helped over the hurdles. If you are clever, your potential will be assessed and you will be punished if you don't fulfil it. Your spare time will be spent fagging for older boys, and if you don't do what they tell you, or any of the staff tell you, you will be punished. But I wish you good luck. You are going to need it.

From an address to the new boys by **Claude Elliot**, Head Master of Eton, 1933–49

Eton, Sometime in the 1970s

The new boy still felt strange. The stiff collar chafed his neck and the tailcoat made him feel much older than his thirteen years. He had not got used to being photographed by Japanese tourists on his way to Rowlands[1] to buy sweets, or 'sock', as he was starting to say. He was glad that the older boy in his house was walking with him and was deigning to talk to him. The pavements teemed with boys and beaks carrying books to their next divs. Here and there, members of Pop in brightly coloured waistcoats strutted like cock pheasants among jackdaws on a stubble. They filled both pavements and a number were jaywalking in the road despite the rush-hour traffic.

His eye was caught by a liver-and-white spaniel that seemed linked by an invisible lead to an older man, to whom the boys seemed to pay more than the usual deference as they 'capped' him by touching their non-existent top hats in salute. A curious paradox of a man, he seemed to be both upright and hunched, with one shoulder slightly lower than the other, and to have the stride of someone three inches taller. He marched along with his head tilted back and inclined to one side, one arm swinging in a soldierly fashion. This, together with a rather haughty expression, lent him a patrician air, which was reinforced by immaculate black brogues and a well-cut suit in the type of assertive pinstripe favoured by mafia godfathers and chairmen of FTSE 100 companies. In fact, he might have been taken for the latter, but for the winged collar and white bow tie, and the gown hanging casually from his shoulders.

Suddenly the dog darted into the road.

'Dougal! Dougal! Come here, sir!'

There was a screech and a hiss of brakes and the crowd gave a collective wince as they turned to see whether the dog had been hit by the truck or not. He had not and he was making his way back to his master pretending that nothing had happened.

The dog's owner made his way towards the lorry, an apology was forming on his lips, but the driver got his oar in first: "Oy! You want to keep that fucking dog on a lead, mate, before it causes an accident.'

The beak paused, drew himself up to his full height and, looking over his spectacles at the man, reasserted his authority with a practised ease: 'Come along, Dougal, we don't speak to lorry drivers.'

And with that, he turned on his heel and strode off, the dog sauntering along behind him.[2]

'Who's that beak?'

---

1 The school tuck shop, then by Barnes Pool Bridge, since moved.

2 There are at least five different variations on this story, which I have merged together to form this one. In fact, I think it happened on several occasions. Sometimes he would bark, 'Lorry driver, stand still!', as he launched himself across the stream of traffic in Keates Lane.

'That's Kidson – MGMK – good man. He's a history beak. My brother says he wouldn't have got into Oxford without him.'

In a school noted for its eccentrics on both sides of the lectern, Kidson stood out as a larger-than-life character. He did not tend to have many dealings with boys in the bottom years, and as one progressed through the school, one became dimly aware of him. The first indication of his presence was probably being given an imperial rocket by him for being incorrectly dressed on the golf course – sorry 'goff' course – or for some lapse of good manners in the street. He seemed on first impressions a rather scary, austere figure. Later it would dawn on one that he was generally seen sharing a joke with some of the bigger rogues in the top two years and he must have a human side after all.

Boys can be very cruel in the bestowing of nicknames. I remember a Nutty, a Potty, a Dippy, a brace of Wetties, a Sweaty, a Village Idiot and quite a few that it would be indelicate of me, and probably now illegal, to explain here. Although he was often mimicked, Kidson never, to my knowledge, suffered any such indignity. He was only referred to as Kidson. Until we left, when he became Michael – he was not the sort of chap who would have been a plausible Mike – although when teasing him (he quite liked being teased), sometimes people called him names to his face: Mikey, or Captain Kidson, on account of his time in the Army, or variations like Mr Kidney, in retaliation for his getting our names wrong.

The school where he taught happens to be Eton, but I hope you will not be put off by that and will stick with it. It could be anywhere, the story is a fairly universal one. Everyone has their own memories of their favourite teachers. (Remember the cheesy television ad campaign to recruit teachers a few years ago?)

If you were not at Eton yourself, perhaps because you were disqualified by your sex or because you were not blessed with the precocious intelligence to win a scholarship or the self-sacrificing, once-affluent and probably now-bankrupt parents to pay the exorbitant fees, I will give you a bit of background by way of context. If you *were* there, you can skip this bit and carry on with seeing whether you get a mention. I am digressing from the story here, but I always thought the red herrings were the best part of any lesson and many a sketchy historian has got by on the strength of his philosophical digressions. Like anywhere with a strong and ancient culture, Eton has its own language, I have tried to minimise the jargon, but if you get lost, there is a glossary at the back.

It is almost impossible to open a British newspaper without seeing some reference to Eton or one of its old boys. Journalists always seem to think it is relevant to mention when someone is an Etonian, although they rarely tell us where others have been educated. It is normally referred to as being in the private sector, but it is of course a state school, in fact The State School, as it was founded by royal charter and the Queen[3] still appoints the Provost and pops in from time to time to see how it is getting on.

The founder, Henry VI, by most accounts a pretty moderate king, had the foresight in 1440 to put state assets – the town of Eton itself and various royal manors around the country – into a foundation that would provide a good education for seventy poor scholars, still called King's Scholars, who would go on to form the elite of the church and state. It has been doing that very successfully ever since, gradually added to by boys who could afford to pay (known as Oppidans), so that the school now numbers around 1,300 pupils, of whom about twenty per cent and rising receive some sort of financial help from the school's charitable endowments.

If you will not accept the 'state school' description, then you will at least accept that it is in the 'not-for-profit sector', as there are no shareholders or dividends and any profits are reinvested to maintain Eton as a force for good in the world, certainly by intent anyway.

Eton pervades the national consciousness to an alarming extent. Delegates at the recent Conservative Party conference – even the female ones – were told to 'fuck off back to Eton' by demonstrators outside. A

3 The young Princess Elizabeth was tutored privately at Windsor Castle by the Vice Provost of the day, which makes her a sort of Etonian herself, and she is in fact an honorary member of the OEA. King Edward VII was also tutored by an Eton beak. Although when her grandson, Prince William, ascends the throne, he will be the first British monarch to have attended the school.

friend of mine[4] once attended a church service in the Outer Hebrides and was surprised to hear the 'Wee Free' minister preaching from the pulpit about the iniquities of 'Old Etonians in their Gucci shoes', which seemed a bit harsh. At the time of writing, the first Etonian Prime Minister since the 1960s[5] has just departed the stage and there is a feeling that the high-water mark of Etonians in public life has passed, not for the first time and probably not for the last either.

The Foreign Secretary, the Archbishop of Canterbury, our next-but-one monarch, and national icons such as Henry Blofeld and Hugh Fearnley-Whittingstall are all OEs. But before we get too smug, we should reflect that a generation ago most of these positions were filled by men and women from grammar schools, so much of this success can be attributed to Labour Party education policy of the 1960s and 1970s.

Etonians have had a remarkable influence on the way we think about things. Politicians who would happily raze Eton to the ground are nevertheless happy to profess themselves to be Keynesians, or talk about something being Orwellian, or to support Amnesty International founded by another OE, Peter Benenson. There are many more Christians in this country today, thanks to the work of Nicky Gumbel and other OEs behind the Alpha Course. Conversely, atheists often quote the Etonian philosopher A.J. Ayer. We still have not found an answer to the West Lothian question posed by the unlikely Etonian Tam Dalyell, the socialist MP who gave Mrs Thatcher so much trouble over the sinking of the *General Belgrano*. The Brexit referendum campaign was characterised as a struggle between two Eton contemporaries David Cameron and Boris Johnson,[6] oppidan pragmatism against scholarly idealism. The jury is still out and may never agree on who was right.

Critics say that Eton is elitist, which is to miss the whole point of it. All those state assets were invested all those years ago precisely to

4 My best man, Granny Clowes.

5 David Cameron was the nineteenth OE PM and the school has produced one in four of them.

6 Though they did not actually know each other at school.

create an elite. They also assume that Etonians get on in life through their connections, and I suppose that is partly true, but I do not think anyone seriously believes that Sir Ranulph Fiennes has become the most famous explorer in the world without breaking into the occasional sweat, or that Eddie Redmayne won his Oscar for his awe-inspiring portrayal of Stephen Hawking through nepotism.

Etonians have somehow managed to be successful in every age. Where once they dominated the Church and later the Empire, today there are dotcom millionaires and stand-up comedians among recent old boys. The fact that Etonians seem to prosper in all walks of life must mean that there is some secret ingredient in the education. Although there does not seem to be any correlation between success at Eton and in life after Eton – happily for those of us who were rather indifferent schoolboys. This is, one senses, a source of mystery and probably irritation to a certain type of beak.[7] How we cheered when we read in the OEA magazine that Professor Sir John Gurdon, an eminent OE, had published his school science report:[8]

Science Report ***Summer Half, 1949***

It has been a disastrous half. His work has been far from satisfactory. His prepared stuff has been badly learnt, and several of his test pieces have been torn over; one of such pieces of prepared work scored 2 marks out of a possible 50. His other work has been equally bad, and several times he has been in trouble, because he will not listen, but will insist on doing his work his way. I believe he has ideas about becoming a Scientist; on his present showing this is quite ridiculous, if he can't learn simple Biological facts he would

7 But not to the wise and perceptive David Evans, who explained to me that those who have been a failure at Eton leave with something to prove, and those who have been a success find life after Eton an anti-climax.

8 OEA Review.

> ***have no chance of doing the work of a Specialist, and it would be sheer waste of time, both on his part and of those who have to teach him.***

Gurdon had just won the Nobel Prize for his pioneering scientific research.

It is by any measure a world-class education. Eton differs from most other secondary schools by treating boys more like undergraduates and the opportunities are the same, if not better, than at many universities. There is a tutorial system similar to that in Oxbridge colleges. There is a vibrant after-hours programme of drama, music and lectures, with an impressive array of public figures coming to speak. Right from the start, boys have their own rooms and they are expected to work independently. This freedom is not without its risks. Without the discipline of supervised evening 'prep', there is a temptation to coast along, working the bare minimum to get by, as teenaged boys are prone to doing. David Cameron was often accused of being an 'exam-crisis Prime Minister', only at his best when the pressure is on, but that might equally be said of most Etonians and I remember my five years there as one long essay crisis.

The number of Etonians in public life reinforces the idea of the Establishment, a self-perpetuating oligarchy. But, if it is an oligarchy, it is one formed by ruthless meritocracy, both in the entrance exams and while at the school. There was always an unease about private education. Kidson himself, who was quite liberal behind the façade, used to shake his head sadly and say that because it caused such divisions in the country, it was very hard to justify. At the time of writing, the tectonic plates are shifting under education. The Cameron government's reforms have blurred the boundaries between the sectors. When I visited Eton the other day, the Vice Provost noted with interest the number of Etonian families enrolling children in the new Eton-sponsored Academy at Holyport.

As I enter my sixth decade, and my more successful friends start to be knighted for their achievements, I have a feeling of not having done enough to repay the extraordinary gift of an Eton education, of not giving enough back. My own year group, the class of 82, has started to make its mark.

James Greenwood rode around the world on a horse, then wrote a book about it. Charlie Spencer's eulogy at his sister Diana's funeral made history with the spontaneous ovation that followed it. Snippets of information about my classmates have occasionally caught the eye in newspapers, such as when Mungo Tennant briefly dated Madonna, or Henry Cole directed a film with Liz Hurley in it, or Darius Guppy was sent to prison.

Two of the boys with whom I learnt to march up and down in the Corps[9] are now Major Generals: Ben Bathurst and Ed Smyth-Osbourne, and Andrew Gilmour has reached Three-star rank in the United Nations. Paul Watkins, always the best story writer in our English divs, is a novelist who has twice been shortlisted for the Booker Prize and journalist Sebastian Mallaby has been a Pulitzer Prize finalist twice. Richard Farnes is a celebrated conductor and Director of Opera North. On the sporting front, Matt Fleming played cricket for England, Marcus Armytage won a Grand National, and Cornelius Lysaght is the distinctive voice of racing on Radio 5 Live.

We have had only one prime minister so far – Mark Vejjajiva, known to us as Veggy, was PM of Thailand for three years – much to the frustration, one suspects, of the British frontrunner of our cohort, Boris Johnson. But, as Boris said at our last reunion, with what nearly proved to be uncanny foresight, 'We have the self-confidence as a year group to delegate the premiership to a boy from two years below us *for the time being*.' There have been a number of successful entrepreneurs – George Morgan-Grenville with the travel operators Red Savannah, and Chris Legard with the mail-order firm Joseph Turner – and at our quinquennial reunions at Eton there seem to be dozens of prosperous bankers, most of them looking decades older than their peers.

Writing about Eton a generation ago feels a bit like the man in the third verse of the 'Eton Boating Song':

9 The Combined Cadet Force (CCF) is still known as the Corps after the Officer Training Corps (OTC) that preceded it.

Twenty years on this weather
May tempt us from office stools
We may be slow on the feather
And seem to the boys old fools
But we'll still swing together
And swear by the best of schools

Things had moved on a little from the time of Claude Elliot, although the immutable truths in his remarks at the beginning of this chapter remained. Fagging waned, house by house, in an attritional battle between housemasters and their libraries[10] through the 1970s and finally died out by 1980. But looking back, things really were so different to today in many respects that one might as well be describing *Tom Brown's Schooldays*. For one thing, the nouns health and safety had not been juxtaposed to the delight of the jobsworths and the exasperation of everyone else. I had a coal fire in my bedroom at the age of thirteen. I still love going to sleep in a room with the glow of a real fire and the reflection of the flames flickering on the ceiling. Sparks used to fly out and burn the carpet. It was great for smoking up the chimney undetected.

The school pub – 'Tap' – was open all day to Sixth-formers and the record number of pints drunk by a boy during chambers (the twenty-five-minute, mid-morning break) was fourteen. I don't suppose he learnt much in the div before lunch, but maybe he felt he knew it all already and so could afford to be slightly over the limit.

There was a sink-or-float approach to life and this was taken literally when it came to rowing. I sank. My first summer, I remember being pushed off from Rafts into the broad River Thames in a whiff (a single-scull rowing-boat). I got a bit of a wobble on, lost control and went bottom-up like a duck. I recall being swept under Windsor Bridge and being fished out of

10 House prefects are collectively called the 'Library'.

the water just before I disappeared over the weir.[11] Later that summer, as I had yet to grow, they made me the cox of my house baby-four. It was not a sensible decision. I steered the boat into every stationary object on the river between Rafts and Locks. I once nearly managed to decapitate the boys in the Eight doing their pre-Henley training, when we went too close and had to lift oars to avoid becoming entangled. I can still picture the look of derision on the older cox's face as they glided past. On long summer afternoons, there was nothing better than sculling up the river, negotiating the locks as we went, to Queen's Eyot, an island in the Thames owned by the school, on which there was a bar where we could buy beer and cider. Working out how much Strongbow one could drink before rowing back was an early lesson in how to conduct a risk assessment.

It would be nice to be able to say that all this never did us any harm and the mollycoddling that goes on today will not do the boys any good, and that is probably half-right. But there are records of boys dying in house fires, and I remember seeing sad little memorial plaques on the chapel walls to boys who had drowned in the river, and urban myth had it that the record-breaking pint-drinker later died of alcohol poisoning at Oxford. The Bear Grylls generation of Etonians do not seem to be any less robust either.

Eton was still the default setting for the education of the aristocracy and the landed gentry. The descendants of the historical figures Kidson taught us about[12] – Percys, Howards, Cecils and Gladstones – rubbed shoulders with the offspring of captains of industry and the sons of impoverished backwoods lairds like me. It was before the 'Big Bang' in the City of London and investment bankers had yet to become masters of the universe; the metropolitan elite did not predominate as now. If anyone had suggested that mainland Chinese pupils would be at Eton within a

11 In a strange coincidence by my cousin David Bland, who was 'in the Monarch' – a sort of river prefect – and on duty that day.

12 He would relish making an unhappy comparison between a boy and 'your more redoubtable ancestor'.

generation, they would have been laughed at. The nouveaux riches were not there in any great numbers, as they preferred to bestow their largesse on that place on the North Circular, whose name escapes me.

In fact, it was a miracle that anyone was at Eton at all. When I went there, the Chancellor of the Exchequer, Denis Healey, was 'squeezing the rich until the pips squeaked' in a bizarre economic experiment never repeated since. Income tax was eighty-three per cent on earned income and ninety-eight per cent on unearned. There is a PhD subject there for someone to work out how on earth the fees were still paid. But, as I never tired of telling my father when I was going through the school-fees mill myself, every generation has its cross to bear. The price of wheat in 1973 was £120 per tonne and in 2016 it is hovering below £100. Taking into account the inflated costs of school fees and producing the wheat, it is probably nearly one hundred times more expensive for farmers to educate their children privately now. It perhaps explains why the modern Eton father is more likely to manage hedge funds than hedgerows.

The popular image of Etonians is something like Lord Snooty and his pals in *The Beano* or of gilded youths in films like *Another Country*. But we were just gawky teenagers going through puberty like any other adolescents on the planet. I have noticed that when they make such films, they generally cast actors in their twenties in the lead roles. I suppose no one wants to pay good money to watch a lot of spotty teenagers grunting. We were also dedicated followers of fashion and of the music of the moment. I had a punk haircut when I was about fourteen. It was not a good look, but my parents took it well.

When Kidson arrived at Eton in 1965, the Beatles and the Rolling Stones contested the top of the charts and when he left in 1994 it was Take That and Wet Wet Wet. He could not fail to have heard everything in-between. Walking past boys' houses in my day, you would hear 'London Calling' by the Clash or 'White Punks on Dope' by the Tubes being belted out at as many decibels as stereo speakers could muster. 'Eton Rifles' by the Jam was a particular favourite of those of us in the Corps. While some beaks would show an interest in modern music, Kidson remained a

Beethoven man at heart, and maintained a lofty indifference to the musical *zeitgeist*. He would dismiss it by saying, 'I don't care much for John Lemon and the Falling Stones.'[13]

Despite its antiquity, or perhaps because of it, Eton's heritage caused a few headaches for the school's late twentieth-century management. Just as Her Majesty might choose to locate Windsor Castle somewhere other than on the edge of the M4 under the approach to Heathrow Airport, so might the Provost and Fellows, given the opportunity of a fresh start on a green-field site, choose to put Britain's premier centre of excellence for male adolescent education in a more isolated setting with fewer temptations on its doorstep; ideally, somewhere behind an electrified razor-wire fence, with the full suite of watchtowers and minefields around it.

Within bicycling distance of Eton, the Yellow Pages lists 151 pubs in Eton, Windsor and Slough alone, 24 tobacconists, 109 betting shops, 2 racecourses, polo at Smiths Lawn, and the Slough dog track. I do not remember any cockfighting during my time, there probably was, but I was not invited to join in. It had certainly been a distraction for previous Etonians in less poultry-friendly times, as Eton High Street's oldest hostelry, The Cockpit, bore witness.[14] Sneaking across the railway line into Slough by night felt like escaping across the inner German border. London is a short train-ride away. Getting on the train for an illicit adventure always reminded me of Gordon Jackson and Richard Attenborough boarding the bus in *The Great Escape*.

They might, on reflection, also have made it co-educational, something that would not have occurred to Henry VI in the fifteenth century, but might usefully be considered in the twenty-first. The lack of female company, far from helping us to focus on our studies, meant that there was generally more on our minds than in them. Being Scottish – or Scotch, as Kidson would have said – had its advantages if you could muster the courage and had the requisite proficiency to do a passable eightsome reel,

13 Older pupils remember him saying, 'I don't care much for Clive Richards or Elton Presley.'

14 Tragically closed in the summer of 2016.

as you could meet girls legitimately at 'Cal Soc' – the Caledonian Society, which met in School Hall sporadically. Otherwise, we ranged across the Thames Valley like dog foxes in February. This generally meant dodging the lorries on the A332 on our bicycles for assignations at the girls' schools of Ascot: Heathfield or St Mary's.

At Heathfield, one ran the gauntlet of running into the redoubtable Mrs Parry, a headmistress of fearsome repute, who was married to a garrulous Welshman, Ray Parry, an Eton housemaster and a history beak of mercurial efficacy. She caught me once; I said that my name was Jack Soames, a friend who had conveniently left the school the half before.[15] These assignations were planned either by queuing for hours to use the house's single payphone, only to find that the girls' single payphone was similarly engaged, or by agonisingly drafted letter. Frequently one would bicycle all the way there to find that the object of one's affections was playing hockey against Wycombe Abbey, away. All that must seem hopelessly archaic to the Facebook generation, they do not know how lucky they are.

We used to conceal cigarettes in the tail-pockets of our tailcoats. I was reminded of this the other day when my son was due to attend his first wedding as a teenager. With great pride, I produced my old school uniform from the back of my dressing-room wardrobe and sent him away to try it on. Oliver returned wearing that cocky, deadpan expression that I remember from when he bowled me out in the fathers' match: it generally means he knows he has got one over me.

'I think these are yours, Dad.'

He handed over a squashed pack of Winston from circa 1980. His sister Rosie squealed with laughter and shook her head theatrically, her eyes bright with a worldly wisdom beyond her years, 'Oh, Dad, you're such a muppet.'

15 Mrs Parry was stricter in this regard than her predecessor as Headmistress, who told Andrew Bell, a Kidson pupil who was attending a school dance at Heathfield: 'I always like my girls to leave school having been kissed by a boy, preferably an Etonian.'

The mothers among you will now be tut-tutting at this appalling parenting, but it was an honest mistake, and thankfully, I think he is giving up at last.

The school employed various countermeasures to ensure that we were not exposed to too much of the real world. There was 'Lock-Up' at 6.30 p.m., after which entry back into our houses was solely through the housemaster's 'private side', unless there was a handy drainpipe. At weekends, they employed the old trick, beloved of POW camp commandants everywhere, of making us answer our names halfway through the afternoon at 'Absence'.

The net result was that, aside from the academic curriculum and any sporting or artistic endeavours, there was a constant subplot running, a deadly game of cat-and-mouse with the authorities equal to anything by Ian Fleming, who was at Eton with my grandfather, or John le Carré, who taught there in the 1950s. Fleming, incidentally, had James Bond expelled for 'trouble with a boy's maid' and finishing his education at Fettes.

It is generally understood by historians that this extra-mural activity was at least as vital as anything that we were taught in the classroom. Important lessons were learned in how to smuggle cigarettes in hollowed-out loaves of bread, how to forge a housemaster's signature on a pass, or answer names for absent friends, and crucially, how to sober up fast before an interview. It may be this extra ingenuity is what gives those from boarding schools the edge in the wider world over their competitors from day schools.

It may also be why there is a cunning resourcefulness hard-wired into the conceptual component of our nation's fighting power. Certainly, without the harsh discipline of our great public schools, and the consequent guile of their old boys, the Germans would never have had to convert Colditz Castle into a high-security jail. And if the Battle of Britain had been lost, the German occupation would have been foreshortened and fraught with danger for the Nazi garrison, as many an old squire would have remembered hard-won skills from schooldays, formed the resistance, and contrived to make their lives nasty, brutish and short.

Eton was an energetic, exciting, raucous, and bewitchingly beautiful place. We were treated to a sensory feast: the sight of verdant wisteria leaves against old brickwork, or of beaks hurtling with precarious urgency down the towpath on their bicycles, roaring into their megaphones during the bumping races; the sound of the bell in Lupton's Tower on a moonlit night, or of studded football boots clattering on pavements on November afternoons; the smell of the roses in Luxmoore's Garden in the cool aftermath of a violent Thames Valley storm, or of toast being made in the house on a winter's evening; the taste of our first pint in the Tap garden; the feel of the cold water as we jumped into the Jordan at the end of the steeplechase, with our lungs rasping with stitch.

But it could also be a lonely, confusing place to spend one's adolescence. I had a very vivid dream recently, no doubt a fragment of neural waste spawned by thinking about Eton while writing the book. In it, I am in the Chapel and I get up to read the lesson to find that I am not wearing any trousers. I pull on some pyjamas and hobble sheepishly over to the lectern to find that the text of the lesson is incomplete. I start well, thrilling to the deep tones of my recently broken voice and then, as gaps start to appear in the text and whole sentences seem to be in Latin, it starts to fall apart. I stumble through the Latin translation, I am paralysed by awful silences. I can hear tittering in the pews. I can feel the eyes of my housemaster and the Head Master boring into the side of my head. Somehow, I get through it and I emerge into the High Street feeling relieved but dislocated.

No such incident ever occurred, although I do remember being daunted by reading the lesson for the first time and stuttering, poorly prepared as usual, through Latin construes in class. However, it seemed a powerful allegory for the journey that we all took through the Eton maze. For many of us, the journey was made much easier through meeting Michael Kidson along the way. In fact, but for him, some of us might not have made it through to the end.

He was, in that rather over-used modern phrase, a 'Marmite character'. He was not universally popular. Like the unfortunate lorry driver, who could not know that he was every bit as rude to dukes as he was to delivery men, some saw only the image rather than the man. No one ever really knew him completely and he remained a man of mystery to the end. But for those of us who peered through the chinks in the armour, we were rewarded first with a twinkle in the eye and then with a beaming, toothy grin, and finally with an enduring friendship, as he became one of the most important mentors in our lives.

CHAPTER TWO

Abdul the Camel Driver

Kidson in the classroom

It is a great mistake to suppose that small boys demand of their rulers impartiality and justice: like the politically undeveloped races, they prefer a benevolent autocracy given to bursts of passion, because they understand that better; the only things they must have are generosity and humour.

Gerald Brenan, from Kidson's commonplace book

Number 5, James Schools, September 1979

The boys filed in to the div. I have written filed without thinking; we probably slouched or sauntered, according to whatever teenage role-play was going on in our heads that day. First impressions were of a classroom whose incumbent was not persuaded by the modern fad of placing the desks – the old wooden ones with fixed benches – around in a semicircle. Nor had he indented for any new teaching-aids like whiteboards or overhead projectors. There was a blackboard, a map of pre-Versailles Europe, and a simple desk at the front with an odd-shaped hemispherical piece of wood on it. A strong smell, faintly reminiscent of home, permeated the whole room. It was soon identified with the spaniel, Dougal, stretched out in one corner.

Kidson stood up.

'Right, if you are all here, I shall get you to answer your names. Alltrup, is there an Alltrup here?'

The tall boy next to me with a mop of reddish hair glanced up and started to mumble something.

Kidson looked at him. A glint appeared at the back of his eyes, the glint of a man who has prepared carefully for this moment and now spies his woodcock close to the gin.

'Ah, I suppose you pronounce it Orlethorpe, do you?'

We all pronounced it Orlethorpe.[16] His sister was rumoured to be going out with the Prince of Wales.

'Well, it's Alltrup. You must be a fearful ignoramus if you can't pronounce your own name properly.' He let a 'w' hover over his 'r's as he spoke, like a Victorian duke.

Althorp grinned sheepishly. It was the first time that someone outside his own immediate circle had taken the trouble to pronounce his name correctly.

'Bathurst?'

'Sir.'

'Blackett?'

'Sir …'

If you could have picked Kidson's classroom up and turned it into a pop-up theatre at the Edinburgh Fringe, people would have paid good money to watch him in action. He applied the Reithian principles and made sure that he entertained as well as informing and educating us. He was a brilliant teacher, although if any young schoolmaster is reading this in the hope of improving his technique, I would advise treading carefully before mimicking his style.

Every young officer has been told at some stage of his career: 'Sir, I'd follow you if only out of curiosity.'

Well, we paid attention out of curiosity. We always wondered what was going to happen next.

Anyone who has observed teenagers in their natural environment – at

16 So does the BBC. Debrett's Correct Form, the ultimate arbiter on these matters, and probably Kidson's source, recommends Alltrup.

home during the holidays, for example – knows that they sleep during daylight hours and only really come alive just as their parents go to bed. If the Department for Education was serious about planning education around pupils, secondary schools would work a night shift, but I doubt whether the teaching unions would stand for it. The natural tendency in any div, therefore, especially after lunch, was to go to sleep. This would be regretted instantly, as it would result in the piece of wood, which on closer inspection turned out to be half a croquet ball, being hurled at the culprit.

A few days after Kidson's obituary in the *Daily Telegraph*, this letter appeared:

> **Classroom ballistics**
> SIR – In 1976 the weapon of choice for Michael Kidson (the schoolmaster who taught David Cameron history) was a half croquet ball (Notebook, July 6). One morning we hid this missile to prevent further attacks.
>
> In its place he reached for the nearest object, which happened to be an electronic calculator belonging to a wealthy boy in the front row. It exploded into a thousand pieces as it hit the rear wall. All protestations by the owner of the calculator were met with characteristic indifference.
>
> We later returned the croquet ball to prevent further losses.
> **Julian Pullan**
> Bramley, Hampshire

The missile was used for individual narcosis, the counter-measure for collective somnolence was the sneeze. First indications were a twitching of the nose and a large white handkerchief would be produced from a pocket with a flourish. He would close his eyes and start rehearsing half-sneeze noises, gradually adjusting the volume. Finally, he reached climax with a piercing '*Ah-Choo*!', the first bar of which was a glass-shattering scream. Even Dougal would wake with a start.

When Kidson read out our names at the beginning of the half, it was the first and last time he called us by our correct names. From then on, names were cheerfully mispronounced so that divs became more like *Blackadder* sketches.

Jakes Ferguson: 'From the first, he affected not to remember my name and called me McPherson whenever he addressed me; so to this day I bump into OEs who call me that, which is confusing for a second or two.'

Johnnie Boden: 'There was a boy named Foss and Kidson said, "What's your name, boy?"

'"Foss, sir."

'"Well, Phosphor ..." and it was always Phosphor after that.'

David Cameron remembers: 'There were two German exchange students who sat in the front row called Bommel and Hoffman, who inevitably became Rommel and Hofmeister as the half went on. He would treat them with a Fawlty-like courtesy, saying, "I am very fond of your country and I have visited it many times ... after the war, of course."'

John Everett: 'In class, he used to strut to and fro in front of the blackboard with his head held high, enthusiastically discoursing – without notes – on the finer details of the historical event in hand, interrupting himself every now and then to fire a question at one of the boys: "Well, Appleton, why do you think Napoleon decided against this course of action, eh? Come on, boy! Speak up!"

'This was our cue to roar back at him: "Please, sir! It's not Apple*ton*, it's Apple*by*!"

'Stopping for a moment to look at us over his glasses with an air of bemused indignation, intended to convey astonishment that he could have been accused of getting a name muddled up, he would dismiss our protest in a stutter of guttural guffaws, a glint of mischief in his eye as he resumed his line of questioning, "Well, then, Apple*berry*. Come on then, boy! What have you to say for yourself, eh?"'

When we got higher up the school, he started to use our first names. **Charles Rhodes** recalls Kidson going round the div asking everybody what their Christian name was.

'Sinjun, what about you?'

'John, sir.'

'John St John? Highly original parents you've got!'

Darius Guppy: 'On one occasion, I remember him physically throwing me out of the classroom. He had mispronounced my name (Gubbins) for the hundredth time – as he did with all the boys (Adlam was Ordlum, Matterson was Macassa, and so on). This time, though, he had referred to me as "Abdul the camel driver" – a reference to my half-Persian origins – and throughout the class I had called him Mr Kipper, instead of Mr Kidson or "sir", and eventually he ejected me.

'Afterwards he confided to one of my friends, "I hope Darius forgives me, I'm very fond of him you know," which I thought showed his soft side beneath the bluff.

'It is, of course, a very sad feature of modern Britain that for the same behaviour nowadays, Michael would be up before some disciplinary hearing for "offending" me, or some other form of political incorrectness. Michael was old-fashioned. He did not give a damn about all of that nonsense, which is precisely why everybody loved him. That is the Britain I miss.'

Just as the stand-up comics of today thrive on their edginess and tread a fine line that they occasionally cross, Kidson did sometimes go too far and stray into what might be interpreted as bullying. The trick, as Richard Wells found, was to stand up to him and gain a mutual respect:

Richard Wells: I was up to Kidson for History A level in 1979. He was on particularly good and insulting form that day, and after I had made a stupid mistake over a date, he obviously decided to target me mercilessly throughout the lesson. His general gist was: what was the point of him teaching me, when I was so stupid, I couldn't remember anything. This went on for most of the div and I was beginning to take it personally. In the end, he went for me one time too many.

'Wells, you are so stupid, I don't know why I bother to allow you in my div.'

To which I replied, 'Well, in that case, sir, as you obviously don't want me here, I'm off!'

I picked up my books and strode out of the div, with Kidson huffing and puffing behind me in a complete fury and shouting after me, 'Where do you think you're going? I didn't tell you to leave, come back here at once!'

I didn't. I waited on the steps outside for what I thought would be a hurricane of abuse at the end of the div, but none came. The boys all walked out, but not Kidson.

Rather worried that he would go straight to my housemaster, I decided to go and see him at the end of the school day to apologise. I went up the stairs and knocked apprehensively on his door. I remember him flinging it open and then staring at me.

'Yes?' he said, affecting incomprehension as to why I might be there.

There was silence, so I said sheepishly, 'I came to apologise, sir.'

'What for?'

'Um … for walking out of your div earlier, sir.'

Kidson was very calm, but he fired back quickly, 'Walking out of my div, Wells, what are you talking about? No one has ever walked out of one of my divs without my permission – I sent you out.'

And that was the end of the conversation. I walked back down the stairs feeling a lot better about life, knowing that no further action would be taken and marvelling at how clever he had been to turn a rather embarrassing situation for him on its head.

Respect!

Kidson's spaniel was a great prop, which he used with comic effect, as **Will Armitage** remembers. 'This led to more political incorrectness one day when Jomo Gecaga, the grandson of an East African president, was leaning back nonchalantly on his chair stroking Boody, the spaniel successor to Dougal. Suddenly the wooden block was hurled by Kidson in his general direction. Everyone came to attention with a start.

'"How dare you man!! How dare you touch my beautiful dog! Just because where you come from you would put him in a bloody great cooking pot and stew him alive, that doesn't mean that you can touch him. You ghastly, abortionate specimen. Argh!!"

'Jomo roared with laughter and was not offended at all.[17] Michael knew that he was capable of taking such un-PC verbal abuse!'

Mungo Mansfield, then **Mungo Stormont**, also stroked Kidson's dog and was told, 'Don't touch my dog! You'll give it fleas.'

Christopher de Bellaigue: 'Kidson defended his oversexed spaniel for trying to solace itself against our thighs, by saying, "Nothing wrong with a young man wanting a w**k!"'[18]

Kidson often strayed into the canine in his history divs. According to **Jeremy Harbord**, he stated that the reason the Interregnum fell in 1660, the tipping point when the population said 'enough was enough' and brought back Charles II, was the day that the Commonwealth banned people from taking dogs to church. **Edward Novis** recalls Kidson describing spaniels as 'descendants of the Plantagenets'.

Like all great actors, Kidson had perfect timing. **Harley Walsh**, an American who attended Eton for one year between high school and university in the US, will never forget his first day of classes:

'My first class was with Michael. I had not figured my way around the school grounds and ended up turning down the wrong street, which caused me to be late. I finally figured out where I should be and ran through the (now empty) streets and down the hallway towards his classroom. My shoes were new, so the leather outsoles were still smooth. As I approached his door running at full speed, I tried to stop, but my smooth-soled shoes slid along the polished floor and I rammed into the door with a loud bang.

17 Jomo confirms this. He writes: 'Suffice to say, I believe anonymising the anecdote would not do Kidson justice, so I am happy for you to say it as it was!'

18 I can't read de Bellaigue's writing very well and I think this word must be 'walk'.

'I opened the door sheepishly and peered in. The class was silent, and Kidson was standing in front of the students with perfect posture and his back towards me. Still looking away from me, he declared, "That *must* be the American. Please find a seat."

'To this day, my children love to hear my "that must be the American" story.'

And everyone remembers his mastery of historical detail, his use of language and colourful turns of phrase. **David Cameron** was one boy who was captivated, calling him 'an inspirational teacher who made you feel as if you were in the room with the people he taught about.'

Anne of Cleves was 'physically rebarbative'. Mary, Queen of Scots was 'sexy'. Young imaginations were stimulated by tales of Cardinal Mazarin sliding down Anne of Austria's drainpipe, or Gladstone consoling ladies of the night. Where other beaks might have stopped short of discussing the sex lives of historical figures, Kidson positively revelled in discussing the 'Ugandan proclivities' of Victorian statesmen – Palmerston dying after 'rogering a housemaid on his billiard table'. **Andrew Gilmour** remembers Henry VIII being described as a 'concupiscent old sod.' About once or twice a month he would come out with his most famous catchphrase – after describing some epic feat of heroism such as the Charge of the Light Brigade, he would fix his classroom of wretchedly inadequate boys with a withering glare and utter the immortal words, 'They were GIANTS in those days.'

Jack Diggle: 'He would throw in the odd word that the majority of us would not use in day-to-day speech – "vicissitudinal" has stuck in the mind, possibly used in some Gladstonian context – he would then linger on the word, knowing it would draw blank faces and very quickly follow up with, "Please don't tell me, Diggle, that you don't know what vicissitudinal means … you could pull any man off his bike in the street and ask him and he will know the exact meaning of the word."'

Jamie Norman: 'I have so many other memories: his opening comment in eighteenth-century outlines on this being the era of Hogarth depicting a fox hanging on to the Duchess of Portland's tits; of the Secret

Treaty of Dover being hard to unravel for professional historians, let alone for educationally sub-normal boys like us.'

Benjy Mancroft remembers the insults: 'He told me once, when I was hunched in the back of his div not listening, that "you look like a sucked orange", which was pretty much how I felt at the time. He also accused me of "vegetating in squalid inertia", which I regarded as a compliment.'

Johnnie Boden: 'I developed a lasting fascination for Victorian history in his classroom. My imagination was captured by his depiction of Sir Bartle Frere and General Sir Garnet Wolseley, as they bungled and swashbuckled across the empire. MGMK's theatrical delivery of these names was a highlight of each division. There would always be a pause first, then he would mention their hallowed names, his voice marginally raised, his lips slightly puckered and often with a glance into the middle distance. Afterwards there would be another slight pause, followed by a look in our direction to ensure that we, too, had embraced the mild absurdity of the names of these moustachioed characters. I always caught his eye and his gentle smile.

'One of the defining characteristics of Eton is the culture of teasing and mimicry. I can't think of any beak more imitated than MGMK (although there was strong competition – my own housemaster Norman Routledge, John Peake and his famous lisp, 'Dippy' Simpson 'up and construe', and many others). Kidson provided the school a great service in this respect. Whenever you left the classroom, you would invariably hear at least half of the division imitating him.'

Jamie Sainsbury: 'He called me Scaramanga, though he knew my name perfectly well, as there were often assaults on the grocery trade. I was mesmerised by the bravura displays of knowledge and the amazing stories that have remained with me to this day, such as Louis XVI hauling himself into corsets and fleeing in disguise for the Belgian border.'

Rob Peake also enjoyed Kidson's theatrical approach to teaching History: 'When about to explain something important in div, he would deepen and raise his voice dramatically and advise the class, "Hang upon my lips, metaphorically speaking!" I remember an aside in div to one poor boy: "I walked through a graveyard on my way here this morning, Smith. I thought of you."

'More importantly, I remember him as an excellent teacher. I enjoyed his classes for the laughs, but also because I never felt out of my depth. There was a strong feeling of knowledge going in. Not something I would say about every beak. Like all the best teachers, he combined authority and approachability.'

Charles Hulbert-Powell: 'He spoke with no notes in a clear and precise way. He made History live. If he asked a question and a wrong answer was given, he might comment by saying, "Any simple apothecary's assistant would know the answer to that." It was memorable, if only because I still don't quite know why the apothecary's assistant was relevant.'

Timothy Melgund: 'My favourite line was: "Every dog in Newmarket knows the answer to that question."'

Mark Davies: 'I once took a secret video of him teaching. It captures the general hubbub in the div, as he goes through his full repertoire. "Total subjugation! This means total subjugation!" he intones, to explain his arm raised in almost Nazi salute.'

Above all, **Charlie Egerton-Warburton** recalls the humour: 'I was known as Forbes-Cockell, because someone of that name had sat in my seat in div three or four years earlier and also had a double-barrelled name. Cripps was always known as Crisp. The most memorable moment was when Kidson walked in after we had submitted an essay on "Napoleon's Rise to Power, 1799 to 1805". He asked us all to stand for two minutes in silence out of disrespect for Crisp, at the end of which he announced to the embarrassed individual, "Boy, if you can't spell Napoleon, don't include it in the essay!"

'I still tell that story at dinner parties after thirty-five years. I believe Crisp has gone on to make a fortune running Australia's largest removals company, so he has had the last laugh.'

Jeremy Harbord: 'When he organised an exhibition about Gladstone in the McNaughten Library, he placed on a table one of those J-shaped, one-handed branch loppers, and tagged it "Gladstone's favourite chopper". As if he knew! Michael had obviously got it from someone's potting shed, and wanted to remind people and illustrate WEG's love for felling trees. I seem to recall asking him if it was really WEG's favourite? I think he simply said, "Of course," with a raise of an eyebrow and a smile to show he was bluffing!'[19]

Matt Pinsent: 'He used to teach in a fluent monologue, sometimes uninterrupted for a full div – a feat of oratory and concentration that would be beyond almost anyone. No notes, no stumbling, and your only chance was to write copious notes as he went. I remember a sprightly and enthusiastic springer, who would be shut under the desk by his chair and our desks. When Kidson's back was turned, we would conceal an ink cartridge in a handkerchief and wave it enthusiastically under the desk, until the dog could not restrain himself and would tear into the package with gusto, only to emerge at the end of the div with blue lips and dribble on his chin.'

Nicky Dunne: 'He burst into the room and the lesson would begin almost immediately. His well-practised narrative flowing as he hung up his gown, and the first volley of questions fired in our direction. Woe betide anyone not paying attention. He would sit at his desk urging us to answer, his eyes screwed up in anticipation as we struggled to come up with the name of Garibaldi or Cavour. Like any good schoolmaster, he knew his brief inside out, perhaps too well, and his views on the unification of Italy must have been recycled year after year. But for us it felt fresh and dramatic, with the added tension of his verbal assaults or physical anguish at a half-baked or incoherent answer. He loved opinion and clarity and berated us for displaying any woolliness. His lessons were exciting and uniquely I actually looked forward to them. His rhetorical flourishes were hilarious. Each harsh put-down was delivered with a horror you knew to be faux, and almost entirely for show. We all absolutely loved him.'

---

19 In fact this was a double bluff as research shows the chopper was genuine. Kidson had borrowed it from Hawarden whose owner at the time was a former Eton Beak, Sir William Gladstone Bt, later the Chief Scout. The exhibition is still remembered at Eton as a model of its kind.

The moment in the week when Kidson gave back our essays was always eagerly anticipated, partly because he was one beak we wanted to impress and we looked forward to his judgement on our work, but also because this was often when he doled out his best insults. A Scottish boy was informed he was a 'Hebridean cave dweller' and a boy of Welsh extraction was told, 'I make every allowance for your nationality, but really this is not good enough.'

He upbraided another boy, 'I know, it must be very hard for you being at the back of every queue when God gave out talent, good looks and intelligence, but for goodness sake, please *try*!' There was one occasion when he said to someone, 'You are so slack and so idle, I cannot even look at you.' The great man addressed this to a wall.

Henry Hood: 'The cleverer boys got their essays back first, before eventually, "And now we come to Hood. Poor ... old ... Hood. Hood, you make me want to fart!"'

When we had a chance to look at our essays, they were frequently covered in red ink. Commas would be sprayed across the page like sparks in a forge. While some other beaks gave the impression of having done their marking on their knees in front of *Panorama*, putting the odd desultory tick in the margins, then a brief comment and a grade at the end, Kidson went to immense trouble. He questioned every bald assertion and unsubstantiated opinion.

Jamie Norman: 'My first essay was to assess the career of Cardinal Wolsey. With his mistresses in mind, I rather pompously and naively observed that "Wolsey's morals left much to be desired." – "Absurd and irrelevant" was his comment in red biro.'

Tim Thomson Jones remembers being told that his essay was 'like a jackass's penis, long and flaccid'.[20]

You knew what Kidson thought fairly early on by the comments in the margin, such as, 'Oh dear.' One essay had six 'Oh dears' in the margin,

20 As was often the case, his insults paraphrased historical quotes, in this case Sydney Smith on an article by Macaulay.

leading to the conclusion: 'This really is the funniest essay I have ever read on Disraeli – it goes into my archives. There is hardly a serious or sensible thought here. Oh dear.'

Other typical margin entries were:

- I don't think that I've ever read a more RISIBLE opening paragraph on Bismarck
- Rubbish
- Gibberish
- Appallingly incompetent gibberish
- Sheer unmitigated nonsense
- Sheer waffle
- This para reads like a demented parrot
- Another dreadful paragraph

At the bottom, he was liable to write:[21]

- Mostly appalling rubbish, I'm afraid. I suggest that another time you attempt a question that you know a modicum about.
- This is utterly awful. There is no thematic line whatsoever: it is a formless patchwork, gormless, badly stitched together, shapeless mass of unrelated half-truths – of no merit whatsoever. I cannot estimate a grade.
- Horrible piece of work – a lot of it little more than gibberish. There is hardly a careful – even a <u>sane</u> – judgement here, and the 'history' is as gruesome as the Bulgarian atrocities. I don't like this one little bit.
- Nearly all sheer nonsense, this is NOT history.
- I don't think I've ever read a more ludicrous paragraph than the 2nd in this essay. One would infer that you were not right in the head. But, on reflection, I don't think I've ever read so much TRIPE in a so-called essay on Louis Napoleon. There isn't a single sentence – never mind a

21 These are taken from his archive of very good and (mostly) very bad essays by boys over the years.

thematic line – that makes sense. It is simply awful. To be done again for Monday 20th March.

- This is primitive beyond words – from beginning to end the English & style are dreadful: the history a piecemeal of 1/2 truths & poorly supported patchwork illiteracy. I don't like it one bit. You will see me before it is rewritten for lock-up Wednesday 14th March. I will NOT accept work of this utterly dismal standard from an A level candidate.
- I am able, verbally, to ask you what you mean by the things you write – because I need to do so: most of this script is quite incredibly obscure. An examiner cannot do this; he will probably think one of several things:

(a) that you are in the middle of an unfortunate brainstorm.

(b) that you are 'having him on'.

(c) that you are an Oriental gentleman with very little English, who has changed his name to Jones.

(d) that you are inebriated.

I shall charitably assume that (b) is the explanation.

Often, he bestowed a new grade he had invented below an F for Fail: 'G'.

Occasionally there were girls in his divs, the daughters of masters who were admitted to the school as day girls for A levels and Oxbridge. **Charles Rhodes** remembers Joanna Bentley, the Conduct's[22] daughter, being in his div and Kidson's refrain every time he handed their essays back: 'Rhodes, beaten by a girl again.'

The girls themselves were initially scared of this outwardly misogynist eccentric. **Sarah Compton-Burnett** arrived late for one of Kidson's divs, as luck would have it at the same time as one of the boys, and Kidson ribbing her mercilessly. But as time went by, they were impressed by his kindness and his generosity.

Joanna Bentley wrote on her leaver to Kidson:

22 The Senior Chaplain at Eton is known as the Conduct.

Sir, Despite the fact that initially I was stunned, bemused, frightened to death etc. I am now most grateful. Everyone but everyone must plague you with compliments. I am merely a small voice crying in the wilderness. I am under the impression that you run the school. At least no one would contradict you, would they? Periodically I assured the young women at Eton that they had no reason to be alarmed by your presence; a perfect gentleman in every sense. With love Joanna.

Edmund Marlowe was so impressed by Kidson's performances that he based the character of the Classics master Mr Trotter on him in his first novel *Alexander's Choice*[23] – the two anecdotes depicted below are real Kidsonisms:

Eton was rich in colourful schoolmasters, but Mr Trotter, a tall, distinguished-looking man in his fifties with a rather severe demeanour and glinting spectacles, stood out for his delightful eccentricity, though at first he appeared to be gruff and fairly alarming.

'Weed!' he would call out to a tough-looking boy called Meade, and repeat it louder in apparent exasperation until Meade understood he was meant. Similarly, 'Cook, I mean Baker!' would learn to respond to the former name as his pseudonym and Greene soon got used to being called Brown. During their first div, they wondered if he was a little mad, but watching carefully when they giggled in response to his mistakes, Alexander soon noticed the faint twitch of the corners of Mr Trotter's mouth that alone in his deadpan countenance betrayed the intense pleasure it gave him to bring his class to life in this way.

His third Classics div of the half was repeatedly interrupted by the noise of drilling the other side of the div-room window. After a while, Mr Trotter put down his Greek grammar book, strode up to the window and opened it.

23 (www.amazon.co.uk/Alexanders-Choice-Edmund-Marlowe/dp/1481222112)

'I do hope I'm not boring you,' he boomed at the bewildered builder, closed the window and quickly resumed his discourse on pronouns, as if oblivious of the tittering of the boys.

The next div, he suddenly interrupted their Latin construe to command them to write down the Seven Wonders of the World, though they had never been taught them. He would give a sovereign to any boy who got all seven, he said. Each boy then had to mark his neighbour's answers and announce his own score. Nought, one, or two was the invariable score and elicited mutterings of feigned incredulity at the ignorance of modern schoolboys on the part of Mr Trotter, until Alexander said six. Alexander caught the beak's slightly puzzled look, as though the glass of plonk he thought he was sipping had turned out to be fine claret.

Kidson modified his style to suit the years he was teaching. Younger boys in E Block were granted more humour than those preparing for exams:

Hugo Jackson: The classes were incredibly rich in historical fact and colour and lots of fun – he was a great one for playing to the gallery. I could not wait for the next lesson. He was a natural performer and carried off an austere and almost authoritarian manner, which thinly masked his enjoyment of jokes. Michael was superficially highly disdainful of us, and played up how insignificant we were in the overall life of the school. He would pretend not to know who we were – one classmate, Brooke Lyndon-Stanford, was always deliberately referred to as 'Lytton-Strachey'. Actually, he knew pretty much everyone and their qualities well.

Another, Piers Faccini, might be asked by Michael something like, 'Faccini, when Lord Clive met Siraj's army at Plassey, what was the impact on the East India Company …?' Piers would pause for a fraction of a moment, and almost immediately, Michael would step in, 'I suppose I shouldn't ask you, Faccini. You were, after all, born under bluer skies! Anyway, Clive delivered x, or y …'

We used to antagonise him deliberately by being particularly stupid, in order that Michael would run across and pretend to rough us up. There would be a charge and he would bellow, 'If you don't stop being so idiotic, I'll have to immerse my hands in your warm intestines,' as he just about held himself back from pummelling us. There might be an incredibly gentle pantomime wallop, but it was always done with such humour and completely free of actual menace that we laughed and encouraged it.

Another MGMK game ... He used to play up his absorption in the historical topic at hand by adopting the manner of the intellectually aloof academic. He would walk up and down at the front of the classroom delivering an instructive monologue on some topic with his eyes closed and with a detached, cerebral air. This comic, selective blindness to what was going on around him, allowed us to encourage Boodie – then a puppy – to jump up on our desks and run up and down the classroom from desk to desk. Each boy would lure Boodie to jump to their desk by waving bits of paper in turn, like a Mexican wave. Michael would pretend not to notice what was going on – still speechifying through the clatter and barely suppressed hysterics and the dog running up and down the room at table height.

But despite the rudeness, the outrageous humour and the histrionics, Kidson was very approachable, as another American boy relates:

Minter Dial: I did A level History with MGMK and despite the severe handicap of being American and having rather woolly English, I managed to carve out a higher than expected grade. Still to this day, I am wont to mimic his grand arrival in class. After flinging his cape over the coat rack and stuffing good old Dougal under the desk, he would glibly spend the first few moments tidying the papers, cleaning the blackboard and completely ignoring our presence. Then, he would look up and, startled by finding an outfit of bedraggled boys and expectant eyes, would moan, 'Oh no, not you lot again.' This would be followed by the return of some marked papers, starting with the rips, and some qualifying public remarks whose words I can still hear echoing in my head.

After one such harrowing experience, where I was the recipient of some scathing commentary about writing sadly verbose English and using split infinitives ad infinitum, I took Kidson up on his offer to come by his place for some assistance.

When I arrived at the appointed hour, I knocked sheepishly. He seemed not to notice, even though I could hear him talking to Dougal. I knocked again. The door was whisked open and almost as quickly pushed back.

'What on earth do you want, whatsyourname?'

Bumbling and fumbling, I uttered the words 'help, please'. As if checking his mental agenda, all the while shaking his head, he finally and reluctantly let me in with an, 'Oh well, okay.'

Once inside, I managed to lean over and pet Dougal. A most reassuring moment, until Dougal was summarily told to return to his bed and I was asked if I would like something. Certainly, I replied, but wasn't sure if he meant tea or food, or both.

'Well, boy, what would you like?' he barked. Long pause. 'Coffee? Tea? Milk? Water?'

Relieved on hearing the choice, I asked for some milk. Wrong answer (again).

'No, don't be such a fool, Dial,' so he remembered my name after all. 'I mean a proper drink.'

More angst. Mini-hours passed by, as I tried to conjure up what I could possibly order at this point.

'How about a gin and tonic?'

'Er, um, well, yes, sir, thank you, sir …'

Then I was invited to wait in his sitting-room, accompanied by Dougal. Kidson returned brandishing two rather tall glasses.

'Well, cheers, Dial.'

Then, he took the drink up to his lips and eyed me as I did the same. He took a good swig. I followed. The taste of tonic completely escaped me. I had just gulped down what felt like pure gin. Mustering all the stiff-upper-lip I knew how, I managed not to choke. With that rather sly, impish smile, MGMK started on about some anecdote of history and we thence proceeded to spend the next two hours talking about life. Not once did my ripped paper with a sub-par mark surface. Suffice it to say, I was all the same marked for life.

As a PS, I did stay in touch with Michael and corresponded a few times. I also had the good fortune to spend a more adult drink with him in the 1990s.

What Minter didn't know, until now, is that Kidson was following his progress with interest. A letter in Kidson's files survives from the headmaster of his prep school:

From: THE HEADMASTER

The Old Malthouse,
Langton Matravers,
Swanage, Dorset

30th January 1976

Dear Mr Kidson,
We met last summer when I was accompanying Minter Dial to his General List Examination.You kindly offered your assistance on that occasion if I ever needed advice. I am writing therefore to ask if you could recommend a House for Minter.

He is above all an enthusiast, full of energy, a fine games player, an interested musician, and I think fairly adequate in the classroom.

I would be most grateful if you could make a recommendation.[24]

With many thanks.

Yours sincerely,

Patrick Jordan.

It is just one of many examples that have come to light of this very surprising man's capacity to act behind the scenes for the good of others.

24 Kidson recommended John Peake and Minter thrived in JSBP.

CHAPTER THREE

Private Business

Kidson the tutor

He was always on the lookout for any bud which he could warm with a little sunshine.

W.E. Gladstone, of Eton beak E.C. Hawtrey, quoted by Sir Philip Magnus, from Kidson's commonplace book.

There is no other way of making a reasonable being out of sensuous man than by making him aesthetic first.

Friedrich Schiller, from Kidson's commonplace book.

One of the most important ingredients in Eton's formula, perhaps its most potent, is the tutorial system. Many schools appoint tutors to oversee the academic progress of pupils, leaving the housemasters to concentrate on their pastoral care. Their tutors normally operate within houses and are subordinate to the housemasters. However, at Eton, the tutor is independent of the housemaster and often acts as a counterbalance. And critically, once a boy enters the top two years, he gets to invite the beak of his choice to be his tutor.[25]

As well as overseeing the curricular work, the tutor is expected to

25 In the first three years at Eton, a boy has a Classical Tutor, chosen by the school, but thereafter he can choose his own tutor, known as a Modern Tutor.

broaden the education of his pupils. This normally takes place at weekly sessions, known as Private Business, in the tutor's home. The tutor can interpret these guidelines freely and how he did so would affect his reputation. Some would teach their pupils how to play bridge, or introduce them to their favourite music or poetry. A muscular geographer named Mike Town would move back the furniture and have bouts of Cumbrian wrestling with his pupils. Others were selected for their academic reputations in the hope of securing an Oxbridge place. Some no doubt, this being a single-sex boys' school, on the attractiveness of their wives.

It is probably the most important decision a boy makes.

Andrew Dalrymple: 'Like many before me, and knowing that Michael was the most coveted of modern tutors, I left nothing to chance. Foregoing a last day of pigeon shooting, or some other opportunity to kill something, I took the night train to London, arriving on the morning, rather than the usual evening of the start of half. I recall him being somewhat discomfited at being accosted by a boy, whom I suppose he hardly knew, shortly after breakfast. But perhaps this worked in my favour, since he was probably unable to think of any good reason to turn me down. At any rate, it was perhaps as well that I had taken such precautions, because he took fourteen pupils in my year, quite possibly a record number for a modern tutor, and probably more than the rules would have permitted.'

Nicky Dunne: 'I asked him to be my tutor. He looked right down his nose at me, perplexed and bemused. And then stalked off saying he would think about it. Later I discovered that I had been accepted.'

Kidson seemed to follow E.C. Hawtrey's practice of seeking out boys who needed help and they in turn often found themselves being drawn to him. I hope they will forgive me if I say that Kidson attracted some of the more unorthodox boys in the school. One such was **Charlie Mortimer**, later to become famous as the recipient of the *Dear Lupin* letters, who was drawn to Kidson by the magnetism of his eccentric character. Charlie was more than usually confused by adolescence and was both dyslexic and dispraxic. (He recalls being the only boy in the school who bowled backwards, as the ball kept shooting out of the back of his hand). After he left, his housemaster, Norman Addison, caught a boy smoking in the house.

'But, sir, you let Mortimer smoke.'

'Ah, now there was a boy who really needed to smoke.'

Another was **Nat Rothschild**, scion of the famous banking family, who also found Eton difficult. It is hard to keep a low profile in a place like Eton with a name like Rothschild. He achieved a certain notoriety among the beaks, when in one English div, the beak, Jeff 'Twiggy' Branch, told the boys to open their Milton at page sixty-five. He noticed that Nat had a different book and thought he must be reading some trashy novel instead.

'Rothschild, what is that book you are reading? Give it to me.'

He seized the book and was mortified, then elated, to find that he had in his hands a first edition of *Paradise Lost* worth thousands. Nat had borrowed it from his father's library.

Then there was **Dominic West**, brought up in Yorkshire, the son of a manufacturer. Dominic was worried that Eton would turn him into a soft southerner and later he would describe how being sent away to boarding school was a traumatic experience. He hated leaving home, and admits now, 'That had a major effect on me – it was the worst feeling I have ever had, very similar to the grief when my parents died.'[26]

Luke Douglas-Home was another lost soul at Eton who chose Kidson to be his modern tutor:

Luke Douglas-Home: As pupils, from all the things that we know about Michael – the stories of cursing truck drivers, his shy showmanship while bringing history from one hundred years ago to life, his dog drinking from the loo rather than Michael preparing a water bowl ('It is clean water, isn't it?'), his battles with Paddy Croker, etc. – there was one moment that stands out in my mind of real importance. And, in fact, that was when I decided that I wanted him to be my modern tutor.

26 *Radio Times* interview, 26 July 2016.

I could explain at length why his significance was more to me than most (a very sick, and then dead father in my first years at Eton, a completely new-to-the-job housemaster with his own young family, and so on), but that is uninteresting and uninformative about him. Rather, I would like to try and describe this microcosmic event, which probably lasted only minutes, or even seconds; a vignette that, I think, says a lot about him and explains his lasting influence on me.

Try and imagine a history div. It is late in the afternoon. We boys are quite silent, trying to avoid nodding off and incurring his wrath. Sensing this common afternoon stupor, Michael stands up, to return the EWs (homework) that he has marked and to try and re-inject some life into the afternoon:

'Kelly – not bad, but not good either … Church – why didn't you mention Peel at all?! … Griffin, Curtis … ,' as he hands back each paper, placing them firmly on each desk, he walks briskly to the next desk. The effect of him walking the room, declaiming names and returning papers awakens us. And then, facing a corner of the room with his back to the div, he says, 'Douglas-Home, yes …'

He pirouettes around, peering closer at the paper. 'Douglas-Home MINOR!' and then he strides to the front of the room and glares at me at the back (aged fourteen). He holds the paper out, as though it smells.

'This … ,' he pauses, his volume rising almost to an angry shout. 'THIS is why your MOTHER comes down all the way from LONDON and CRIES ON MY SHOULDER.'

Laughter throughout the class is unstoppable.

'Cries on my shoulder,' he then says quietly, and he discards my work on the floor as he walks on. 'Williams, Newton … ,' and I have to walk over and pick up my work, with sniggers.

It was an early lesson: with his sense of theatre, it was not so much about the repeal of the Corn Laws of 1846, but more on taking a surprise humiliation. As a young schoolboy at that time, the idea of a mother being involved in your school life was anathema. I did not know my mum had been down to see him. No one else in that room knew that my father had died just weeks before,[27] except Kidson and me.

I was still consumed by loss, and while not being rough about my shoddy work, he was trying humorously to cajole me out of it. At the end of that div, the imperceptible glimmer of a tiny, wry smile – and then it was gone. When I reminded him of it twenty-five years later, I saw that same, almost imperceptible, smirk. 'You have to try and make people laugh, don't you?'

The perceived wisdom is that he looked after the academically awkward, the indolent and the lazy, by Eton standards. I think that is the wrong way around. We saw (those of us who chose him to be our tutor) someone who would help us to survive in the Eton system, with humour.

I suppose I was similar to Luke in the way that I heard a kind of dog whistle. Like many of my generation, I was struggling to come to terms with my parents' divorce three years before I arrived.[28] As soon as my voice broke, the hormones altered my state of mind and I drifted through my time at Eton in a concussed state that we would now call clinical depression.

Although I never unburdened myself to Michael about it, somehow I knew that he understood how I felt. And that was enough.

* * *

The first thing that any boy noticed about Michael Kidson's flat was the notice on the door, written on Fortnum & Mason headed notepaper. It was a signpost to a hidden sanctuary, a land apart from the rest of Eton.

---

27 Charles Douglas-Home, Editor of *The Times*, 1982–5, died 29 October 1985.

28 Although there were nothing like as many broken homes as there had been two generations before. My father's godfather was at Eton after the First World War, when only two boys in his house had fathers alive.

Fortnum & Mason

Please push open the door and walk in.
If it is not on the latch, knock: there is no need to ring the bell (which is maddeningly strident).

Regrettably – if there is no reply, then I am not in, or not available.

If the dog is outside the door, kindly DO NOT LET HIM IN. Guard against his artfully insinuating himself, or even, in extremis, trying to use force, for he is a tricky and determined character.

Anyone who allows him in will not be welcome.

Nicky Dunne: 'The bland stairwell and cheap door with its ugly metal pull gave no clue to the contents inside. For an adolescent boy struggling with the hidebound rules of a boarding school, it was like entering Narnia. Sometimes there was a key in the lock, sometimes it could be found beneath the mat outside. Music would be playing, quite loudly. Mozart or Handel. "Sir? Are you there?" Silence. "Sir?" Long pause. "Of course I am here, you imbecile." In you would go. "Sir? Where are you?" Longer pause. "I am in the bath, you clothead." His flat was a kind of refuge and an enchanted world. The entrance hall and the small sitting-room beyond were drenched in high culture, an oil painting or drawing covering every inch of wall space.'

To be tutored by Michael was to enter an arcane world that was far broader and deeper than any that the mainstream school had to offer.

It was a very elite club and the other members were invariably kindred spirits. It had its own language. He talked about someone of whom he took a dim view as being a 'very moderate man'. A pupil could be a 'constant disappointment'. A favourite term was 'I dare say'. Someone with a bloated ego would be 'full of hot air' or a 'fat fool'. A hero would be 'of the first rank'. BP was 'an excellent company – I would recommend it to anyone to work there.' One's efforts were invariably 'perfunctory' or 'trite'. One aspired in one's essays to be 'trenchant'. It was important to broaden one's vocabulary, but only if one was able to pronounce words correctly in accordance with 'Fowler'.

Although he was a History beak, he would have been just as comfortable teaching English Literature or History of Art. In fact, he did sometimes teach an O Level English division and **Andrew Joicey** remembers his opening remark on their set text, *Pride and Prejudice*: 'This is a delicious book and I have read it fourteen times.'

As well as History, Private Business encompassed classical music, nineteenth-century sporting art, a love of antiques, golf of a very Wodehousian sort, great literature and numerous anecdotes about interesting people 'who died the other day'.[29]

Time spent in Kidson's company was never dull. He was remorselessly didactic, determined to improve every aspect of our beings at every opportunity: 'Don't say hopefully, it makes you sound like a football manager,' or, 'I hope that's not a Windsor knot in your necktie, is it?'

But whereas this would have been tiresome coming from most other beaks, it was always conducted with such humour and withering lightness of touch that it seldom grated. He taught us important lessons in life: how to give and receive a bollocking, the value of a well-turned insult. He corrected our pronunciation and commented with asperity on our dress but, above all, it was his mission to civilise us that made life interesting. He was always hinting at a hinterland that we should aspire to inhabit.

The quote at the beginning of this chapter, about needing to make us aesthetic first, which I only saw when I read his commonplace books after his death, struck a chord immediately. He took the *Spectator* and four

29 The definition of the other day was generally taken to be any time during Kidson's lifetime.

Sunday newspapers and would encourage us to read obituaries and book reviews to broaden our knowledge. He was always making comments like, 'Of course, I go to Venice every year,' or, 'Yes, well I read all of Jane Austen's novels every year,' as if this was the usual *modus vivendi* of a gentleman of taste.

Often, he would read to us. Jamie Sainsbury particularly remembers excerpts from Huxley's *CromeYellow*. Others remember Somerset Maugham and Saki short stories. I have a very vivid memory of Kidson introducing us – mostly, I suspect, for the first time, stoutly Philistine country boys that we were – to Beethoven's 6th, or Pastoral Symphony. I remember, as if it were yesterday, Michael explaining the composer's thinking behind the work. How we were to imagine walking in the countryside beside a babbling brook and then getting caught in a storm and finally the shining tranquillity of the scene when the sun comes out again. Then he put the record on his old gramophone, turned the lights off, and we sat back and listened. I still do, when I have had a hard day, and find myself transported back to the sanctuary of his flat. And when I took the first faltering steps along the road of parenthood, I played it to my children, when they were babies, to try to get them to sleep.

He was of that wartime generation who lived almost in the dark, either through thrift or for fear of the Luftwaffe. His flat, while furnished with a masculine utilitarianism that interior designers might sniff at, was full of interesting things: ticking clocks, leather-bound books, good Georgian furniture and – his passion – sporting art. He gave the impression that he was a dilettante, a connoisseur of the finer things in life, who just happened to be our tutor as well; studied amateurism that probably infuriated his colleagues, but helped to endear him to us, wannabe gifted amateurs that we were.

One time he asked us all what we wanted to do when we finished being educated. I remember saying that, after following the rest of my family into the Coldstream Guards, I wanted to go home and farm, but – and I probably blushed at this point – I thought I might try my hand at writing as well, to help make ends meet. He gave a little half-smile, which I took to mean that he didn't think this was an entirely ludicrous proposition. But then he sighed, 'Ah, we would all like to write, but it's so hard to make a living out of it, the hardest way of all, I think.' Nothing more was said about my literary aspirations, but months later, before the holidays, he pressed two books on me: *The Great Gatsby* by F. Scott Fitzgerald and *The Leopard* by Giuseppe di Lampedusa.

There was no tiresome instruction to write an essay, or prepare to discuss them on my return, I was just to read them. He said something about my needing to read something well-written to improve my deplorable English, if I was ever to pass any A levels. But years later, I made the connection with the earlier conversation, and wondered if it was his way of trying to hitch my wagon to the literary firmament. The books, which I enjoyed very much, both had Kidsonian overtones when I later reflected on them: one about a man with a mysterious past and an unrequited love affair, the other about a man struggling sadly but humorously to come to terms with a changing world.

My own children went to Ampleforth, and Michael was very similar to a Benedictine monk in his commitment to his boys,[30] his worldliness and individual, but nonetheless strict, moral code that accorded with a higher authority, but ignored the conventional pettiness of school life. Although he didn't attempt to proselytise[31] and he wore his faith lightly. He wasn't in the slightest bit churchy, but was probably a more effective Christian for it. Most of us would think of him as the ultimate Good Samaritan.

Going to see him, one was frequently offered a stiff drink, usually gin and tonic, with an elaborate ritual of hunting for ice and lemon and a paraphrased aphorism of Churchill's that 'no gentleman would ever drink gin and tonic without lemon'. It must have cost him a fortune in gin over the years. He wasn't a great boozer himself – it would have been disastrous

30 The first of my son's outstanding housemasters, a monk named Father Chad Boulton, told me that he had sixty-two boys in his house and sixty-two beads on his rosary, 'and boy, do I have to pray hard for some of them.'

31 There would have been little point in a school where we went to chapel every morning by Henry VI's edict.

if he had been – and it was another way that he civilised us, helping us to learn to enjoy a drink in an adult fashion.

He once unwittingly, though, contributed to a near-fatal accident through his generosity. Richard Pilkington and I called in to see him on our way back from Tap. Michael, not realising that we were already quite tanked up, suggested we try some excellent malt that he had. It was the first time I had tasted Laphroaig (another gap in my education filled by MGMK). I can still taste its unique, seaweedy flavour now. It must have been very special, as it came in an earthenware bottle. We chatted and then headed back to our house, somewhat the worse for wear. On our way back, we decided to pull into the bike shed for a quick fag.[32] The first drag of nicotine had a catalytic effect on the beer from Tap and Michael's malt and I passed clean out on the concrete floor, giving myself quite a dent on my forehead.

Later on, I did join the Army, partly on Michael's advice. He said that as I was very idle, and liked drinking gin, the Army and I would be well-suited to each other. Perhaps his own very brief spell in the Army had imprinted something on his character. Looking back, I think part of the secret of Michael's success as a tutor was that his relationship with us was more like an enlightened senior major with wayward subalterns, than that of tutor and tutees.

Sitting in his flat, with Michael perched on the bum-rest[33] beneath an oil painting of hunters at grass, was like being in an officers' mess with the same good-natured banter. He had a Rabelaisian wit; any suggestion of sexual bravado by a pupil was met with a withering glance from him and the comment, 'You wouldn't know what to do with it, you probably think it's for stirring your tea.' Of more diffident pupils, he would say, 'He needs rogering by a big black woman – that would sort him out.'

Michael did much to develop the strength of our characters, as we learnt that we had to stand up to him to earn his respect, and I am sure

32 American readers may be confused by this – it means a cigarette!

33 Ditto, this means a club fender.

that his dry sense of humour also rubbed off on his pupils. The formality of the classroom was relaxed a little, but he would maintain a comfortable distance by teasing us with mock severity.

Hugh Roche: 'I was even shorter then than I am now and I couldn't sit straight in his armchairs with my feet touching the ground. He would always put me in the highest one then say, "Will you sit straight, man! Sit with your back against the back of the chair and put both feet on the ground." And I would be pulled into all sorts of contortions!'

We were forgiven almost anything except being boring or smelly. Pupils who failed to have an opinion, even a daft one, or who thought that a grunt sufficed for conversation, were liable to be subjected to a tirade of abuse: 'You're so boring, why can't you just say something, anything!' Likewise anyone who appeared still smelling as if they had crawled out of the bottom of a rugby scrum was given a painfully detailed critique of their personal hygiene.

Ed Smyth-Osbourne recalls: 'He sometimes gave me a hard time, but I can say that his rather unique blend of ostensible criticism was directed with the best of intentions, though whether to improve or to instil backbone I was never quite sure! Both were valuable in their own way.[34] My inadequate knowledge of the arts, born no doubt of my dubious West Country heritage, prompted an all-too regular refrain of "You Philistine, Smyth-Osbourne", but seeing that I was beyond hope, he despatched me with Sir Edward Creasy's *The Fifteen Decisive Battles of the World* and talked of Fuller[35] in a rather more elucidating way than many Staff College instructors over a decade later. I remember him to this day walking into a History Division and telling us to take out a sheet of paper and write down everything we knew about Robert Nairac, the morning after his posthumous George Cross was announced. Suffice to say, whether

34 Ed was later a distinguished SAS officer, so if any work on his backbone was required it certainly did the trick.

35 Major General J.F.C. Fuller, who with Basil Liddell Hart became the guru of armoured warfare after the First World War and codified the principles of war. His theories still permeate military doctrine today.

it was Palmerstonian Gunboat Diplomacy, Gladstone's foibles or Nairac's heroism, you never forgot it, because he made it interesting.'

Private Business with MGMK became one of the highlights of the week:

Andrew Dalrymple: Thus began a very happy two years of being one of Michael's pupils, a period that entirely transformed my enjoyment of Eton, and made them especially happy. He was a very charismatic and engaging person, and there was something particularly comforting about his study. Perhaps it was the highly congenial surroundings, the books, the paintings, and good furniture, or maybe it was his ever-present springer spaniel, Dougal. Or on second thoughts, the not-always present Dougal, because of the notice on his door.

But it was also the fact that being with Michael was never dull, and his 'privates' were invariably fun. We would often discuss current affairs; our opinions were expected, his were characteristically robust, and of course, always right. 'That silly little boy who is now our Foreign Secretary (a young David Owen), the Russians will eat him for breakfast!'

Of course, this would be followed by unhappy comparisons with a 'giant like Palmerston – what on earth are we coming to?' He also loved reading us passages from his favourite books: Tolstoy's account of death in *War and Peace*, or the treatise on Pride – 'by far the worst of all the deadly sins' – we were warned darkly never to be proud.

The dictionary game was perhaps his favourite. Extracting some improbably obscure word from one of the two volumes of his Oxford Dictionary, we would all be invited to manufacture a plausible definition. These would then be read out by Michael, including one of his own, as well as the genuine article, and we had to judge which was correct. There would be much screwing up of the face and comments of 'how absurd', 'how could it possibly be that', or hooting with laughter, as he read out ours, while his own was, of course, attended with gravity and conviction, so that he was invariably victorious. But even without such trickery, he would naturally have won handsomely, since he was a consummate wordsmith and grammarian.

His kindness was legendary, and it was always fun to call in unannounced, which many of us were inclined to do in the late afternoon, when you could be sure of a bit of tea, some toast, and a happy half-hour. At least, this was certainly so, provided you did not let Dougal in if he was outside, or use a buttery knife to extract your jam or honey. If that happened, the jar, however full, was deemed to be unusable thereafter: 'You might as well just take it away with you now, damn you, I certainly can't use it again!'

Nicky Dunne: 'Tutorials were unusual. He performed, but more "piano" than the "fortissimo" of his divisions. I remember one long evening discussing Oscar Wilde. He hinted at a way to live and to think beyond the conventions of a public school. His dismissive attitude towards the school rules and those who enforced them was like manna from heaven. Being included in his inner world was an intense privilege. He made no concessions to us. He barked out his opinions on painters, writers, composers and challenged us to disagree. This was trust, and it felt like the world was ours, and that with his approval we were finally mature enough to make it our own.'

Martin Humphreys: 'He was my Modern Tutor for one term (seventh term Oxbridge). I vividly recall his crowded flat and that green mini, which he filled with boys to visit Hughenden Manor.

'One day a fellow tutee and I knocked nervously on his door for a tutorial. "Come!" was the bellowed command. We were somewhat taken aback to find that Michael was in the bath, door narrowly ajar. We retreated. Not wise. He insisted we conduct the tutorial through the bathroom door. Surreal.'

Ian Marr: 'About half-a-dozen of us would go round to his flat for a tutorial, which could be anything from a general-knowledge quiz – nobody ever got more than two out of a hundred: cue massive histrionics of disbelief from Michael, at the end of which we were dismissed and he would decide if we were ever allowed to return – to a pronunciation test (combat should be pronounced "cumbut", solder as "sodder", and so on).'

The most abiding memory for **Eliot Woolf** is the day he was sent to meet Kidson, ahead of him becoming his tutor the following year: 'He asked me what A levels I was proposing to take. I told him that they were History, Geography and Spanish. In his inimitable way, he responded that I would not be taking Spanish, I would instead be doing History of Art … and in that single moment, I found myself embarking upon a study of History of Art, which became my favourite A level by a long distance, my subsequent choice of degree, and triggered a love of art that has stayed with me ever since. Spanish would have been a disaster!'

Tom Birch Reynardson: 'I spent quite a lot of time with Michael in his flat, chatting away, often with Migs Greenall in attendance, who at that time was a close friend of his. They seemed to me to have an excellent relationship, mobbing each other up, sometimes being quite rude, but always having a laugh, Migs smoking copious numbers of cigarettes ("disgusting habit", as Michael was only too keen to point out to her, with a grin). Sadly, they fell out. I think Michael found the close companionship of a woman quite trying.

'An important obsession of his was pronunciation and the use of English and, of course, his extremely well-thumbed Fowler's *Modern English Usage* was never far from his chair, so that he could point out to us how abominable was our grammar and pronunciation. This always gave us the opportunity to wind him up by mispronouncing "combat", for example, or splitting an infinitive, which normally provoked a huge explosion, but I do not think he ever threw the revered Fowler at us.

'Of course, he was quite liberal with his drink and "Help yourself, dear boy" was a familiar cry. I remember visiting him once with a streaming cold and he told me, "For God's sake, boy, have a hot whisky and stop that ghastly snivelling." The cold disappeared pretty well immediately and this has been the answer to any ailment ever since!'

Harry Nuttall: 'Frequently he would be in the bath with a suitable beaker of whisky, while we, his motley pupils, were arranged around his drawing-room listening raptly to his frequent musings. Not very PC, but then he wasn't.

'He was an enormous help during A level revision. I was allowed to sit surrounded by his books in his dining-room in the evening – he provided beer, sandwiches, and an ashtray (in case I felt the need to smoke).'

Hugh Graham-Watson: 'You may remember, if you ever had tea with Michael, that he cooked his boiled eggs for six minutes and, somehow, they always came out perfectly and he also seemed to have a constant supply of eggs with double yolks. A six-minute egg and a double yolk was a wonder to me!'

Simon Broackes: 'I was extremely fond of Michael. At our first meeting, he commented, "I see your mother is called Joyce ... my cleaning lady is called Joyce!"

'He was also a shareholder in my father's company,[36] and would berate me if the share price had fallen.'

Michael was always the person to go to if one needed help writing a difficult letter, as another boy remembers: 'I was very grateful after I had received a rather handsome amount of money at the age of seventeen from a godmother – £5,000, quite a sum in 1970 – when he helped me to draft a thank-you letter, which started with a classic Michael informal introduction, "I just wanted to send you a note to say ..." It can't have gone down badly, because she gave me another £20,000 forty years later. (But please don't quote my name with this!)'

Maurice Fermoy tells of an amusing moment in his second year of the Eton Corps: 'We had to don a disguise and try to bluff our way to the central Corps office in New Schools Yard, with the cannon guarded by the "enemy". Kidson lent me his deerstalker hat, tweed suit, stalking stick, half-moon glasses *and* Boodle, his dog. Anyway, I set off, head down, up Eton High Street from his flat, going for the direct route, dragging this bloody dog along with me. Unsurprisingly enough, I was rumbled and

36 Sir Nigel Broackes was chairman of the Trafalgar House group, which included the Ritz Hotel.

turned and fled, tweeds flapping, with Boodle cantering alongside!'

And, of course, Kidson was a man of the Turf, as **Cornelius Lysaght** remembers: 'It was because of Michael that I did not win anything for what should have been an early "winning" bet. It was the January half and we were walking down Eton High Street for some reason or another. Knowing my love of racing, he asked me if I had been at Kempton on Boxing Day for the King George. I replied that Kempton was a little too far away from my family home in Herefordshire, so instead my father and I had been at Wolverhampton (this was 1970s Wolverhampton, before the artificial "all-weather" track was in place).

'I can hear his words now: "No, I can absolutely assure you, you were not; there's no jumping at Wolverhampton."

'"But I was, sir," I insisted maybe two or three times, and growing ever more emboldened, I asked for a £5 bet on the matter. After a moment considering, he gave a reply I so often use myself in such circumstances when doubts begin to arise.

'"No, certainly not; I wouldn't want to take your money."

'I think of MGMK every time I say it.'

Michael's greatest gift was his companionship, which he offered to so many boys attending school at Eton – often very different people:

Tom Goff: Michael was a complete breath of fresh air to so many of us. He injected enthusiasm and joy into our lives and helped us to understand the human condition: he kept on saying to me that love of, kindness to, and knowledge of other people was the only true way to understand the world and to unlock the door to one's own fulfilment and happiness.

He was incredibly good to me and to countless others. Much is made of Michael's wit, which was often hilarious, but among his various arts was his empathy and kindness that he imparted to so many of us – not only those in his own tutorship. I feel we all recognised in Michael someone who could bring kindred spirits together; he made us feel that we could walk on water. 'Politeness,' he always said, 'costs you absolutely nothing.' How right he was.

He offered good advice. 'Follow your heart. Only that organ which God has given you will lead you to happiness. Your life is yours to live. No one's going to do it for you.' He also said to me umpteen times: 'Please don't come back and see me in fifteen years and say, "If only I'd worked harder!" Superb advice, which I do not think I totally heeded!

Private Business with MGMK contained many unusual events. His particular favourite was *The Muppet Show*. He would instruct you to, 'Turn on the telly, put on the Muppets, and then make yourself a good whisky and soda.' Meanwhile Michael turned to his desk for at least a quarter-of-an-hour's writing. He would then comment, 'Do tell me when Kermit's coming on. I LOVE him. And PLEASE stop smoking so much, your parents would not approve!'

In the early years, to Dave Ker and his contemporaries, Kidson was like a cool, young uncle. As he grew older, the role changed subtly to one of dottily benevolent great-uncle, and so did the relationship with his boys.

Hugo Jackson: 'Will Pease and I used to see if we could get a rise out of him outside Chambers. By this time, we were in the later part of "C" or early "B" block. We had got to know him very well and were very close to him. Anyway, Michael used to walk with a slight stoop – leaning a bit to one side – which I am sure he used to exaggerate at times for the "Ministry of Funny Walks" comic factor. When he left Chambers in a cloud of other beaks, if we happened to bump into him, we would walk alongside him and very gently imitate his stride. When he noticed, he would ham it up with a mock-injured tone, and would chide us for insensitivity to people who have to struggle with their misfortunes and disabilities.

'Taking things a bit further, we would say, "Oh, come on, give us a hug, sir, it's only because you're really like a father-figure to us that we feel we can tease you …" We would mob him a bit and put our arms around his shoulder. Naturally, there would be a sharp theatrical start and he would hiss with exaggerated embarrassment that we were humiliating him in front of his colleagues and we were immediately to go away. He would then try to stride off as we followed in his wake, making up reasons he needed to stop and talk to us. All through this, whilst pretending to be affronted and appalled at the lapse in standards, he would have a delighted twinkle in his eye and be holding back a laugh.'

Kidson's generosity and wide-ranging education were not confined to Eton's campus:

Andrew Dalrymple: One week, he announced to us all that he had never been to the cinema, which he insisted on pronouncing with a hard 'c', despite our protestations. So we arranged to take him, and the next week, we trooped across Windsor Bridge to the ageing establishment that was more-or-less opposite the Old House Hotel. There was the usual long advertising programme, which caused him some impatience, but was much enlivened by the advert for a local estate agent, whom we were told would be able to advise us on all aspects of our property purchase. Michael immediately, and rather too loudly, said that someone needed to advise him on where to find a decent tailor, causing a certain stirring amongst the immediate audience.

Anyway, we watched Clint Eastwood in one of the quite violent *Dirty Harry* films, much in vogue at that moment, and which, rather reluctantly, he was forced to admit he enjoyed, saying, 'He makes that James Bond fellow look like a complete patsy!' Of course, therefore, he must have been to the 'kinema' before.

Most of Michael's pupils were taken to prominent local houses in an attempt to civilise them, since we were habitually described as 'complete Philistines', and I well remember being taken to Waddesdon Manor one fine Sunday afternoon, in the summer half. We set off, crammed into his green mini, lunched well at a local pub, where a certain amount was drunk and even smoked, despite his admonition of the 'deleterious effects of smoking', and then went on a tour of the house.

We were about halfway round, in one of the innumerable, treasure-filled rooms, overseen by elderly women, when **Hugo Guinness** said, 'Hey, sir, you know with only these old women sitting around here, we could have half this stuff out of the house and be gone before they even wake up!'

Audible sigh. 'Guinness, you must first consider whether you would ever be able to enjoy possessing anything which you had obtained nefariously. I know I couldn't.'

Jeremy Harbord: 'When I was taken with two others to see *Dr Zhivago* (Michael: "The best novel written since the war … etc.") at the ABC Cinema in Windsor, two girls sitting behind us were whispering rather loudly and rustling sweet papers, immediately getting on Michael's nerves. So he got up, physically turned round, and almost shouted, "WILL you stop making so much noise!" Hoots of laughter from us boys, of course.'

Richard Forwood: 'A classic Kidson tale was when we bullied him into taking us to see Dame Edna Everage perform in London. We sat in seats close to the stage. From the start, Dame Edna was picking on the audience, particularly those just below him, and his eyes kept falling on the incredibly disapproving face of Michael. I think it was at first a steely stare from Michael at Dame Edna, and then his spending the rest of the performance sleeping or pretending to be asleep, that kept them apart. I have always wondered what reply Dame Edna would have received if "she" had been unwise enough to pick on Michael.'

Anthony Whitaker: 'Michael took a group of us to London in about 1970 to see the epic film *Waterloo*. Robin Smith-Ryland bought an ice cream in the interval but, by the end of the film, most of it had somehow ended up on the floor. When the lights came up, Michael said, in a loud voice, "Smith-Ryland, why have you ejaculated on the carpet?"'

Hugo Jackson continues: 'Once, Michael got a minibus to take the tutorial to Hughenden – there must have been eight or ten of us. When we got there, I got in trouble for letting Boodie jump out of the window of the van and run around the grounds out of control. So, Boodie and I were both shut in the van and I was forbidden from getting out, as a penance, while the rest of the tutorial toured the house and grounds. But, of course, after a ceremonial wait of about five minutes, I went off and found the group.

There was a certain amount of pretend shock at my disobedience and then everything was forgotten.

'On the way back to school, however, Michael described how nice it would be for us to go to the pub for a pint, as it was a beautiful afternoon. We all got geared up for this treat and then, with perfect comic timing, he pulled the rug from under us while blaming me: "Well, it really would be pleasant to be able to visit a nice pub for a glass of beer, but I'm afraid that with Jackson's Lilliputian stature none of us would get served at all … so, that plan's off! I'm afraid, Jackson, you've let us down again."'

Finally, **Tom Goff** has fond memories of a night at the opera: 'Of many experiences with MGMK, which included Ascot, Windsor and Kempton Races, Michael very kindly took us on one magical night to Glyndebourne. It was a beautiful summer's evening in June of 1984 – Mozart and *The Magic Flute*. Michael loved it – as did all of us. But it was very hot in Black Tie. Nonetheless, MGMK had it all covered with at least four bottles of ice-cold Chablis, prawns, salmon, and plenty of water in a cold box, and a driver.

'He looked after us all superbly and he obviously took such pleasure in taking us there. But he reminded us firmly on our return to school that A levels were but two weeks away, so, "Get to it!" A happy night.'

CHAPTER FOUR

Crime and Punishment

Distrust all in whom the impulse to punish is powerful.

Nietsche, from Kidson's commonplace book

It was very good of Kidson to take me on as a pupil when he was heavily oversubscribed. You will have gathered by now that I was not a model schoolboy. My poor mother lived in constant dread of the telephone call asking her to come and take me away. My father was equally concerned, but a bit conflicted: part-way through my time there, it emerged that neither he nor my uncle had quite stayed the course at Eton, which added piquancy to the issue. I was beaten three times. The third occasion was one of the last floggings in Eton's history. It was in Michael McCrum's last half as Head Master, before handing over to the altogether more genial Eric Anderson, an Enlightenment figure who banished the cane forever.[38]

It was Ascot week and my friend Peter Stanley and I were leaning on the counter in a haze of smoke, filling in betting slips in Joe Coral's in Windsor like men of the world, fifteen-year-old men of the world. Suddenly, from nowhere I felt a hand on my shoulder. I turned to find the President of Pop, who told us both to follow him outside.

We were sent to see our housemasters, then left to stew for a few days. It was quite a stew, as we were both on final warnings. The President of Pop, Duncan Beardsley, later sent an apology via a senior boy in my house. Apparently, the manager of Coral's had been aggravated by losing money

38 Actually, had he not done so, it would have been banned by statute anyway in 1999.

to boys (we always had very good tips: those Eton connections again) and had telephoned the Head Master to drop us in it – hence Duncan had been dispatched to make an arrest. I have never darkened the door of a Joe Coral's since.

I have always thought that the Armed Forces are pretty good at handling the theatrical dimension of summary justice, but they have nothing on Eton, not since the time of Hornblower anyway.[39] After nearly a week of pondering our fate (actually the authorities were probably doing a fair bit of pondering as well, but we didn't consider the problem from their angle), we were 'on the Bill'.

The door of my English div crashed open and a Praeposter[40] strode in.

'Is Blackett in this division sir?'[41]

'He is.'

'He is to see the Head Master in the Bill now.'

It is not a long walk from Alington Schools up Common Lane to the Head Master's classroom at the other end of Upper School from the Chapel – about 300 yards – but it felt like the retreat from Moscow. Once there, I met up with other miscreants, Peter among them, and we were made to wait, and wait. Eventually it was my turn and I was marched in front of the Head Man by the Praeposter. He sat behind a desk on a raised dais, so that he towered above me like the judge in a Bateman cartoon. I began to feel rather small.

I never thought McCrum was a barrel of laughs, but I suppose I would say that, wouldn't I? Given that we had what you might call an Arnold–Flashman relationship. Maybe he was a mine of filthy stories when he was with his cronies at the Athenaeum, after a second decanter of port, but I doubt it somehow. Kidson thought very highly of him and McCrum's son

39 Eton was a little behind the times. The Royal Navy and the Army had abolished corporalpunishment in 1881.

40 A senior boy with silver buttons on his waistcoat to denote that he was one of the twenty brainiest boys in the school.

41 Although we talked about being 'on the bill', Praeposters always used the correct terminology of 'in the bill'.

Steve was my house captain in my first year; a renaissance man, he would stand at the top of the stairs in a gold lamé Pop waistcoat playing the theme to *The Pink Panther* on a saxophone. So, because I have respect for Kidson's judgement of character and because he was Steve's dad, I'm prepared to give him the benefit of the doubt and say that he was a good man, just on the wrong side of history on this occasion.

He scared me shitless.

I cannot remember exactly what he said, but you can probably imagine the gist of it. As he went on, it looked as if there was a chance that I was not going to be expelled after all. So when he finally said, 'You are going to be beaten, go and wait outside,' there was a huge sense of relief, rather like being told that you are not going to face a firing squad, you are going to have your balls chopped off instead.

There was another long wait. I daresay the Head Man went and had a cup of coffee or maybe he needed to limber up.

Act 3, Scene 1: The Praeposter opened his third door of the day for me and I began the long walk down Upper School. The sight before me was rather like the one that greeted Anne Boleyn on that last, fateful walk across Tower Green. At the far end, there was the large oak block in the middle of the floor. Behind it loomed the Head Man, the executioner, glaring at me like a particularly lugubrious funeral director at a dropped coffin.

Other people say that they saw one of the school chaplains in the corner, like a sort of UN observer, but I never saw him, I was too busy focusing on that damn block. Or maybe it was a ghost they saw, like the sly shade of a rural dean, and I could not see it. The block was always placed about level with where my grandfather had his name carved on the wall. I thought the old rake would have been grimly amused by my present predicament.

When I finally reached the scene of my nemesis, McCrum pointed to the block and told me to kneel and hold onto the bar. The first thing that struck me was that, whereas the block itself was of oak so ancient that it had turned almost black, the bar must have been broken by a previous occupant and replaced in brand new pine. I wonder what the joiner thought when he came from Slough to fix it.

I have always had very knobbly knees and it was sore kneeling on the wood. The step was just too far above the ground so that my feet scrabbled for a toehold on the polished wooden floor, like a man dangling on the end of a rope in a spaghetti western.

I heard McCrum walk over and select a cane from the portable rack that had been placed to one side, rather as a Sunday morning golfer pulls a nine-iron from his bag. He came back and I felt the tip of the cane flick my tails up over my back. Then he took two steps back.

The sound of the cane whistling through the air and the thwack of it across my body was like the crack and thump of a bullet passing overhead. The initial shock was followed by a pain so sharp that I could not tell whether it was hot or cold. Root-canal surgery does not come close. The received wisdom was that if you cried out he hit you harder. Whatever, I was determined not to let the bastard hear me yelp. But the pain had to go somewhere. An animal howl started somewhere deep inside me, coursed through my body, and bouncing off clenched teeth, escaped through my nostrils with a muffled squeak.

He paused for effect, then took two steps back again with the fluency of a ballroom dancer and had at me again. He had perfect rhythm, backwards and forwards like a metronome. The effort of kneeling, head down, holding my breath to avoid making a sound, started to make my head swim.

The seventh stroke is the worst. It means that he regards six of the best as a hoary old cliché and means to go on.

After the eighth stroke, he stopped.

'Now get up.'

I shuffled to my feet, relieved that I could stand on jelly legs and forced myself to look him in the eye as I shook his hand.

'I hope that will teach you to behave in future.'

Some hope.

Hey ho, what doesn't kill you makes you stronger. At the time, I remember a feeling of elation as I walked back to my house. There was still the messy technicality of a final warning, my third as it happened, but otherwise it was over. The alternative might have been hours of community service, which would have been far less palatable.

My wife likes to shock dinner guests sometimes by revealing that she can still see the scars where the wheals have turned white on my skin. But the scars are certainly not mental. I do not need counselling and nor, since I know you are dying to ask, has it turned me into some sort of sado-masochist. Although there was something fascinating about the pain, it was not remotely erotic.[42]

I cannot speak for the Head Man, but I do not think it turned him on either. It was just what headmasters did in those days. McCrum had served in the Royal Navy in the war and after the horrors of Atlantic convoys, his definition of hardship was probably rather different to what ours is today. I think in his old-fashioned mindset he believed he was doing me a favour, which in a funny sort of way he was. I was later able to reflect, when confronted by the tender mercies of the Guards Depot, that it is quite good to get some really bad experiences over early in life, so that the other ones do not seem so tough.

Michael McCrum beat boys quite regularly. He once beat a boy for riding his bike down Judy's Passage at night without showing any lights. One old boy I spoke to had been given twelve strokes of the cane, possibly a post-war record. He had been admitted to the sanatorium shortly after being caught and his co-defendant had been beaten and had contrived to have a tape-recorder concealed on his person, which he much enjoyed playing back to his friend in his sick bed.

Perturbed by this foretaste, he had gone to see the Head Master wearing protection. McCrum gave him six strokes, then stopped and asked him if he was wearing padding. The boy denied it at first then, under pressure, confessed. He was sent outside to remove the padding, before being brought back in for another six.

---

42 I visited Eton the other day and Andrew Gailey, the Vice Provost, showed me the block. I knelt on it for old times' sake and to ensure accuracy in my account. I fear he thought me a bit weird.

Despite this record McCrum was, in fact, viewed in some quarters as a dangerous liberal when he banned the practices of boys beating boys during his tenure.[43] Charlie Mortimer, who was there ten years before me, was beaten by his house captain,[44] and there must still be lots of awkward encounters at drinks parties when injured parties bump into their beaters. Dave Ker, one of Kidson's early pupils and one of his closest disciples, was the Chairman of Pop in 1969[45] when its members decided to put a stop to 'Pop tanning', a form of gang-beating where boys who had stepped out of line would be summoned for an interview without coffee in the Pop Room and prefects would line up to take a swipe one by one.

In marketing terms, I am one of the last of the baby boomers and, although the boundary was set for purely demographic reasons, it seems there really was a change in attitudes around that time, which made the experiences of baby boomers very different from Generation X's. It was a time of progress or decline, depending on which camp you are in, change anyhow, and one should not leap to judgement about something considered as normal at the time.

Kidson had clear views on the matter. After he was beaten by the Head Master, **Charlie Mortimer** wrote to his sister Jane to say that he was heartened by his tutor, Mr Kidson, 'saying that he thought beating was anachronistic, barbarian, repulsive and very revolting'.

Looking back, it was a blessing that I was not thrown out. My life might have turned out very differently if I had been. I have often wondered if Kidson spoke up for me and helped to swing the decision in my favour on that occasion. I was up to him for History, but he was yet to be my Modern Tutor, so I cannot be sure that he was involved; but he often acted as a sort of guardian angel and usually we were completely unaware

43 Housemasters were still allowed to beat, but by the end of the 1970s all of them chose not to. McCrum is also sometimes credited with banning fagging, but in fact this was done either by housemasters or by house captains on a piecemeal basis.

44 An Indian prince, the Maharajah of Jodhpur, just to add a little post-Raj glamour to the historical footnote.

45 Readers may be confused as to why Pop needs a Chairman as well as a President. The reasons are lost in the mists of time.

of his help. In his papers, I came across a copy of a letter he wrote about another boy:

14th October 1987

134–135 High Street,
Eton

Dear Head Master,

Your immediate reaction to this is likely to be 'Why doesn't he mind his own business?'

******* ****** *came to see me late yesterday evening looking for help and advice. He has been up to me, I know him well, and I suppose he was at a loss whom to turn to.*

Is it really right to send him away from Eton just because – so far as I can see – he's a difficult boy having a rough passage (and emerging from it), but guilty of relatively trivial offences? Is the criminal record much more than a catalogue of petty misdemeanours, and are they all authenticated? What do they add up to?

I feel that we have a responsibility to try to get boys like ******* *back on the right track – to persevere, not to take the easy route and say 'You're too difficult for us to handle: I'm afraid you must go.'*

Could it not be that we aren't very good at making the best of him – that we lack the character and skill to turn him round?

Why are we schoolmasters, ubiquitously alert to boys' faults and failings, sometimes so slow to recognise our own limitations?

To send this boy away at this stage is to condemn him – almost certainly – to inferior keep and worse temptation. He is too young and inexperienced for us to be able so lightly to say 'It's his own fault, etc. etc.'

His future is what matters, not our comfort and peace of mind. We should try harder with these boys.

Am I wrong?

Yours sincerely,

Michael Kidson

P.S. He is very well liked in his house. A pupil of mine tells me he is a tower of strength in the play they are producing. He is also, I gather, one of the editors of the Arts Review. He is well over the worst of his problems.

P.P.S. Though, no doubt, he will never be very punctilious, and may often dismay by his manner.

Sometimes these letters were successful, other times not. On such deliberations, whole lives were hinged. I can think of dozens of my contemporaries who fell by the wayside, many never to be heard of again. Equally, I can think of at least one Prime Minister who would have been unlikely to make it to Oxford, let alone Number 10, if the cards had fallen differently. This letter from Eric Anderson was in reply to one of Kidson's pleas in mitigation that did not succeed:

From: THE HEAD MASTER
To: M.G.M.K
7 July 1984

Dear Michael,

Thank you very much for your letter, which raises a very important point. I do not like getting rid of boys before their time is up, but I do not think that the School has a duty to put up with bad behaviour indefinitely. Whenever possible, we try to give a boy who is troublesome a number of chances; but when the point is reached that I have written to parents to say that, if there is another major misdemeanour I shall ask for the boy to be removed (as in the case of X), it is inevitable that I have to do what was threatened or such letters lose all credibility. There are several boys in the School whose parents have had such letters and who have behaved magnificently since – and one would imperil that by not acting as one said one will for the boys who step badly out of line.

I have also to consider the reputation of the School, and a party rowdy enough to attract the attention of the Windsor Castle Police and to cause them to send me the sort of report they did, is not something which one can consider trivial. Conversation with the Deputy Ranger makes it clear, too, that these boys, with others, have been a very great nuisance to the Windsor Great Park authorities for some time. If they had told us sooner we might have been able to nip it in the bud, but unfortunately, they did not.

Yours sincerely,
Eric Anderson

Sometimes Kidson was presented with a *fait accompli*, but it did not stop him writing (to McCrum in this case) if he thought there had been an injustice:

2.vii.80

Dear Head Master,

I am sorry that I couldn't be in Chambers today to speak for Bossom (I had to take my dog to the vet as I wasn't teaching) – especially as he seems to me to have been pretty fiercely treated.

I examined on this Board for five years, and never recall a single instance of a candidate's ending his paper with a sentence left in mid-air. In my opinion the law is indubitably an ass if a great issue has to be made of a boy wanting to write three words to end what he has to say.

I believe that the Board would not expect us to interpret their instructions quite so literally or unimaginatively – not, heaven knows, that much imagination is needed. Surely we can observe the Board's regulations reasonably and adequately within the rubric without administering them like a Borstal institution?

However, if this is your considered policy, then might I suggest that, in future, invigilators be instructed to tell candidates when ONE minute remains (not five): then there would be no doubt.

And, for the record – as I gather you asked Bossom – I have always told boys up to me to finish a sentence in an exam, & I shall continue to do so. It is as much up to us to administer the law sensibly & equably as it is for candidates to obey it.

Yours sincerely,
Michael Kidson

Kidson had a very well-oriented moral compass, it is just that it was not always aligned with the school rules, which he regarded as petty and unduly restrictive.

One boy remembers attending Windsor evening races, something for which he would have been beaten or worse. He watched the horses in the paddock, placed his bet, and hurried excitedly up to the stands to watch the race and … ran straight into Kidson. As they caught each other's eyes and with nowhere for the boy to run in a packed grandstand, Kidson simply said, 'I believe I teach your twin brother history,' then put his binoculars up and watched the race. Nothing more was said.

He was quite relaxed about drinking and smoking, reasoning, I suppose, that boys will be boys and it was better done in his presence than elsewhere. Although he would sometimes pretend to be horrified and dramatise the situation:

Hugh Boscawen: 'During a Private Business session in 1970 or 1971 – not a very interesting discussion that evening – Johnny Parry said, "Sir, did you know that Dougal has a tick on his throat?" MGMK replied, "Nonsense," and went on reading, before looking at Johnny, the dog and the tick, and in great horror and panic, exclaimed, "How do we get rid of it?"

'J. Parry reached for MGMK's cigarette box, coolly took out a cigarette and lit it, saying rather quickly and quietly, "Hope this is all right, sir," and started to apply it to the tick. Horrified at the sight, MGMK rushed to the curtains and looked round the edge of them, saying, "I don't want the Head Master to see you."

'Johnnie efficiently removed the tick and then calmly smoked the rest of the cigarette …'

James Murray Willis: 'On one occasion, he took his modern tutor group to London to see *Lady Windermere's Fan*. Once on the M4 in the school Bedford Dormobile, from the back of the vehicle Jonathan Clyde asked, "I say. Do you mind if we smoke, sir?" "Oh hell!" exclaimed Michael. A memorable outing, snooker and dinner at the Oxford and Cambridge Club, then the theatre.'

This relaxed attitude sometimes brought him to the attention of the authorities:

From: THE HEAD MASTER
To: M.G.M. Kidson Esq.
21 December 1971

Dear Michael,

Can you tell me something about the party which I understand was held at The Corner House on the last night of last Half. I am told that a number of boys were there and did not leave until the small hours, and some of them were drunk and others were smoking. I dare say that this has all got exaggerated, but I should like to know the true story if you know about it. If you do not, perhaps you can tell me who was giving it, so that I can ask him.

Yours sincerely,
M. McCrum

Kidson was something of a barrister manqué; he had abandoned his idea of reading for the Bar, but was nevertheless able to fulfil in part his legal aspirations by regular advocacy on behalf of his motley collection of outlaws.

Paddy Dodd-Noble: 'Even before he became my tutor, Michael had intervened and stopped me from being sacked for throwing eggs at Joan Lestor (the Labour MP for Slough), who was canvassing from her car driving around Eton. He secured me the possibly more palatable punishment of being beaten by the Lower Master F.J.R. Coleridge instead.'

Geoffrey Carew was another of Kidson's pupils who needed his help. He awoke one morning in the middle of the garden of a smart Belgravia square. Unable to recall how he had ended up there after leaving a night club, he became acutely aware that he needed to catch a train to Yorkshire for the next party of the holidays and his things were still in Alex Cohane's flat.[46] Being a bit of a country mouse, he did not know his way around London, but managed eventually to find the flat in Fulham.

Banging on the door to no avail, it became apparent that Alex had not made it home either. Then Geoffrey spied an open window. He hauled himself up and was halfway through when he found himself caught at the navel. Looking down, he spotted a smart leather writing-case on a desk and he reached down to pick it up, so that he could write a message. At that moment, a woman appeared in the room. He did not recognise her and, as she reacted with indignant fury to his questions about Alex, it gradually dawned on him that he was trying to break into the wrong flat.

As the affronted householder began to talk about calling the police, Geoffrey reassured her that it was all a huge mistake and to prove his innocence wrote his name and address down and gave it to her before resuming his search for the right flat.

Several days later, he was lying by the pool in his parents' garden in Somerset when the police arrived to arrest him for burglary. He spent two days in a cell as the police tried to extract a confession from him. His parents employed the most famous solicitor of the era, Sir David Napley, to defend Geoffrey. Napley decided that Geoffrey needed a character witness and Kidson, ever the advocate, swung into action with a promise to appear in court and a character statement:

46 Alex was another pupil of Kidson's.

I have known Geoffrey Carew very well for nearly four years. I am his tutor here and have also taught him a good deal: our tutorial system has always encouraged an informal and yet disciplined relationship between masters and boys.*

I am entirely confident of Geoffrey's honesty. There has never been the slightest suggestion since I have known him of any deceit or dissimulation – indeed, when he is doing something wrong, his openness and frankness are often disarmingly casual. It is true that he does not relish some of our pettier school rules, but he is in good company in this respect.

He has outlined to me the circumstances of this charge against him. Implausible as his story may be, I see no reason to doubt any part of it. I once described him in a tutor's report as 'muddled as a chimney jackdaw'. He frequently doesn't stop to think; he is careless and often hurried. But the good side of him more than compensates: he is cheerful and good-natured, and very well liked. As I have said in an even more recent report, he would be a good man to find oneself in a slit trench with.

His irrational behaviour in this matter is very much his style, and even more explicable if he were still a little befuddled by wine. It is the kind of silly thing he would do.

However, to bring him before the courts in this way and over this matter, seems to me not less than ludicrous. Daft he may have been, but to call it burglary is nonsensical.

M.G.MacD. Kidson

** I mean that he has been in my division, not that I've actually taught him much.*

The case was thrown out, thanks in part to Kidson appearing as a character witness in court and the school never got to hear of it.

And then there was Lupin. **Charlie Mortimer** survived being caught poaching the Queen's pheasants in Windsor Great Park, but was later expelled and then reinstated after another incident. He and another boy went up to London to visit one Denise Bunny, a professional lady in Soho, who they hoped would relieve them of their virginities.

Unfortunately, their night of passion was thwarted by her refusal to take a cheque, even a Coutts one. Worse, at that moment their housemaster decided to have a fire practice and they were discovered to be missing. They were going to be expelled when by chance the other boy's godfather, Field Marshal Viscount Montgomery of Alamein, arrived to take him out to lunch. Monty mounted an assault on the authorities and the Head Master proved to be no more of a match for him than Rommel's Afrika Korps had been, and caved in. Although he was beaten, Charlie lived to fight another day.

Then he was caught riding a motorcycle down Maidenhead High Street. It was what is known in the trade as a 'full house': speeding, no insurance, no helmet, and a passenger on the back. Thrown into a cell, he made his one telephone call to Kidson.

Kidson arranged bail and then set about mitigating the effects of the impending court case. He thought it best not to inform the school under the circumstances and took a considerable risk in acting independently. When the dust settled, Charlie's father Roger Mortimer wrote his son a *Dear Lupin* letter and also this one to Kidson:

Budds Farm,
Burghclere,
Newbury *13 January*

Dear Michael,

I hope you will permit me to address you in this familiar fashion, but I feel you know most of the members of my family fairly well. I trust the tiresome affair of Smith's motor bicycle is now over. Charles was fined £12 this morning; his licence received various endorsements and was suspended for three months. But for your help, the outcome might have been far more serious. Smith was not charged; Clarkson was represented by a solicitor and was fined in his absence. I did not enjoy a morning spent among the younger members of Maidenhead's thriving criminal class.

I agree with everything you said in Charles's report, except for the comparison with a chimney jackdaw; I thought that was unfair to the bird. As you say, he is a sort of inverted Lord Rosebery. I suppose Rosebery was spoiled at Eton, possibly for life, and no doubt his tutor – was it the poetical Cory?[47] *– was a bit too keen on certain aspects of the Greek way of life. I have heard it suggested that Rosebery was a repressed homosexual. He was a frightening father and the present Lord Rosebery, who in his prime was harsh and overbearing himself, was always scared of him and never sat in his presence unless given permission.*

Old Rosebery much preferred the younger son Neill, who was killed in the war. Having married a Rothschild, old Rosebery, unreasonably in the circumstances, used to upbraid his offspring for possessing Jewish traits and would dismiss them from his presence with the words, 'To your tents, O Israel.' In my youth, I used to visit the old man's house, long since demolished, in Berkeley Square; it was crammed with Napoleonic relics.

After which uncalled for diversion I will revert to Charles. He has been scruffy and amiable in the holidays and has confined his reading to his younger sister's 'comics'. Running this dreary discotheque has compelled him to organise himself to a slight degree as he has had long and complicated train journeys accompanied by the impedimenta of his trade. To start with he was always landing up in Bournemouth or Swindon, when his destination was Bath or Billericay, but latterly he has been rather more competent. Except in one unfortunate incident he appears to have given satisfaction.

Yours sincerely,
Roger Mortimer

47 The lyricist of the 'Eton Boating Song', William Johnson Cory, mentor of Rosebery, Balfour and Asquith, now thought not to have been 'a bit too keen on certain aspects of the Greek way of life', but he resigned suddenly from the school, possibly under suspicion, all the same. He is one of a very select band of Eton beaks to have had books written about them. The others are Oscar Browning and A.C. Benson, the lyricist of 'Land of Hope and Glory'.

Julian Colville was another Kidson pupil who nearly landed him in the witness box. Julian was an ardent Chelsea supporter. He and some friends had gone to Stamford Bridge to watch a match. Julian remembers that he was hobbling along with a broken toe from playing in a house Sine[48] match. He was on the terraces in 'the Shed', chanting at the opposing fans and at the police, as only Chelsea fans can. There was a crowd surge and Julian, handicapped by his toe, lost his footing and went down. He felt someone help him to his feet and was alarmed to find that his rescuer was in fact a policeman, who twisted his arm behind his back and led him away. Though completely passive, he was arrested and charged with obstructing the police and incitement to riot. Aged seventeen, Julian felt very intimidated and worried that he would also be prosecuted for under-age drinking, as he had been in the pub before the match.

Julian's parents instructed Sir David Napley's firm – by now probably rather grateful for the steady stream of work provided by Mr Kidson's pupils – to defend him. Once again Kidson was the obvious choice as a character witness and he gave up a day of his Easter holidays to go with Julian to the initial hearing at a Magistrate's Court. Julian remembers that, although his parents were determined that he should plead not guilty, he had it in mind to plead guilty and pay a fine, in order to get it over with and save everybody any further trouble. It was at this stage that he saw a very different side to his tutor. Kidson took him off to one side and with deadly seriousness told him not to be a fool.

Julian recalls: 'He said very forcibly, "You are not guilty and you cannot go through life with a criminal record and this stain on your character. You are to plead not guilty."'

The next hearing was set for the summer holidays and once again Kidson accompanied Julian. The prosecution rather over-egged their case and alleged that Julian had led a charge of two hundred hardened football hooligans against the police. The judge took one look at Julian, who by

48 Sine was a second XI of senior boys in the house who did not have their house colours – hence Sine (without).

his own account looked about eleven and was wearing a 'butter wouldn't melt' expression, and very sadly threw the case out before Kidson could be called to the witness stand. We can only speculate on how he would have performed on the stand and feel sorry for those assembled, who surely missed a great courtroom dramatic performance.

Julian is eternally grateful to Kidson for his advice; he now works for a hedge fund and recently had business in America, where any sort of criminal record would have prevented him getting a work permit. Indeed, before he went, he had to obtain a statement from the Metropolitan Police affirming that there was no trace of any crime on his record.

Mark Wiggin had been caught drinking before. Already on thin ice, he had a very narrow escape when he had had rather too much to drink at the Windsor Horse Show.

Charlie Brooks takes up the story: 'Mark used to come on Pop patrols with me[49] – not that he was in Pop – but we both liked the same pub in Windsor over the bridge and down to the right. This arrangement used to drive the President of Pop, who was a dry old stick, mad. Anyway, things got out of hand one night and we got drunk – I think our evening also involved a trip to the Chairman's tent of the Windsor Horse Show – and Mark's housemaster became aware that Wiggin had gone missing.'

At around midnight, Mark was lying in the gutter in Common Lane, unable to make it back to his house. A middle-aged woman approached and Mark – *in vino veritas* – proceeded to proposition her. Big mistake: it turned out to be his housemaster's wife. He sobered up quite quickly at that point and was sent to bed and, realising that he was in big trouble, had the presence of mind to pretend to be unable to be roused when his housemaster came to interview him.

The next morning, he explained that he had spent the evening talking to his tutor in his flat. He then hurried round to see Kidson at the earliest opportunity to secure the alibi. Mark had started to plead his case when

---

49 A patrol of local pubs by members of Pop, to ensure that there were no boys in them, of course. A case of *Quis custodiet ipsos custodes*.

his housemaster telephoned. Mark remembers what happened next as pure slapstick comedy. Kidson pretended that he could not hear, 'John, hello, John … are you there? It's a very bad line … Can you hear me?' He tapped the cradle at the top of the telephone. 'Hello, is that better? … No, I'm sorry, I still can't hear you … Can you speak up?' He put the receiver down, then lifted it off so that it would be engaged.

Kidson then gave Mark one of the biggest rockets of his life and made him realise that it was only because he considered having to lie to one of his fellow beaks was a lesser evil than Mark's certain expulsion, that he would help him. He took responsibility for both boys' drunkenness the night before. Once again, he had put his career on the line to save one of his boys. Charlie Brooks was kicked out of Pop,[50] but both boys were allowed to stay and sit their A levels.

Hylton Murray-Philipson risked being in serious trouble by going off to St Mary's Wantage[51] to see his girlfriend. Kidson tried to talk him out of going, but realising he had gone, he found out which train Hylton was catching and went to Slough station to pick him up, so that he was not caught returning to school.

Miles Montgomerie was another boy who had outgrown school. He was caught going up to London to see his girlfriend. Miles remembers Kidson's reaction: 'Miles, you are a bloody fool. If you need to see your girlfriend, just invite her round to my flat and I will make myself scarce for a couple of hours.'

Despite Kidson's help, Miles did not quite make it through to the end. He had secured an unconditional offer to an American university so did not take his A levels seriously enough. The final straw was when he took a pillow into an exam and went to sleep, provoking the ire of the invigilator.[52] Asked to leave, he went round to say goodbye to Kidson, who

---

50 But Charlie writes: 'The adorable, kind, understanding Eric Anderson slipped me back in, much to the fury of my housemaster …'

51 A girls' school that no longer exists.

52 Barnaby Lenon, later Headmaster of Harrow.

said, 'Miles, I am worried that you will end up sleeping rough in London, so I have arranged for you to be a member of the Lansdowne Club and paid a year's subscription so that you have somewhere to go.'

Nat Rothschild was asked to leave before A levels, but Kidson allowed him to stay in his flat, so that he could continue his revision and sit the exams. He then helped him successfully to apply to Oxford.

Sometimes expulsion was inevitable and there was nothing Kidson could do about it. The letter below was written to a boy who had just been expelled:

1st March 1992 *134–135 High Street*

My dear Edward,[53]

I am very sorry that you got yourself in this pickle, & departed so suddenly. It's a consolation that what's happened must now bring out the best in you, for you are thrown much more on your own determination and resources.

First of all, to keep cracking away at your work in the next few weeks so that A levels turn out respectably. There's no reason why you shouldn't do just as well as though you are still here.

Memories are very short when people make mistakes; and we all do. These days, people are tolerant and understanding and only want things to work out well. You needn't fear that your friends will desert you: they aren't friends if they do.

You are lucky to live among a loving & helpful family. You must now get on with life quietly and sensibly & feel that the best days lie ahead. I don't want to sound too much like a schoolmaster: but this is a challenge, & I'm sure that you can take it up.

53 The name has been changed.

Meanwhile if you need any help or advice, always let me know. Some of the immediate problems that arise can easily be settled in the next several weeks.

Best wishes,

Michael Kidson

You may have formed the impression by now that Kidson rather flouted the system. Not a bit of it, he upheld the authority of the governing power on every occasion, except when he did not agree with it. Once he was teaching in his classroom when there was a knock at the door and a Praeposter opened it hesitantly and came in. It is the conventional etiquette that the beak stops talking and stands aside to allow the Praeposter to issue his summons. He had barely started when he was furiously interrupted by Kidson.

'How dare you, sir! You are here on the Head Master's business and you are to deliver his message with authority! Get out, man, and do it again!'

The next time, the door almost flew off its hinges and smashed against the wall.

'Much better,' he purred.

He was also not automatically on the side of the underdog. **Jamie Sainsbury** hoped that Kidson might get him off what he regarded as an unfair charge. He had been out with parents in London with other boys from his house on St Andrew's Day. Special dispensation had been granted for them to be away from Eton on the day. The boys[54] had given the parents the slip for a few hours and had repaired to the Ritz for a few sharpeners before going back to school. Unfortunately, there had been a spy in the Ritz, who had told the boys' dame.

54 The party was a cosmopolitan one: it included a Habsburg Archduke, a Chinese boy, and Piers Flint-Shipman, later a famous actor who starred in *Another Country*, before being killed in a car crash.

None of the boys was quite eighteen and they were accused of not having permission to be 'not with their parents'. Kidson, outwardly at least, sided with authorities. Probably he would have found it hard to go against a housemaster on an issue where there were three other boys who were not his pupils. Also, Jamie was a first offender and therefore not in danger of expulsion. Nevertheless, he may have made an appeal for clemency, as Jamie was given the choice of six strokes with the cane or six hours' moss-picking in School Yard. He chose the latter.

And in cases where Kidson believed boys had acted immorally, he viewed the facts with a searing clarity and was unwavering in his support for the Head Master. This is a letter to a father who had written to him appealing for assistance:[55]

Dear Andrew,

Many thanks for your letter etc.

I'm very sorry: but, frankly, I fear you have comprehensively got hold of the wrong end of the stick.

John has done very badly indeed in this matter. He has not been misjudged at all. I personally have spoken to the police; old boys and old pupils have given me information; the Head Master and all concerned are well satisfied of his complicity.

When he has his back to the wall, John seems quite unable to distinguish fact from fiction; and it is clear that – like me originally – you are far too credulous. In being so, you are doing him a disservice: it encourages him to believe that honesty is not the best policy.

In fine, Andrew, there is no 'dastardly judgement'. The solicitor's report does not 'clearly vindicate' John, and certainly could not do so if they were made properly cognizant of the facts. You must not be beguiled by legal casuistry: those of us who have access to privileged information

55 The names have been changed.

are not in the slightest doubt that John has behaved deplorably.

It is now unpleasant history; and Eton wishes to forget it. I hope that John will remember it only with disgust, and think and behave differently in future.

With all good wishes,

Yours,

Michael

CHAPTER FIVE

A Shropshire Lad

My life possessed no Spring.

Harriet Martineau, from Kidson's commonplace book

I have employed the old obituary-writer's trick of putting the details of Kidson's birth and early life midway through, in order to avoid losing you in the early chapters – so often one tires of a biography simply because the subject's childhood was ordinary. Although Michael's was anything but, as you are about to find out.

Like all legendary schoolmasters, Kidson had an interesting back-story, or at least that was the impression he gave – but like a good artist, he left it up to us to decide what it was, merely leaving the odd clue so that our imaginations did the rest. His detractors, and he had a few, thought him phoney and said that he invented himself as he went along. Although he was a good friend to many people, no one really got close enough to Kidson to find out much about him.

He projected a slightly dilettante image, a gentleman schoolmaster who left grubby careerism to others, and there was an assumption that he must therefore have considerable private means. He spoke airily about Scotland, leaving an impression that he had antecedents and property there. The cover story was that he came from Shropshire, where his grandfather had been a parson, and we were allowed to assume a conventional background of Shrewsbury, the King's Shropshire Light Infantry, and Cambridge. But in the small world that we inhabited, where everyone seemed to know something of everyone else, the fact that there was an absence of corroboration led to suspicion. He had an air of mystery about him and he liked to keep it that way.

None of us could have guessed at the true story. In fact, Michael's childhood could have been used as the plot in one of the Victorian novels he so enjoyed. Shortly after I agreed to write this book, a parcel arrived with the contents of his desk: letters, newspaper cuttings and his discharge papers from the Army, plus two photograph albums. The detective story had begun.

Writing a biography is a bit like doing a large jigsaw puzzle and as I sifted sadly through the flotsam and jetsam of his life, I observed gloomily that there were remarkably few pieces. The various genealogical websites produced tantalising snippets and then came a breakthrough: his executors, who had been given power-of-attorney before his death, were able to request his Army records from the Ministry of Defence. Within days, a triumph of bureaucracy – 263 sheets of A4 – arrived, hot off the photocopier in the Army Personnel Centre in Glasgow, with more pieces to provide enough of the jigsaw to be recognisably Michael.[56]

He was born in London on 24 August 1929 to George Kidson and his wife Mary, née Gillies. They lived in Wilbraham Place, off Sloane Street, in the comfortable surroundings of Belgravia, then as now a smart part of London. He was christened Michael George MacDonald Kidson. Mary had been born in Scotland, but may have been brought up in South Africa, the daughter of Norman Gillies, a civil servant there. Gillies and MacDonald, Michael's middle name, are both Scottish names from the Hebridean Islands, so it is probable that Mary's parents came originally from Scotland and her mother may have been a MacDonald. George Kidson's middle name was Fleming, also a Scottish name, although the Scottish connection in the Kidson family is less clear. It would explain Michael's close affinity with Scotland, and especially with Mull, in many ways Michael's spiritual home and his final resting place, where the MacDonald and the Gillies clans have been inter-marrying for centuries.

---

56 There is a splendid cover entitled THE WAR OFFICE – THIS FILE WILL IN NO CIRCUMSTANCES BE SEEN BY THE PERSON TO WHOM IT RELATES. Well, it has not been.

George had served as an officer in the First World War. He had graduated in mechanical engineering from Manchester University before the war and was commissioned as a Second Lieutenant and rapidly promoted to Lieutenant in the Manchester Regiment in 1917. It must have been desperately worrying for his parents, who were still mourning the loss of their only other child, their daughter Edith, who had died the previous year aged twenty-eight.

George's medal records[57] indicate that he served in the 2nd Battalion in France. This was the battalion in which Wilfred Owen was serving when he was killed one week before the Armistice on 4 November 1918; the poet's mother received the telegram informing her of his death as the church bells were ringing out to celebrate peace. Although he was wounded twice, George was more fortunate and returned to Manchester after the war.

It was there that he met Michael's mother, a married woman, Mary Brisbane (née Gillies), the wife of a chemist, James Brisbane. They fell in love and an affair started. When the Brisbanes moved to Enfield, it seems that George also moved south. Matters were brought to a head when James Brisbane filed for divorce in April 1922. In the National Archives in Kew, I found the petition for divorce, which stated:

> *That on 15th, 16th, 17th and 18th days of April 1922, the said Mary Agnes Brisbane committed adultery with George Fleming Kidson at the Cosmo Hotel, Southampton Row, Russell Square in the County of London.*

Presumably, in those days the evidence would have been provided by a private detective in a grubby mackintosh and a fedora hat, with a flashbulb camera.

Mary did not defend the suit and costs of £70.8.11 were ordered against George as the co-respondent, who appealed against them unsuccessfully.

57 He was entitled to wear 'Squeak and Wilfred', but not 'Pip', as he had not served from 1914.

George and Mary were married in 1923 in Paddington Registry Office. Mary left two sons, aged five and three, behind with James, who had won his application for their custody. What Michael did not know was that he was not an only child. His elder brother Ian was born five years earlier, in 1924, but suffered from some form of mental disability, possibly severe autism, and was sent to live in an institution before Michael was aware of his existence.

Michael's parents employed a nursemaid, Roberta May Batten, to look after him and it seems that Mary fell foul of Sir James Goldsmith's dictum that 'when a man marries his mistress, it creates a vacancy': George fell for the nanny and started an affair, which was discovered. It appears that Batten was swiftly moved on, but that George was infatuated and continued their affair at her next addresses in Trebovir Road, Earl's Court, and at a farm in Hertfordshire. It also seems that in the wake of the Wall Street Crash in October 1929, George was out of work. In August 1930, he embarked on the *Guildford Castle* for Cape Town. Mary filed for divorce in October, signing in an educated, rather masculine hand, stating:

> *That the said George Fleming Kidson has frequently committed adultery with Roberta May Batten a nurse lately in the employ of himself and your petitioner and with other women whose names are unknown to your petitioner.*

George is shown as 'a farmer … at Tark Farm near Craddock, South Africa' and Mary as now living at 199 Queens Gate. Mary applied to have custody of her two children.

George came back from South Africa in February 1931 and immediately filed a response to the divorce. Mary's solicitor filed notice again, but nothing more seems to have come of it and the divorce decree appears not to have been granted.

The 1931 census might have provided a snapshot of the family unit at that point, but historians will never be able to access it. The entire records were destroyed in a fire, apparently started by a cigarette, at the

Office of Works store at Hayes, Middlesex, on Saturday, 19 December 1942. I wonder how many frustrated researchers will be thwarted in their attempts to find out about their grandparents, as a result of that moment of carelessness. It appears, however, that George went off the rails at this time and spent six months in prison for an incident in Croydon in December 1931.

Whether Mary was a serial bolter, or whether she had some sort of breakdown is not known, but later, while he was still quite small, she walked out on Michael and by all accounts she was never heard of again. Michael told Nigel Jaques that he thought she had gone to the United States and he possibly had half-siblings there, though we do not know why he thought that. Certainly, Mary has not shown up in any on line records of marriages or deaths in the United Kingdom.

In 1963 the following notice was placed in the newspapers:

> Mary Agnes Brisbane (otherwise Kidson).
> Last heard of London area 1922/24. Will
> she or anyone knowing her whereabouts
> communicate with Richardson and Sweeney,
> solicitors, Sunbridge Road, Bradford.

As James Brisbane lived in Bradford and died there in 1966, it is likely that he or his surviving son Cyril put the notice there, hoping for a reconciliation before he died. Maybe one of his descendants will read this book and find some sort of comfort.

For a child's mother to die early in their lives is tragic, but children are amazingly resilient and generally learn to adapt to the situation. But what if your mother simply disappears? Michael must have gone through life thinking, hoping, that she might suddenly reappear. Without the grieving and catharsis of a normal bereavement, if there is such a thing, there can be no closure. As far as we can tell, he had no photograph of her, and he must have struggled to remember what she looked like as the years went by.

Michael never forgave his mother and hardly ever spoke of her. When he did, in his dotage, it was with great bitterness:

'What sort of woman abandons her child? What sort of bitch does that?'

Abandoned by Mary, and with his father unable to cope with bringing up a small child, Michael went to live with his elderly grandparents.

The Reverend Herbert Kidson, by then in his mid-seventies, had retired to Shropshire with his wife Kate. He had been the vicar for thirty-four years of St Margaret's, Prestwich, which was then a village rapidly becoming a suburb on the north side of Manchester. Photographs show a rather severe-looking man with enormous moustaches, in a black frock-coat with a dog collar; he could have stepped out of an illustration in the *Barchester Chronicles*. Prestwich was a large parish, with a handsome church and a commodious vicarage. The living was in the patronage of the head of the Egerton family, the Earl of Wilton, who lived at nearby Heaton Hall.

The Kidsons were relatively well-off. They had been tailors in Manchester and had profited during the cotton boom, which made the city one of the richest in the world in the nineteenth century. The Reverend (Joseph) Herbert Kidson's father, also Joseph, is described – or presumably described himself – in the 1861 census as a 'Merchant Tailor, Dresser & Nailor[58] employing 23 men & 1 boy'. The following extract from a history of Manchester describes his business:

> In few things have we changed more during the last seventy years than in the matter of dress. Joseph Kidson, of 37 Piccadilly, was a fashionable tailor, popular with his well-to-do neighbours. One of these has left us some interesting reminiscences. He says: 'I remember quite well in the year 1835 being one of a wedding party, our clothes having been made at Kidson's, in Piccadilly, each of us being dressed alike, a claret swallow-tailed coat with black velvet collar, a yellow Valencia vest, and light grey trousers, the

58 A nailor maintained the teeth (nails) on the carding machine used on wool and cotton before weaving. (http://rmhh.co.uk/occup/n-o.html).

> cost being £6 10s. Mr Kidson recommended white satin waistcoats, which really at that time would not have been out of the way, and were indeed often worn in evening dress. Of course, there were also stiff stocks round the neck of a gay colour, and high chimney-pot hats.' Such a costume would indeed be a sight to see in Market Street now, but in 1835 would excite no notice. In those days, unless a man was in mourning, coat, vest, and trousers were all different, both in material and colour, and the tailor's bill was no doubt increased in consequence.[59]

It is interesting that our Kidson, always so dapper – one pupil remembers his purple socks – should have this lineage. Perhaps he inherited some sartorial gene that skipped the black uniformity of his Victorian clergyman grandfather and surfaced in him. The shop no longer exists and 37 Piccadilly is now a camera shop. Joseph Kidson was the son of another Joseph, a 'draper and tailor' from Salford, Lancashire, and his wife Jane, and probably the trade goes back in the family beyond into the eighteenth century.

Joseph Kidson – the one who sold white satin waistcoats – was married to Hannah, the daughter of Joseph Adams, a schoolmaster. The 1841 census shows the Adams family living in relatively humble circumstances in Church Terrace in Wisbech, Cambridgeshire. So perhaps Michael was genetically predisposed to be a well-dressed schoolmaster.

It would appear that the Kidsons made enough money from tailoring to move up the social ladder and to send their sons to university. Michael's grandfather, born in 1856, was at Hertford College, Oxford, and married into a slightly higher social milieu. Michael's grandmother was born Kate Dickinson at Wimbick House, Aughton, near Ormskirk in Lancashire, to John Dickinson, a Liverpool cotton broker and his wife Elizabeth, née Underwood.

59 Source: *Manchester Streets and Manchester Men*, J.E. Cornish, 1907. Reproduced on Google.

The one surviving photograph of their family home shows an imposing, ivy-clad country house, which suggests that it was probably the big house of an estate, and old man Dickinson may also have been a landed gentleman. Kate had been educated at a boarding school in Bedfordshire. Perhaps the Earl of Wilton knew Kate's family, or maybe he had his suits made by Kidson's and knew Joseph senior, at any rate in 1892 the Oxford-educated Herbert was given the living and the opportunity to enter the Trollopian world of life in the vicarage at Prestwich.

On his retirement in 1926, Herbert Kidson wrote *Records of St Margaret's Prestwich 1849–1926*. It is not a riveting read, but it gives an extraordinarily detailed account of every parochial, architectural and ecclesiastical detail; Kidson's grandfather was clearly also a dedicated historian.

Inside the front cover, Michael has written in pencil: 'Surely one of the most boring books ever written. Painstaking and infinitely thorough, it illustrates dramatically how far the Anglican Church has fallen from grace – from this climate of communal trust & devotion to the existing world of malaise and indifference. Michael Kidson, July 2006 – 60 years after my grandfather's death in 1946. His vicariate was a model of love & devotion.'

Michael's grandparents had retired to a house called St Margaret's, presumably after Herbert's church, in Church Stretton, a village near Shrewsbury, where they set up house with Herbert's brother, Arthur Kidson, who was a widower, a retired schoolmaster and an historian.[60] It is possible that the reason these two Mancunian brothers retired to Shropshire was that one or other of them had taught at Shrewsbury School nearby and the expectation seems to have been that Michael would go there. By Michael's account, his grandfather had strict Victorian views on bringing up children, but he was fond of him, and for a time he appears to have had a happy rural boyhood, learning to fish, which became a lifelong passion.

60 He was commissioned to write *A History of East Retford Church* amongst other blockbusters.

In February 1970, he had an article published in *The Field*:

> My grandparents, who lived in an old mill house in the village, seldom fished themselves, but they encouraged my interest, and were careful not to cut down the banks and spoil the best lies in the stretch that ran through their grounds ... I was initiated by a native of the village, who knew every stream for miles around and who had perfected the technique of catching these trout.

Here he probably also developed his love of hunting by following the local hunt. *Baily's Hunting Directory* lists Church Stretton as one of the South Shropshire Hunt's best meets, although Michael spoke about following the neighbouring Ludlow. And he may have had his first taste of racing at the local point-to-point. He was a lifelong supporter of Worcestershire Cricket Club and perhaps he was also taken to watch cricket by his father or grandfather. It must have been difficult, though, for the small boy, living with his grandparents, who had only moved to Shropshire recently themselves. Neither fish nor fowl, not one of the village boys nor fully accepted by the sons of the local gentry, he was probably always the outsider, with his nose pressed to the glass, watching the county set at play.

Michael later told Nigel Jaques that his father George was a ne'er do well, who sponged off his own father, Herbert. He lived in Over, a village near Almondsbury in Gloucestershire, where Michael spent some of his time, but they did not have a good father–son relationship. He was ever afterwards very critical of those he felt were being poor parents. It appears that at some point his father had a close association with a woman named Amy and may have remarried, although possibly he was unable to do so with his first marriage still technically extant. We know little about Amy, but not long before he died, Kidson did once mention to Julie, his housekeeper in retirement, that he had had a wicked stepmother.

In 1938, at the age of nine, he went away to preparatory school at Grove House in Surbiton, near Kingston upon Thames in Surrey. A year later, war broke out and we can imagine Michael and his schoolfellows being issued with their gasmasks and trooping down to the school's air-raid shelter. He never spoke about this period of his life, but he must have experienced the Blitz at close quarters – 447 high explosive bombs fell in the locality, including several in the area of the Grove.[61]

Michael probably also watched the Battle of Britain going on in the skies above London. One of 'The Few' was his elder half-brother, whom he never knew existed. Pilot Officer Norman Brisbane was a Spitfire pilot serving in 65 Squadron. On 7 July 1940, he scrambled with two other pilots, Flying Officer George Proudman and Sergeant Patrick Hayes, to intercept a large formation of Messerschmitts attacking a convoy of ships in the Channel. They were never seen again. Another RAF section in the area thought that they had been ambushed in the clouds and shot down over the sea. Officially still posted as missing, Norman's name is on the Runnymede Memorial for airmen with no known grave, just down the Thames from Eton. He was twenty-two and had been commissioned three months. The other half-brother, Cyril, survived the war and died in Northumberland aged seventy-two – again Michael and Cyril were unaware of each other's existence.

Happy country upbringing as it was for a time, any stability that it provided in Michael's childhood was not to last. In the winter of 1941, his father died suddenly on 20th January. His will names his widow Amy as sole beneficiary, to whom he left £900. Five weeks later, his grandmother also died, and eleven-year-old Michael was left living in St Margaret's with the two octogenarian brothers. A decision was taken to send Michael away to an orphanage, the Royal Orphanage of Wolverhampton.[62] His grandfather, unable to cope without his wife, moved into the Quarry Nursing Home nearby, where he died in 1946.

Before he died, Michael's grandfather took the decision to tell him about his brother Ian's circumstances, something which, by Michael's

61 http://www.bombsight.org.

62 The name was changed by command of King George VI to the Royal Wolverhampton School in 1944. The school is still going.

account, he struggled to do. Sixty years later, after Ian's death, Michael told David Pease about his brother and broke down telling him the story. His Uncle Arthur also died in 1946, leaving sixteen-year-old Michael without any family at all, save for poor Ian in his asylum.

When Michael wrote to boys in difficulty telling them, 'It's a consolation that what's happened must now bring out the best in you, for you are thrown much more on your own determination and resources,' he knew what it is to be alone in the world.

The register of wills shows that Herbert left £6,592 and Arthur left £7,595 – both around £500,000 or even £1 million, according to some calculators, in today's money. But, according to Michael, his grandfather had not changed his will to enable him to inherit and he did not receive very much money. It seems that there was also a trust of some kind for Michael's benefit, administered by a firm of solicitors in Lancashire, Dickinson & Parker (probably the partner was a cousin on his grandmother's side), and another trust was set aside to look after his brother Ian in his mental hospital.

Amongst Michael's possessions was a heavy, leather-bound photograph album. There is an inscription in the front of it:

Herbert
from May
on his 21st birthday 1877
to
Michael Kidson
his grandson

Inside there are portrait photographs of the Kidson family going back to Joseph Kidson, the prosperous tailor in a frock-coat and mutton-chop whiskers, and his wife in a heavily embroidered crinoline. Under each one his grandfather has carefully written who all the people are in neat copperplate handwriting. One can imagine the orphaned boy going off to boarding school with this prized possession, the only remaining link with his roots.

At this time, the Royal Wolverhampton School was a charitable foundation dedicated to the education and maintenance of children who had lost one or both parents. Possibly the most overused word in the English language these days is 'austerity'. Perhaps if people could go back in time and visit Michael at school during wartime rationing, they might revise their definition of the word.

The Monty Python star, Eric Idle, who is fifteen years younger, was enrolled at the school after the war by his mother when his father was killed, and remembers:[63]

> I remained there for twelve years. The living conditions were Dickensian and the teachers were allowed to beat us. We were given sixpence a week pocket money, which we spent in the tuck shop. Having little money to spend was a valuable learning experience. My schooling also shaped my work ethic, because while other children were listening to the Goons, I was studying, which enabled me to go to Cambridge University.

In another interview, Idle is quoted as saying:

> It was a physically abusive, bullying, harsh environment for a kid to grow up in. I got used to dealing with groups of boys and getting on with life in unpleasant circumstances and being smart and funny and subversive at the expense of authority. Perfect training for Python.[64]

I do not know whether Kidson and Idle ever met, but it is interesting that they shared the same command of the English language, anarchic sense of humour, disrespect for authority and sunny outlook. 'Always Look on

---

63 Interview with Angela Wintle, *Sunday Telegraph*, 10 January 2016.

64 Bob McCabe, *The Pythons' Autobiography By The Pythons*, Orion, 2005: ISBN 978-0-7528-6425-9.

the Bright Side of Life', Eric Idle's hit from *The Life of Brian*, summed up Kidson's approach. Maybe it is based on their school song.

Hard as it must have been, it seems from references written later by the headmaster, Colonel Gibbs, and a mistress named Miss Selina Brooks, who remembered him fondly, that Michael made the best of his time at Wolverhampton and thrived. He was captain of cricket, boxing and soccer, and a sergeant in the Army Cadet Force. He also did well academically.

Kidson left in 1947, after passing his higher school certificate, and was called up for National Service in 1948.

A boy with his background and education might have expected to be an officer, but there is no record of him attempting the War Office Selection Board[65] to go for officer training. He may have harboured ambitions to be commissioned into his county regiment, the King's Shropshire Light Infantry, but with no family and precious few contacts, he would have found it very hard to pull the necessary strings to be sponsored by the regiment. After two wars, most regiments had plenty of sons of fathers who had served, and the Royal Wolverhampton School may not have been very helpful. As a result, he was swept into the Royal Artillery and spent two years in the ranks.

Various next-of-kin forms that Michael filled in during his military service mention a guardian named Frank Kidson, who lived in Cheshire. His relationship is listed as uncle, although genealogical records indicate that he was probably a distant cousin. A letter from Frank Kidson to the Army, returning Michael's mail, states that he has not heard from him for a long time and does not know his whereabouts, so probably Michael cut his ties with him as soon as he was of age. Later he listed his next of kin as Mrs A. Kidson, who is shown as 'mother', and this must be Amy, his stepmother or possibly his father's common-law wife.

Whilst many would have been happy to keep their heads down and get through it all, it appears that once again Kidson thrived in a tough

65 Familiarly known as the 'wozbee' after its acronym WOSB.

environment. After basic training, he was posted to 57 Heavy Anti-Aircraft Regiment at Orsett Camp, Grays in Essex. The barracks was near the Thames, between what is now the Dartford Tunnel and Tilbury Docks, the home of Essex Man and, no doubt of more interest to the young Michael, of Essex girls. Michael once told Julie that he was engaged to be married while he was in the Army, but that he had broken it off.

No doubt the regiment, with its searchlights and ack-ack guns, had been put at Grays to counter the Luftwaffe and then forgotten about. Within two years he was a Bombardier[66] at the very young age of twenty. His records show that he was an OFC, a Fire Control Operator trained in the use of radar. Fire Controller's jobs are very responsible – the risks of shooting down friendly aircraft are clear – and not given to the second-rate. He was highly thought of, too, as his commanding officers, Lieutenant Colonel Wright and Lieutenant Colonel Tailyour, later provided glowing references. One can imagine that Kidson excelled in the regimental sports teams, which would also have brought him to their attention.

It would undoubtedly have been where he first developed his teaching skills. He would have been taught 'methods of instruction' on his junior NCO's cadre. It would have been ingrained in him to construct lesson plans of 'explanation … demonstration … imitation … practice' and to keep his soldiers on their toes by frequent bouts of 'question … pause … nominate'. Probably he stood on one leg on the drill square and uttered the immortal words, 'Continue to look this way and I will demonstrate what to do on receipt of the word of command TWO.' Cadences of soldiering and life skills, once learnt, that are never forgotten.

In later life, Kidson kept his time in the ranks quiet; perhaps he was slightly ashamed that he was not commissioned like the majority of his colleagues, but in many ways Bombardier Kidson's brief career was more of an achievement than if he had spent his time in the Officers' Mess.

66 The Gunner equivalent of a Corporal, two ranks up the ladder.

CHAPTER SIX

Toiling Upward

Kidson finds his vocation

The heights by great men reached and kept
Were not attained by sudden flight
But they while their companions slept
Were toiling upward in the night.

From Kidson's commonplace book

On being released from National Service in 1949, Michael Kidson took himself off to a crammer, Turret Court, at Westgate on the Isle of Thanet in Kent. Evidently this was to prepare for the Oxbridge exam. He also got a job teaching at Moffats School, a preparatory school at Bewdley, in Shropshire.

In 1950, according to his Army reservist records, Michael had passed the Oxbridge exam and was all set to go up to Oxford University to read English Literature at St Catherine's Society, not then granted the full status of college that it enjoys today. Possibly he had applied to Hertford, his family college, but had been rejected and then found his way to 'St Cats'. However, there is no record of his matriculation, and he must have dropped out in the first few weeks. On coming down again, he got another prep-school teaching job, this time at Dunchurch Hall, near Rugby, where he taught from 1951–2. While there, he must have reapplied to go to university, this time to Cambridge.

In early 1953, Kidson went to work as a 'mud student' at Ardnacross on Mull, owned by the Forresters, an Etonian family. Perhaps he was drawn there by a desire to find his Scottish roots.

Rory Forrester recalls: 'This was a dairy farm and I do remember thinking that farming was not really what he was cut out for. There would have been other students here with him and we all lived together. I remember Michael was quite forthright in his opinions and as we all had meals together, we saw quite a lot of him. He got on very well with my parents and came back to stay on a number of occasions, both before and when he was a master at Eton.'

It was the start of a lifelong love affair with Scotland in general and Mull in particular.

Kidson went up to Cambridge in 1953 at the relatively advanced age of twenty-four, even by the standards of the National Service era. He was at Gonville & Caius College (pronounced 'Keys'),[67] a beautiful, cloistered college in the heart of the town, between King's and Trinity. Doing my research, I noticed that Kidson is now on the College's Wikipedia entry as a notable alumnus of Caius, presumably on the strength of his obituaries – he would have liked that.

After enjoying a very good lunch with the Fellows of Caius in their splendid Dining Room,[68] I was given a library card and took myself off to the University Library to find out more. The records show that Kidson read Economics for a year as the first part of his Tripos before switching to History. The History dons at Cambridge in that era included the Marxist Eric Hobsbawm at King's College, the Christian historian Owen Chadwick at Trinity Hall, and a visiting lecturer Nikolaus Pevsner, of architectural fame. The great G.M. Trevelyan, a hero of Kidson's, had recently handed over as Master of Trinity and gone to be Chancellor of Durham, but he still appears on the lists of lecturers, so we can probably assume that Kidson attended some of Trevelyan's lectures. Amongst Kidson's contemporaries, the only one I could see who has become a household name was one

67 I'm sure I am not the only one of MGMK's pupils to have looked in vain through the Cambridge prospectus for Keys College.

68 The Fellows' Dining Room is an unique and interesting room with details from the Temple of Apollo at Bassae. The design of the room includes a large and complex painted ceiling along with painted and gilded column capitals, frieze and altar: www.gonville-and-caiuscollege.ac.uk.

T. Dalyell of the Binns – Tam Dalyell of the West Lothian question, who was at King's next door.

Kidson specialised in Modern History and developed a fascination for the Victorians. Philip Magnus's biography of Gladstone came out in 1954 and this book became a seminal influence on Kidson. Bits of it are copied into his commonplace book and would find their way into his prose in letters and reports. Possibly part of the attraction was also that Magnus lived at Stokesay Court, ten miles from Church Stretton, and Kidson may have been aware of him as a local figure. Gladstone, that most complicated and intellectual of Victorian statesmen, became in Kidson's mind the greatest of the 'great men' he apostolised.

Pupils who were excoriated by Kidson for their idleness will be gratified to learn that he got a third in his Economics examinations and emerged after two years of History with what my contemporaries would know as a 'Desmond': a 2:2.[69] Perhaps the Kidsonian view of 'great man' history did not accord with the left-wing dogma of many dons at the time, or maybe after the deprivations of Wolverhampton and the hardships of National Service there were too many distractions at Cambridge. He may have spent rather too much time at Newmarket. Possibly he spent three years on a Byronic rampage. I do hope so.

It would have been the first time in his life that he encountered girls on an equal footing and it is nice to think of him, after his miserable childhood, punting along the Cam on long summer afternoons. The MOD have records of him serving in the Cambridge University Officer Training Corps and his curriculum vitae of the time reveals that he played cricket for Caius, but did not win a Blue. However, he was later elected to the MCC and wore the distinctive red-and-gold tie with pride thereafter.

Some colleges maintain tutor files on their alumni in their archives forever; even to the extent of keeping Porter's Reports along the lines of 'I was doing my rounds when I encountered the young gentleman emerging

69 After Archbishop Desmond Tutu.

naked from the fountain.' Caius, alas, does not – so we do not know who his tutor was, or whether he was a refractory undergraduate. It may be significant that later he did not use his tutor as a reference. We do know that he was happy at Cambridge and that it was the most formative period of his life, particularly in developing his love of History. He spent most of his working life trying to help boys to go there.

On graduating in 1956, he divided his time between staying with Amy at her house, Stead Vallets, a farmhouse on the Earl of Plymouth's Oakly Park estate near Ludlow, and London, where he stayed at the Oxford & Cambridge Club[70] in Pall Mall, rather appropriately in his case, which he gave as his address when he re-enlisted in the Army.

At a loose end after Cambridge, it seems that Michael decided to combine his interest in teaching with his military experience and apply for a short-service commission in the Royal Army Education Corps. He applied before he left Cambridge, but then asked for his application to be postponed so that he could travel across Europe on a belated gap year, or in Kidson's case, no doubt, a Grand Tour. He travelled across Holland and Germany and made his first acquaintance with Italy and his favourite city, Venice. In 1957 he finally took the plunge, perhaps in the absence of a better option, and in late summer attended an RAEC interview board and a WOSB, both of which he passed with flying colours.

He was ordered to report to the King's Shropshire Light Infantry Depot in Shrewsbury, where he spent a week being kitted out and no doubt being marched up and down the square at the rate of knots. After his time in the Bombardiers' Mess and Cambridge, he probably found the privations of the barrack-room rather irksome.

Kidson then spent eleven weeks at Eaton Hall Officer Cadet School in the Duke of Westminster's vast gothic pile in Cheshire, where it had resided since the war. He was excused the first six weeks of the course, which consisted mainly of drill and basic training, on account of his previous service. He was commissioned as a Lieutenant[71] on 22 February

70 It may be more than coincidence that this was also Gladstone's club when he first went to London.

1958. He achieved a respectable C Grade[72] and his company commander's report is good: 'Kidson has made sound progress throughout the course. He has an alert, enquiring, mature attitude, which should ensure success in his next appointment. He will make a very effective young officer in the Corps of his choice.'

He was posted to the AEC Training Centre at Beaconsfield and seemed set fair for a promising career. Alas, in Michael's life of snakes and ladders, somehow he had hit another snake:

To: The Commandant,
Army School of Education & Depot RAEC,
Wilton Park, Beaconsfield. *11th April 1958*

Sir,

I have the honour to submit my application to resign my short service commission in the Royal Army Educational Corps.

I find myself quite unfitted by attitude and ill-prepared by training for the work of the Corps. This was brought home to me very clearly during my two weeks' instructional attachment at Salisbury.

I had originally intended trying to convert my S/S commission on to a regular basis: since I no longer wish to do so, this S/S engagement only has the effect of preventing me from going ahead with my future in another direction.

I regret having to reach this decision, which I only do after very careful thought and after a broad and comprehensive view of the work of the Corps. I am firmly convinced that I made an error in accepting this engagement and beg that it should be terminated at the earliest possible date.

I have the honour to be, Sir,
Your obedient servant,
M.G.M. Kidson,
Lt. RAEC

---

71 His degree was taken into account, so that he was automatically promoted from 2nd Lieutenant to Lieutenant on commissioning.

72 The Army does not go in for grade inflation and most officer cadets would have received a C and many a C− or worse.

From: Army School of Education
To: The War Office AG 14 (o) *11th April 1958*

Lt MGM Kidson (455526) RAEC

1. *The above-named officer has been attending an Officers Initial Training Course at this School since 3rd March 1958. This course would be due to end on 30th May.*
2. *Attached is an application by this Officer to resign his commission together with an Interim Report by his Company Commander.*
3. *I am of the opinion that Lt Kidson is unsuitable to be passed out from here as an Instructor Officer RAEC and I do not recommend his retention. He has neither the aptitude nor the outlook required for the job and he will not be an asset in any unit in an educational capacity.*
4. *Will you please issue instructions regarding the disposal of this Officer.*

F.K. Hughes, Colonel,
Commandant

It appears that Beaconsfield had unrealistic expectations of him. His report states that:

> He has no professional training as a teacher, and very limited pre-graduation teaching experience in a preparatory school ... Lacking both professional training and experience, he finds considerable difficulty in getting down to the instructional level of the soldier ... his lack of teaching skill precludes his employment as a specialist instructor which carries superior rank ... This report is in no way intended to cast doubts on his integrity, his character, his personality or his genuine qualities. He is smart and soldierly in his training, he has a good manner and address, and his military duties have been satisfactorily carried out.

It begs the question why they bothered having a School of Education if they expected their teachers to arrive pre-trained. One also wonders why the Board accepted him the previous summer, knowing he was not a qualified teacher, or why they could not put right any perceived deficiencies in a Cambridge graduate.

The Army allowed him to resign his commission and he was transferred to the Regular Army Reserve of Officers. Thus the Army was deprived of the service of a schoolmaster later to be lauded by a British Prime Minister as the most inspirational teacher of them all. There followed a protracted and one-sided correspondence as the War Office tried to make him pay back his uniform allowance. Kidson came off best, simply by ignoring it.

Dr Johnson said that 'every man thinks meanly of himself for not having been a soldier' and it is clear that Michael did think meanly of himself after this experience, which must have been bruising. It made him reassess his vocation as a schoolmaster. He joined the oil company Shell on a graduate training scheme. Little is known about his time working for the company in London and Rotterdam. Photographs survive of him standing on the docks in a British warm overcoat[73] and a hard hat, grinning for the camera. He remembered his spell as 'an oil man' with affection, but a few months of corporate life were clearly enough to persuade him that his vocation lay elsewhere. Later in 1958 he was offered a job as an assistant master at Papplewick by the headmaster, Peter Knatchbull-Hugessen, while he read for the Bar.

Papplewick is a preparatory school in the heart of Berkshire's stockbroker belt, across the road from Ascot Racecourse. Photographs in his album show that Kidson renewed his interest in racing. He would go and watch horses at early morning exercise on the course on race days, before going back across the road to spend the day teaching and umpiring cricket matches. While there, he realised that his vocation did lie in teaching after all, and he dropped his law studies.

73 Possibly still contested as their property by the War Office.

Rupert Hancock, who was taught by Kidson at Papplewick and Eton, remembers his time there: 'At Papplewick in those days, an otherwise dismal seat of learning, attention frequently wandered and, of course, if he had thrown those wood-backed blackboard dusters, he would have done damage with consequences. My recollection is that they were carefully loaded with more chalk (a quick wipe of the board) and then lobbed at the miscreant, landing with a bang immediately in front of his face, waking him with a start and covering his face with chalk to the enormous amusement of everyone else.

'In the Papplewick classroom, his sensitive readings of Maupassant and others have never been forgotten, illustrating the effectiveness of his teaching and the enduring impact that he had on this and, no doubt, other pupils. In Stuart history, his constant emphasis on the thoroughness of Thomas Wentworth, served both to make the historical point and to sow the seeds of useful values for later life.

'The assistant matrons were selected, apparently, for their looks (an attribute that was not wasted on the boys). Amongst these was one gorgeous girl, who was the best-looking of them all, and who attracted MGMK's attention. My recollection is that he made his "approach" in the most traditional manner, and again and again, but sadly without success. Whether she was linked elsewhere is not known to me, but makes little difference either way.'

Another Papplewick boy, **Andrew Warren** writes: 'Michael George MacDonald Kidson (loved those initials!) was a technicolor star in a monochrome 1950s staff room. His generosity to his pupils was legendary – both in terms of regular sweets from Charbonnel et Walker, but also kind gifts, like obtaining a desperately sought, just-released Bentley Dinky car (with independent suspension) and refusing reimbursement. I still treasure his words of encouragement on my otherwise mediocre final school report – they remained my leitmotif throughout my career.'

In 2013, an American pupil at Papplewick, **Mike Watts**, went to enormous trouble to write to him, shortly before Kidson died, from the USA:

Dear Mr Kidson,

It is going to take some considerable feats of memory to dig back fifty-five years ago when you were teaching us history at Papplewick School in Ascot, but those times are still very vivid for me and I wanted to make sure you knew what a profound influence you had on me and my brothers (in Papplewick parlance Watt I, Watt II and Watt III). We were part of a very large contingent of children whose fathers all flew for Pan American World Airways and were probably the first wave of 'Yanks' to pass through the school.

I can still remember you reading aloud from the works of Thomas Babington Macaulay (among others) and how vivid and compelling you made the study of history. I also remember your fondness for chocolates and the custom boxes you would have shipped to your quarters at The Lodge.

Those Papplewick years were easily the most formative of my life and influenced everything that came after. We returned to the US in 1959 and I went on to college and graduate school and have spent most of my work life in television production and advertising.

Please know that you influenced and shaped all that my brothers and I have accomplished over the years.

With every good wish,

Mike Watt

Others remember that Kidson was a glamorous character, 'a dapper dresser in his sports coat, cavalry twills, cravat and highly polished brown shoes' with 'a brand new Mini Cooper, which we all vied to be driven in'. Even then he was showing maverick tendencies. During an interminable service in the chapel, he was seen to have substituted a hymn book for a novel with a similar cover and to be reading *A Tale of Two Cities*. **Tim Stevenson** dug out his old school photograph, showing Kidson 'detached from everyone else, deliberately not looking at the camera with a silly grin on his face.'

Two young assistant masters at Papplewick at the time went on to be distinguished headmasters of preparatory schools: Gerald Barber, who taught there between Eton and Oxford was later headmaster at Ludgrove[74] and Nigel Talbot Rice, who became headmaster of Summerfields. **Gerald Barber** was amused by Kidson's behaviour when Knatchbull-Hugessen, who had founded the School in 1947, was transferring ownership to a charitable trust. Kidson affected to be very concerned by this and concealed a recording machine behind some books in the library to bug a governors' meeting, so that the staff would know what was going on.

Nigel Talbot Rice says that 'Kidson had a strong influence on younger members of the staff: 'He introduced me to his Savile Row tailor and would give us his firm views on certain matters. He would rubbish the *Daily Telegraph* versus *The Times*, and he had a very low opinion of *Country Life* compared with his favourite, *The Field*. It was the era of *That Was the Week That Was* on television, which Kidson liked. He had quite a liberal, David Frost-type view of life, he was very scathing about the Douglas-Home government and I would not have been surprised to learn that he had voted Labour. He really hated the school photograph and was as uncooperative as he could be, sitting almost sideways on to the camera, looking bolshie with a scowl on his face and dark glasses. He affected to be a misogynist, but this was very far from the case, as he conducted an affair throughout much of my time there.'

The youngest member of staff was John Penney,[75] who was teaching there between Radley and Oxford. He recollects being rather dazzled by Kidson:

John Penney: The articulacy with which he delivered his forceful views and his stylish manner made him an impressive, even alarming, figure, but I soon learned that he could also be very kind, and once we had found common ground in a contempt for the *mens sana in corpore sano* attitude, then still sadly prevalent in independent schools, we became good friends.

---

74 Where he was headmaster to the author and later still to TRH Princes William and Harry.

75 Now Dr John Penney, University Lecturer in Classical Philology and Fellow of Wolfson College, Oxford.

I owe to Michael an introduction to Meredith's *The Ordeal of Richard Feverel*, the first volumes of Osbert Sitwell's autobiography (Michael had a taste for lush prose), the short stories of Aldous Huxley (accompanied by fulmination against H.E. Bates, then much in vogue), and G.F. Bradby's *The Lanchester Tradition* (a neglected minor masterpiece about a reforming headmaster at a public school facing down entrenched opposition).

Those of us who lived-in would have dinner together, and Michael would dominate the conversation, keeping us up to date on any gossip. The boys' mothers all seemed to adore him and they would pass on to him various salacious details they had gleaned about each other's marriages. And Michael would duly repeat these for our delectation. Or it might be the rather intimate medical problem of the Head Master, whom Michael had been driving to a hospital appointment that day. There was no malice in any of this: Michael simply could not bear to have a good story wasted.

Mischief rather than malice prompted some of his more outrageous social performances: he rather enjoyed embarrassing those he was with. I remember visiting Papplewick after I had left to go to Oxford. We went out to dinner at our usual pub. We were served by the daughter of the house, whom I had got to know well, and as my first course was being placed before me, Michael suddenly said, very loudly, 'When two lovers meet after a long absence, it is usual for them to kiss over the prawn cocktail.' The poor girl fled to the kitchen and did not come out again. Michael beamed happily.

Michael could be contemptuous of some of our colleagues (not without reason, it must be said). he used to say of W. that he must have been hiding behind the door when the brains were being doled out, and one evening he reported with glee that he had attended the evening chapel service that W. had conducted as Master on Duty, and had heard him lead the school in a prayer for the games equipment.

In chapel, Michael would sit with the rest of us in the back row and would sing all the hymns with enthusiasm. He had a good voice, and was aware of it – when complimented, he would say complacently, 'Yes, it's a great gift.'

And then various isolated memories: Michael arriving in the Common Room one tea-time with a bundle of silk ties that he was discarding from his wardrobe, flinging them on the table for the rest of us to pick over; or Michael operating a reel-to-reel film show, which included a film about David Livingstone bringing Christianity to the African natives, which provoked sardonic comments such as: 'Fat lot of good it did them!' He was never one to respect conventional pieties, and that was one of the things that made him so memorable.

Knatchbull-Hugessen made Kidson Second Master,[76] something the other masters felt was perhaps a vain attempt to make him conform. But Kidson was already feeling that Papplewick had served its purpose as a stepping stone to teaching at a public school. He successfully applied for a job at Bradfield under the headmaster, Tony Chenevix-Trench. Unfortunately, the vacancy did not materialise after all and Chenevix-Trench later moved to Eton. In 1965, when Kidson applied for a position at Eton, he was accepted. It was an inspired appointment and is a tribute to Chenevix-Trench's judgement. Even a CV writer with Kidson's skills could not have disguised some gaps and inconsistencies, the 2:2 and a somewhat tortuous career path. The letter offering him the job finishes: 'I should be grateful if you would let me know if you would like to come to Eton in September. I hope you will, as I believe you would be very happy here.'

Perhaps Chenevix-Trench, who had suffered in a Japanese prisoner-of-war camp, recognised another tortured soul, and a precious talent that had been suppressed by life's snakes and needed to be given a ladder.

After a long search for his vocation, false starts and dark tunnels, Michael arrived at Eton and found his niche. His life may have had no spring, but by early summer it was back on track.

---

76 Deputy Head.

CHAPTER SEVEN

The Corner House

'Oh, Chips, I'm so glad you are what you are. I was afraid you were a solicitor or a stockbroker or a dentist or a man with a big cotton business in Manchester … Schoolmastering's so different, so important, don't you think? To be influencing those who are going to grow up and matter to the world …'

James Hilton, *Goodbye, Mr Chips*

We remember the best and the worst of the people who taught us. Looking back, they seem polarised into stereotypes: bad like Wackford Squeers from *Nicholas Nickleby* or Captain Grimes in *Decline and Fall*, or good like Mr Chips or the bloke in *The History Boys*, or the Robin Williams character in *Dead Poets Society*.

As we go through life, we change our view of teachers. In early schooldays, we are in awe of them, and as this passes there is a short time when some of them become quite cool in our eyes. As puberty kicks in, we look on them with mounting disdain, and the cool ones are ridiculed and the ones we were in awe of are seen in a nasty light. Most of us, at that stage, would say that the last thing on earth we wanted to do was to be a teacher. Through the sixth-form years they achieve a modicum of rehabilitation, and some might gain our respect and even lasting affection, but I suspect, for many of us, when the moment comes to say goodbye to quite a few of them, it is with ill-disguised relief on both sides.

It is only when we have children of our own that we begin to think of teachers collectively again. In what seems no time at all we are back at schools, as prospective customers rather than as pupils, meeting potential headmasters and housemasters. They invariably seem to be nice people with a similar outlook on life to ourselves. They are tanned having spent the long summer holidays on the beach in Cornwall with their children. They radiate fulfilment from leading interesting and rewarding lives, shaping the characters of young people. They live in a comfortable house, in bucolic surroundings, in a community of kindred spirits. They are not besieged by doubts about being able to complete the education of their own children privately.

We interview them – and they interview us – in a study that is full of the tools of their trade: copies of *Wisden* and historical biographies that we would like to read ourselves but never have time, golf clubs, racquets for every known ball game, *The Times* crossword half-done, a temporarily suspended game of chess, and so on. The contrast with our own Stakhanovite struggles in the middle caverns of corporate life starts to look stark. In short, we wonder whether, somewhere along the way, we have missed a trick and maybe a teaching career might not have been such a bad idea after all. As we go through it all again as parents, we look upon the good teachers with admiration and gratitude for helping our children through the difficult years, and feel short-changed and affronted by the mediocre ones, but in general we are in awe of them again for the wonderful job that they do. The wheel has gone full circle.

For Eton beaks, the advantages of a teaching career are particularly rewarding. Henry VI's munificence, conserved and increased by more than five centuries of beady husbandry, allows the school to pay more than other schools to get the people they want. There have been instances where beaks have wanted to leave Eton, to accept promotions to become heads of departments elsewhere, and have been crestfallen to find that they would actually be taking a drop in salary. Eton has sometimes made up this difference in salary to allow them to move on and maintain a bit of movement in the ranks. If we were to accept, crudely and probably wrongly, that market forces are the sole determinants of these things, then Eton masters are like the Premier league footballers of their profession.

The school has always had interesting people teaching there *en route* to stardom elsewhere. I was taught divinity, in a very lively and theatrical fashion, by the Conduct, Roger Royle, who went on to perform a similar role at the BBC and have his own television show. Sir Jeremy Greenstock taught there before joining the Foreign Office and ending up as our Ambassador to the United Nations.

Some of them seemed to the outsider to resemble a very exclusive club with a vaguely discernible academic flavour. Quite a high proportion were Etonians themselves. In fact, some of them had only been away from Eton for long enough to get a degree, normally at either Oxford or Cambridge, before returning to a semi-monastic vocation by the Thames.

One housemaster was a baronet, another was married to the daughter of a marquess. Being a beak at Eton was still seen by some as an agreeable way of life for a gentleman of private means, rather than anything as vulgar as a career; although these attitudes were gradually giving way to a more meritocratic organisation and a new breed of beaks was appearing, particularly in the sciences and newer departments like geography.

Some housemasters still ran their houses very much as their own private fiefdoms. Housemasters at Eton have a tradition of autonomy, stemming from the time before the First World War when they ran their houses as private businesses, independently of the school – even to the extent of the Head Master, until recently, needing the housemaster's permission before entering a boarding house. There is the famous story of Michael McCrum being embarrassed to discover, second-hand and several days later, that the Queen Mother had taken tea in a boys' house as a guest of the housemaster, her friend Giles St Aubyn.

Though it was not apparent to the boys, in many ways the real power in the school rested with the OE housemasters, who saw themselves as guardians of Eton's traditions. It is said that Michael McCrum used to tell a story against himself of a meeting where David 'Dippy' Simpson, (who taught me Greek for two years in a soporific monotone), upbraided McCrum for imposing some change with which he did not agree: 'Head Master, of all your crass decisions, this is the worst one.'

Starting on the princely salary of £1,540 per annum, Kidson was put to live in a 'colony' of young beaks in The Corner House on Eton's High Street, between College Chapel and Barnes Pool Bridge. Michael Meredith, an energetic young English beak, who had arrived on coming down from Balliol at the same time, was in nominal charge of their arrangements as 'the coloniarch'. The others were Howard Moseley, Mark Philips and Jeremy Greenstock. James Cook joined later, when Greenstock moved on.

Jeremy Greenstock: Michael's presence in The Corner House gave the colony a very special character – of humour, intellectual banter, an apparent worldliness and a refreshing independence from Eton's rather overbearing traditions. He was immensely kind to me as a new beak, so long as I could put up with the occasional teasing, and an important source of advice on how to cope with the mysteries of effective teaching. Like so many of those who knew and loved him, his streak of iconoclasm was central to his charisma, even though we knew it was partly invented, and concealed some raw inner sensitivities. His 'sister', for instance, was the regular subject of speculation amongst the other colonists.

Michael was instrumental in bringing Jane Mortimer (as she then was) to The Corner House. The housekeeper for my first two terms was a rather sour and difficult widow called Mrs Stabb (we never knew her first name), whose struggles in the kitchen and frustrations with us bachelor beaks eventually exhausted both her and us. Michael suggested turning to the alumnae of the Cordon Bleu cookery school at nearby Winkfield, I suspect because he already knew of the possibility of Jane from his racing connections with the Mortimer family. Although Jane, by design, only lasted one term, the experiment was successful enough to continue with younger housekeepers from then on. When I later introduced my girlfriend (and later wife), Anne, to the colony, Michael insisted on calling her Jane, something she quickly accepted as one affectation amongst many of a man with too many positive qualities to be regarded as offensive.

His satisfaction on the housekeeper front came in spite of his increasing reluctance to turn up for communal meals with the rest of us. I think he just valued his own privacy. But he gave a scurrilous assortment of reasons for avoiding our company, one of which was that he could not stand the way a colleague peeled his oranges in a single whorl from top to bottom.

His dogs were part of his make-up and of his set of instruments against the outer world. On one occasion, his spaniel, a subservient creature we referred to as Wuggles, got into Meredith's room, settled on one of his Hepplewhite chairs and, when discovered and admonished by Meredith, peed on it. Meredith immediately dispatched the valuable piece to the rubbish tip and rejected Kidson's half-hearted attempts to compensate him for it. Yet the relationship between the two of them did not suffer for long, as each was aware that the other, for all his eccentricities, was an outstanding teacher of Etonians.

For this was what really marked Michael Kidson out as exceptional. With outwardly unimpressive academic qualifications and with a constant disdain for the traditions and arrogances of the Eton culture, Michael gave his pupils the highest priority. He read their characters with accuracy, addressed their faults with immense sympathy, and regularly gave them the benefit of the doubt against other beaks.

Michael Meredith remembers that they each had a study and a bedroom and shared a communal dining-room. There was a spare room, in case any of them wanted to invite a guest. Kidson, perhaps because he was older, was the only one to have a double bed in his room. All the beaks complained vociferously about their living quarters, except Kidson, who seemed quite satisfied. The five beaks all got to know each other very well. They knew the others' girlfriends and, after a while, their families as well. They all remember, though, that Kidson never spoke about any of his past and they never knew a thing about him. Until one night Kidson announced that he was inviting a guest.

Michael Meredith: 'A slightly raffish character named O'Riordan, who had been in the Army with Kidson, arrived for dinner and to stay the night. We had a convivial evening and as the wine flowed O'Riordan's tongue loosened and he started to let slip stories about Kidson's past life, to Michael's obvious discomfort. O'Riordan was never asked again.'

Jane Torday, the eldest daughter of Roger Mortimer, and sister of Charlie 'Lupin' Mortimer, takes up the story of life in The Corner House:

Jane Torday: I had waved Lupin off to school many times, but the start of the summer half in 1967 was the first time that my brother, then fifteen, had accompanied me to a room of my own at Eton, in a household of men – not boys.

'Don't talk too brightly at breakfast,' advised my father as he retreated to his car, my brother ambling beside him.

But what on earth was I doing there?

Only someone as kindly disposed towards the young and inexperienced as Michael Kidson could have offered a dippy eighteen-year-old girl the job of cook for this little colony of five single beaks, living at their recently renovated The Corner House.

Michael, aged thirty-eight, seemed positively ancient to me. His jacket tweed, his trousers grey-flannel, his MCC tie in place, his hair short, he served sherry from a tray in his book-lined study, where the remaining walls were hung with sporting pictures – he loved horses, and paintings by Stubbs in particular. Bachelor he may have been, but there was absolutely nothing confirmed about it.

There was one telephone in the house and it rang often. The shout would go out: 'Michael, it's your sister.' On occasion, Michael was visited by a tall, beautiful brunette, a married lady with several children. As he did not have a sister, she was not introduced to me as such. Over time, some years later, he spoke of this captivating woman – obliquely, but conveying a certain longing. Rightly or wrongly, I always felt there was a sadness at her ultimate unavailability.

Of other mothers, and parents in general, Michael was often disparaging. All too often, he felt, they did not understand the needs of their offspring and how best to steer them forwards. I only learned from his obituaries that his own mother had deserted the family in his infancy, and his father died a few years later, leaving him with his grandfather who also died, intestate, not long after. From this bleak childhood grew a man who did not care to see misguided or unhappy children.

In 1967, without rancour and with a degree of accuracy, Michael might address me as a dim little filly. But not in front of a room full of pupils, thank you. My first week there, eager to engage him in literary conversation, I gazed at the narrow, printed spine of one of his history books, which seemed to read 'Planet Agent', and enquired if Michael was interested in science fiction ...?

I was never allowed to forget my misreading of Plantagenet.

Michael's good looks were enhanced by his quirky smile – he was determinedly deadpan, but his own humour frequently got the better of him. His mouth was often twitching at the corners as he delivered some salvo to one of his pupils – or indeed to myself.

Michael also knew boys were invariably hungry and he was regularly seen in the high street, purchasing paper bags full of sticky buns and doughnuts for visiting pupils.

Living conditions in The Corner House were positively luxurious. I had two light and airy rooms, with polished parquet floors, which I proudly called 'my flat'. Unbelievably, I was permitted to smoke in them. Or was it just a blind eye ... it was the 1960s. However, apart from dear Lupin's visits for tea, biscuits, and fags behind my sofa, my sitting-room door would suddenly fling open without warning and Michael would stride into the room. He was sometimes disposed to shout 'Boo!' and disappear.

How did Michael, a maverick, relate to his fellow beaks in a household that included highly intelligent characters of future distinction, notably Michael Meredith and the youngest at twenty-three, (later Sir) Jeremy Greenstock. Michael was a passionate historian, a sportsman and a good conversationalist. He was a committed – and demanding – teacher, who cared sincerely for the wellbeing of his boys. He commanded respect, as well as raising laughter. That he would help boys in trouble, and if necessary cover-up for them, was probably not immediately known to his colleagues.

What Michael thought of some members of the teaching staff at that time was another matter. Of the pernicketiness he often encountered, he would mutter, 'He's such an old woman.'

The beaks in their subfuscs fluttered round the house like so many black birds, dashing from one destination to another. Pupils came and went all day long. There was a certain glamour, a sense of Eton's long history, about the boys in their formal black tailcoats with the blaze – as on a horse – of white collar and shirt. I do not think my sons, among other Old Etonians, would agree. It is an uncomfortable uniform.

Mealtimes were a respite for the beaks, but often eaten at speed. I prepared cooked breakfasts, which sat in a Belling warmer oven, solidifying, ready for consumption after a starter dish of tinned grapefruit. This appetizing combination was eaten after what was called 'Early School' – a tradition of lessons before breakfast, long since abolished.

Lunch was brisk. Dinner was more leisurely. I think I may sometimes have been permitted to join them for that ... they were all, on reflection, very sweet and indulgent to me. My organisational skills were not conspicuous, but perhaps they enjoyed the presence of a young female who could cook tolerably (I love food. I read and cooked from Elizabeth David's *French Provincial Cooking* in my Eton kitchen). They routinely dropped into the kitchen for a gossip.

At the end of that summer half, when I took off to live and work in London, Michael – and the others – still kept a kindly eye on me. I went down occasionally and spent the weekend there. After dinner (who cooked it?), Michael would insist that we took his beloved spaniel for a post-prandial walk before bedtime, regardless of weather or season. I dreaded these little forays. Namely because Michael had spotted that I had no sense of direction and could be led in circles around Eton with no clue as to how to get home without his assistance.

He took a certain pleasure in winding me up to the maximum. My conversations with Michael veered between genuine exchanges and sustained teasing. He was able to pinpoint and reveal so many of my zones of ignorance, giving him countless opportunities for merry mockery.

James Cook arrived in 1967 and started in another smaller, less well-appointed colony, 'Overbank'. For those bachelors who sought to climb Eton ladders, membership of a smart colony was almost essential. So, when Howard Mosely asked Cook to join the The Corner House, he leapt at the opportunity:

James Cook: I had scarcely encountered Michael Kidson before, and I had to get used to his (feigned – I would like to think, but I am not sure) dismay at having to share accommodation with a chemist. To him, Chemistry was definitely not a serious subject, a judgement all the more easily reached by the fact that my predecessor in the colony had been a respectable classicist, a notably fine rackets player, as well as being destined to become a distinguished diplomat and the British ambassador to the United Nations. I also had to get used to the fastidious pronunciations, to being called 'Charles' or, more disconcertingly, 'What did you say your name was?'

While I quite understood Michael's admiration for Tom Graveney, the Gloucestershire, Worcestershire and England batsman, I was a little nonplussed by his failure to recognise me in the street as he sailed past, backbone bent to the wind, and his misplaced concern for the amount I ate and the effect it would have on the colony bill! One quickly realised, however, that these were games he was playing.

What remained a mystery, however, was Michael's past. A portrait, we supposed it was of an ancestor, hung in the colony dining-room, a portrait of a man in traditional clerical dress. But was it really an ancestor, and might it not be hanging there merely as a means of establishing some spurious nineteenth-century respectability? I did not dare to ask. And what about Michael's preference for batting without batting gloves? Was this a genuine eccentricity or an act of pointless bravery performed to establish a reputation for carefree courage in the minds of boys?

And then there were his dogs, a succession of Jack Russells and springer spaniels, that accompanied him everywhere, but never on a lead. Michael was enormously fond of them and fiercely loyal to them (except when their behaviour embarrassed him; at such times, he contrived to disown them). Inevitably, they were not always as popular with the rest of the colony as they were with boys, and I once had the temerity to complain to Michael about the then present incumbent.

A sensible man would have made his point with a few vehemently expressed words and then fled. Foolishly, however, I had not planned an exit strategy and, having made my point, as I thought with sweet reasonableness, stood there watching helplessly as sails and masts came crashing down about my head in Michael's withering and repeated broadsides. When it came to his dogs, Michael did not do sweet reasonableness. I did not make the same mistake again.

Another spotlight on life in The Corner House is shone by a characteristically descriptive thank-you letter to Michael from **Grizel Hartley:**[78]

8 December 1970 *Dorney*

O my dear Michael,

I sort of despair of this letter ever reaching you. I ought to have written at once, and you will be a million miles away, and never know how much we adored your dinner party. I don't think, in all my life, any time has gone so fast. It was all so utterly congenial, and that isn't the word, but it will have to do. Hubert, who got home late and dog-tired from London, was as completely refreshed as if he'd had a bath of champagne.

It wasn't only that it really is a great honour to be asked to a colony, but all the endless fascinations, a horse in the hall and a Herring on the wall, and Howard's great aunt's super-tablecloth, and far too

78 Quoted from *Grizel: Grizel Hartley Remembered*, edited by P.S.H. Lawrence, (Michael Russell, 1991). Grizel was teaching at St George's Ascot at the time, her husband Hubert Hartley had been an Eton housemaster before Kidson's time.

Above left: His grandfather, The Reverend Herbert Kidson

Above: Michael in prelapsarian days en route to prep school

Left: George Kidson, Michael's father who served in the trenches

Below: Wimbick House, Lancashire, Kidson's grandmother's family home

Above: Eaton Hall where Kidson completed his officer training

Left: Kidson as a subaltern shortly after leaving Eaton Hall

Below: Kidson (on right) the oil man with Shell in Rotterdam

Michael Kidson shortly after his arrival at Eton in 1965

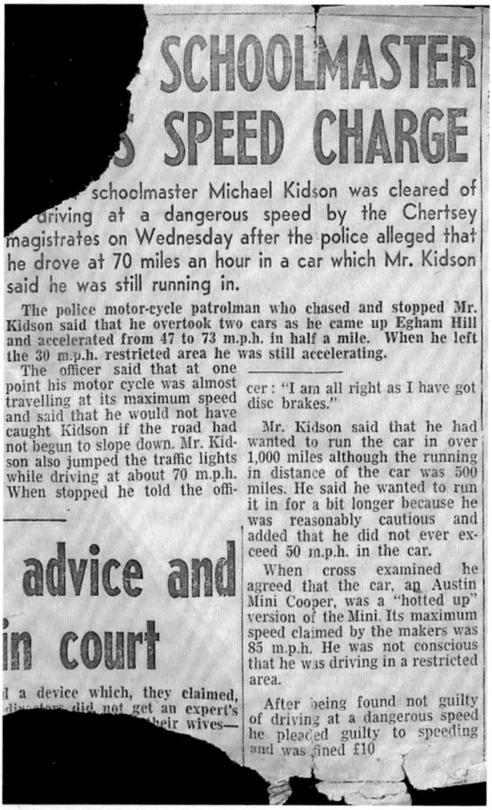

SCHOOLMASTER
S SPEED CHARGE

schoolmaster Michael Kidson was cleared of driving at a dangerous speed by the Chertsey magistrates on Wednesday after the police alleged that he drove at 70 miles an hour in a car which Mr. Kidson said he was still running in.

The police motor-cycle patrolman who chased and stopped Mr. Kidson said that he overtook two cars as he came up Egham Hill and accelerated from 47 to 73 m.p.h. in half a mile. When he left the 30 m.p.h. restricted area he was still accelerating.

The officer said that at one point his motor cycle was almost travelling at its maximum speed and said that he would not have caught Kidson if the road had not begun to slope down. Mr. Kidson also jumped the traffic lights while driving at about 70 m.p.h. When stopped he told the officer: "I am all right as I have got disc brakes."

Mr. Kidson said that he had wanted to run the car in over 1,000 miles although the running in distance of the car was 500 miles. He said he wanted to run it in for a bit longer because he was reasonably cautious and added that he did not ever exceed 50 m.p.h. in the car.

When cross examined he agreed that the car, an Austin Mini Cooper, was a "hotted up" version of the Mini. Its maximum speed claimed by the makers was 85 m.p.h. He was not conscious that he was driving in a restricted area.

After being found not guilty of driving at a dangerous speed he pleaded guilty to speeding and was fined £10

advice and
in court

d a device which, they claimed, directors did not get an expert's ... their wives—

Above: The Corner House, his first lodging. He later resided at 134-135 High Street just to the left of the photograph

Left: Historical evidence of Kidson's driving

Below: The desk where Kidson composed his many supportive letters and acerbic reports

Right: His study at Eton. 'The entrance hall and the small sitting-room beyond were drenched in high culture, an oil painting or drawing covering every inch of wall space' *(Nicky Dunne)*

Above: Ivy Cottage, Westonbirt, Gloucestershire. Kidson's bolthole in the holidays and later his home in retirement

Left: Kidson's Gloucestershire friends outside 'The Cat': Jeremy Sinker, June Goatley, Julie Wodecki, Aly Walker, Julie Spruels and Ken Grey

Below: In Nat Rothschild's private jet bound for India

Far left: Dougal on holiday, River Tweed and Floors Castle in the background

Left: Joseph Yeboah, hall porter outside the Army & Navy Club. Joseph would look after Kidson's dogs for him while he was in London

Above: Rick Hewitt, Kidson's gardener

Below: A rare photograph of MGMK in his later years with Nat Rothschild watching the racehorse named after him, *Modern Tutor*

Kidson's portrait, painted by Georgina Barclay, now hangs at Eton

delicious wine, and all the superb dinner cooked by one pretty little girl quite unfussed, as if she'd just strolled in without a care. The beautiful rooms, and the warmth and comfort, and the Personnel. It was a teeming rich mixture, the other Michael the fount of all wisdom, James with his mediaeval scholar's face, Howard with the innocent choir-boy expression, and Mark with the wonderful Foreign Office manner, the Vice-Marshal of the Diplomatic Corps.

And if I hadn't been brought up like Alice in Wonderland, not to make personal remarks … but I'll tell you the rest when I see you again. It was an unforgettable, life-giving evening. No one has ever enjoyed anything so much. I don't think, Michael, if you had thought for a hundred years you could have made it more heavenly than it was. Thank you with all our hearts, and I hope this may be in time to wish you a happy New Year.

Love from Grizel

Some beaks were obviously gay, although there was no question in those days of that being openly acknowledged. Years later, I heard that a few had 'come out' to no one's great surprise or disapproval. There is a disgraceful slur against schoolmasters in the public's mind because of the crimes against children of a few warped individuals and the assumed link, often, but tragically not quite always, erroneous, to homosexuals. We are apt to forget that the very best teachers are often single because a married teacher cannot possibly give the same devotion when they have a spouse and children to worry about.

One of the greatest housemasters of the era was 'Nutty' Norman Routledge, a brilliant mathematician who had been a Cambridge don before teaching at Eton;[79] he was a highly eccentric bachelor and, as it was

79 It is said that he was persuaded to leave Cambridge for Eton by Archie Nicholson, who told him that 'Eton is one of the few places where it is not a disadvantage to be thought amusing.' I hope that is still the case today.

later acknowledged, though the boys in his house had long assumed it, gay. He was worshipped by his boys, who adored his quirky sense of humour – he once appeared in one of their house plays dressed as an angel.

One of them, **Johnnie Boden**, who gave the eulogy at Norman's funeral, recalls: 'Eton was briefly besieged by a paedophile called Mr Andrews. At House Prayers, Norman warned us about him: "Gentlemen, there is a pervert called Andrews who will offer to take pretty boys out to tea, pretending to be a friend of your parents. If he comes close or tries to chat to you, simply say, no thank you very much, Mr Andrews, not today – and send him to see me."'

When I told friends that I was writing a book about a schoolmaster, some of them gave me a knowing look and said, 'Ah, and I suppose HE NEVER MARRIED,' that being the code at the end of an obituary, a polite way of saying that the chap danced at the other end of the ballroom. (I have noticed, instead, that these days they say he was consoled in his later years by his partner, Terry Somebody-Or-Other). But Michael certainly was not gay, he simply never did marry. It was only when we found out about his motherless childhood, most of us for the first time in his obituary, we could all understood why.

In fact, amongst the boys, who generally have a good nose for these things, Kidson had the reputation of being quite a swordsman in his day. No names, no pack drill, and I will spare their blushes but, judging by the list of those reckoned to have been his conquests, when Kidson discussed the 'Ugandan proclivities' of Victorian statesmen with his pupils, he was not talking from a position of virginal ignorance. He could be quite shy with women and gave the impression, to us at any rate, of being rather a misogynist. But women, or some of them anyway, clearly detected more than 'a thin bat's squeak of sexuality' in him.

Fi Carpenter, whose parents were friends of Michael's, remembers hearing her mother and a friend comparing him to the actor Patrick McGoohan, a heart-throb of yummy mummies of the time. Maybe women like the challenge of a confirmed bachelor, one without the gay connotation. I have seen normally demure women going all fluttery and giggly over monks – same sort of thing, I suppose. On the reader's behalf, I asked some of his female acquaintances what they thought women – other women obviously – might have found attractive about Michael. Some sensed his vulnerability and thought he needed mothering. One thought that there might have been a bit of the Mr Rochester about his manner. Another spoke of his charm and yet another of his gentleness. One lady gave me a sphinx-like smile and said that he could be very persuasive and had an outrageous sense of humour.

So, there we have it: good looks/challenge/vulnerable/needed mothering/Mr Rochester/charm/gentle/persuasive/GSOH – he seems to have had all the bases covered, bar Heathcliff and Mr Darcy.

Perhaps his outward misogyny was only another layer of armour that protected him from the world. Some of his colleagues have said that he made friends more easily with women than men. One of Kidson's closest friends at Eton was the school librarian, Helen Garton. Miss Garton was a spinster of indeterminate age by the time I knew her. She ruled the library under its great baroque dome with a rod of iron. Woe betide any boy who raised his voice or was caught eating in her demesne. Always very well turned-out from her perm down to her patent-leather court shoes, she was another of Eton's enigmas and one could never tell what was going on behind her thick, black-rimmed spectacles. It was rumoured that she had arrived at Eton after being jilted at the altar by an Italian lover. She would often be seen enjoying a glass of sherry in Kidson's flat.

Keith Wilkinson lived next to Miss Garton at Willowbrook and remembers observing Kidson coming and going. One day, he happened to be coming out of his front door just as Kidson was going in to Helen's house: 'Kidson saw me, paused and, quite unruffled, turned to Helen as she opened the door, "Ah, Miss Garton, there you are, I'm looking for a book ..."'

His friendship with Miss Garton gave rise to a certain amount of teasing by his pupils and his love life was the cause of endless speculation. I remember once going round to his flat to discuss an essay and pretending not to notice a strange woman hiding in his dining-room.

Rupert Hancock recalls: 'Returning from one of our golf (pronounced "goff") games in Fleet, Hampshire, around 1967, we made a minor detour via another village, where I waited in the car while he made his visit. Why and who remain a mystery.'

CHAPTER EIGHT

Beaks

Their perpetual enmity was like mice in the walls.

Laurie Lee, ***Cider with Rosie***, from Kidson's commonplace book

Whilst Kidson was gregarious and clubbable with boys, those who found their way into his gang, anyway, he was generally aloof with his colleagues. In some ways, he was something of a Peter Pan character, remaining a teenager rather than one of the grown-ups. They felt, with some justification, that he was not entirely loyal to the side of authority on occasions.

Some of them found him difficult, off-hand, rude and petulant. Perhaps these traits rubbed off on him through his constant association with a bunch of bolshie adolescents in some form of reverse Stockholm Syndrome. At any rate, with some notable exceptions – John Peake, Charles George, Jeremy Nichols, Michael Meredith, Nigel Jaques, James Cook, David Evans, and later Andrew Gailey – most of them did not 'get' him. They either had a run-in with him and bore a grudge, or judged Kidson's book by what they saw as a rather pretentious cover, and did not read further.

Michael Meredith writes: 'A word about Michael and other beaks. Those of us who knew him well held him in great affection, realising that under the badinage and eccentricities there was a warm heart. I think "affection" is a good word, because Michael avoided emotion where possible, and required nothing more. Mark Phillips, for example, heard that he was in a care home, and, a week or two before Michael died, went to visit him. Michael was very ill. He could not speak and so communication was difficult. Mark had brought with him some Eton photographs and gently talked Michael through them. When he had finished, Michael looked at him and managed to whisper, "Thank you. I very much appreciate that." I think the story speaks so well of both men.'

'Those who disliked him thought him offensively rude, snobbish and a show-off. Of course, it is true that Michael could be intolerant of those he (often wrongly) considered in some way 'inferior'. It took time and patience to understand Michael, and a willingness to stand up to his pejorative comments and attitudes.'

David Evans: 'Boys accepted the abuse because they felt that it was a sign that he liked them and they interested him. I remember a boy in my house (Harry Lopes) telling me that he had received the highest possible praise from Michael, "If I was stuck with you on a train to Inverness, I would not find your company entirely tedious." Beaks were far less likely to take this attitude.'

It was very difficult in a place like Eton, where everyone worked in a close intensity, for beaks to conceal their feelings for other beaks, but Kidson frequently breached the covenant of solidarity between beaks and would say to a boy having difficulty with one of his colleagues, 'He's just a poor little civil servant.' Or he would mutter about the way some of his colleagues held their knives and forks, and of one unfortunate beak, he would say, 'I can't bear watching the man stuffing his face with some disgusting pudding, which he insists on calling "sweet".'

It did not help matters, either, when he deliberately got their names wrong. While boys played along with this running gag, adults were less inclined to find it funny.

Jeremy Nichols,[80] who did appreciate Michael's sense of humour, was a great friend of his and made Michael his son's godfather.

80 English beak, housemaster and later Headmaster of Stowe.

Jeremy Nichols: He had some of us round for drinks (including some pupils) and had run out of tonic. So, in some flusterment, he rang C.J. Reid (the chemist halfway down the High Street, half of whose emporium was given over to drink and other things).

'Hello, this is Kidson calling. Is that Mr Sunderland?'

'Is that Reid's the chemist then?'

'Well then, that's Mr Sunderland.'

'Oh, Scarborough, Sunderland – I knew it was one of those north-eastern towns ...'

We had to go and get the tonic from elsewhere!

Maybe Kidson's spiky exterior was in part explained by his desire to keep people at arm's length. As a newly arrived beak, he would have been pitched into the social whirl of the Eton community. Michael Meredith, who arrived at the same time, remembers that there were formal black-tie dinner parties on most nights of the week. He had arrived at Eton with only two dress-shirts and quickly found that he needed more. Kidson had nothing to be ashamed about in his past, but he had good reasons for feeling a little vulnerable. For one thing, whilst most beaks had, if not a first-class degree, at least a 2:1 – many had PhDs as well and quite a few were published authors – Kidson's academic credentials were less impressive.

David Evans: 'There was quite a bit of intellectual snobbishness among the staff – though beaks were not themselves snobbish (about class) – you had to have a First and probably one of the top prizes at Oxford or Cambridge to teach Classics to one of the top divs. It was said of Michael that he had been parachuted in from a prep school, because it was thought that he would be good at teaching the dimmer boys.'

Then there was his equivocal military service. In the mid-1960s, almost all teachers would have either served in the war or done National Service, and most, if not all, would have been officers, often in some of the smarter regiments. There is the story of a housemaster asking a boy how far they had got in their history syllabus. He replied, 'We have reached the point when Mr Parry enters the war.' Kidson's own National Service in the Gunners and short-lived career in the Education Corps were not things that he would have wished to discuss.

He might also have been uneasy about his background and education. Class was still a big issue – the most enduring comic sketch of the time is the one with John Cleese, Ronnie Barker and Ronnie Corbett on *The Frost Report* in 1966. One beak remembers walking into College with a briefcase and hearing a boy say, 'Here comes the grammar-school boy with his satchel.' (And then being pleased to watch Naomi Johnstone, the legendary battle-axe and Matron in College, grab the boy and give him a savage telling-off).

For Kidson, with his Oliver Twist boyhood, it was probably a source of unease. He would not have wanted to talk about it to avoid being pigeon-holed as 'other ranks', or worse. Indeed, he may well have found it painful to talk about his past and probably found it difficult to do so. I guess he pretended the nightmares had never happened, blanked any questions and stuck to the cover story, which was the life he felt he should have had, if tragedy had not intervened.

Part of his cover was sartorial. In matters of dress, Kidson laid a justifiable claim to be the best-dressed beak around. He lived within 100 yards of the tailors Welsh and Jeffries, a marvellous institution run by Sidney Boddy,[81] one of the great Eton characters of the era. Sid liked his drink and one soon learnt to get there early in the morning for a fitting. Suits cut after lunch never seemed to fit nearly as well. While we waited for Sid to find our trousers (which he had invariably lost), we would chat to Zita, a large and talkative Italian lady with a heart of gold, who ironed and sewed in the back rooms and allowed us to smoke in the Hoffman Press shed. Kidson was always having a new suit run up. He would breeze in like a Regency buck and say, 'Now Boddy, it's time I had a new suit ...'

---

81 Welsh and Jeffries is still there, but Sidney has long gone. I was told that when he retired in 1990 he bought a pub in Ascot, where he died eight years later.

To those beaks who affected a donnish anti-fashion in their dress – shapeless suits with lace-up moccasins or even, I remember, grey socks with sandals – this peacock in their midst probably seemed frivolous and pretentious. No doubt his one-upmanship also grated. Paddy Croker, who was well, if rather conventionally, dressed, once complained that he had spent seventy pounds on some new brogues, a sizeable sum in the early 1970s. Kidson replied, 'I presume that's seventy pounds each?'

Kidson's standing among his fellow beaks was not helped, either, by jealousy over his popularity with the boys.

Giles St Aubyn, Kidson's initial Head of the History Department, wrote:

8th November 1968 *Angelo's*

Dear Michael,

At the meeting on Saturday we went fully into the question of pupils amongst History masters. It became clear that certain masters were seriously under numbers. They partly accounted for this fact by saying they thought that other masters were seriously over numbers. Consequently, I thought it only right to make an analysis from the Calendar of the present distribution of pupils. Unless I have calculated wrongly, it appears that you have thirty! I seem to recall some time ago that you did mention that you were having trouble, but I must admit that I did not realise the matter had not been put right, nor did I imagine that you were fifteen over numbers.

At certain times, some tutors are considerably more popular than others, for good or bad reasons, and if pupils are to be equally distributed amongst the whole staff, this can best be achieved by rationing.

Although at the meeting no names were mentioned, it was clear to me that there was some ill-feeling amongst members of the Department directed towards those who grossly exceeded their statutory number of pupils and hence deprived others of the opportunity of taking any.

If I am right in supposing that you have thirty pupils, I would like to know how this has come to pass. At first sight it appears to be an unprecedented breach of a regulation which originates with the Head Master.

Yours ever,

Giles

A protracted negotiation followed, with attempts to get Kidson to 'jettison' some of his pupils. However, to the ultimate benefit of those of us who were his pupils, Michael continued cheerfully to disregard the regulations and regularly had to split his tutor groups into two, so that more of his evenings were taken up with Private Business than any of his colleagues.

To many of us, Kidson seemed to be the best housemaster we never had. Rummaging through his papers I discovered why:

From: THE HEAD MASTER *24th October 1968*

Dear Michael,

I know you will appreciate the difficulty in which I find myself in the allocation of House Lists. There are well over twenty members of staff who are now over thirty years old and have not begun making lists. It is clearly impossible for many of them to start lists with any prospect of taking over Housemasterships at a reasonable age, and I have been obliged to take age very seriously into account in inviting masters to open lists for the future.

After careful study of the position over the next four or five years, I must write to tell you that, simply on the grounds of age, I shall not be able to invite you to open a House List.

I hate to disappoint you and so many others who deserve better news; alas I just can't please all whom I'd like to!

Yours ever,

Tony

So, that was it. While other beaks could climb the greasy pole from assistant master to housemaster and then, maybe, go to be headmasters of minor, then major, public schools before, if they were very fortunate, becoming Masters of Oxbridge Colleges – or these days, a lucrative post running an educational trust – Kidson was to be consigned to the also-rans. He would always be given a pokey flat to live in, while his contemporaries could look forward to life in an agreeable Georgian 'private side', a large garden and a salary increase. You might like to think that the news would have been broken over an interview with coffee and biscuits, but evidently not. It must have come as a bitter blow. After so many reverses, just as he was making a success of his life, the ladder was removed.

Perhaps Michael had been led to believe that he might be given a house, but it was really a formality, and should not have been a big surprise to him that he missed out on grounds of age. A number of other beaks were also victims of the hopelessly incoherent system of house lists, which has since been modified, and received the same letter. Boys used to be put down for the school at birth and entered on a house list. The result was often, thirteen years later, that the housemaster in question had moved on to be a headmaster elsewhere and someone completely different was in charge, leading to five years of festering resentment for all concerned. There were instances of parents going to great lengths to research houses only to find that they had a girl. The other side of the coin was that there was such a long lead-time that housemasters were appointed on age – or in fact youth – rather than purely on experience and suitability.

It seems a bad HR decision, but perhaps we should be grateful. Kidson would not have had so much opportunity to focus on teaching. Nor would he have been able to carve out his unique niche as a tutor, if he had taken charge of a house. He would have had to conform and cope with the tiresome administrative minutiae of running a house of fifty boys and dealing with their parents. With hindsight, he might not have enjoyed it that much, although it must have been a great disappointment at the time.

Probably it was at this point that the maverick side of his nature took over. With his brilliant gift for teaching and his extraordinary empathy, he could see that he had an important role at the school, and he was determined to interpret it and pursue it as he saw fit, whether it accorded with the conventions or not. Mavericks perform a very important role in organisations. They are generally people who are not being motivated by the thought of promotion.

While some people go through their careers focusing on the next post rather than the one in hand, mavericks are often the ones who do their jobs best, when you stop to analyse it, although this is often camouflaged by their attitude. They are also the ones who are not afraid to speak their minds or bend the rules, and in doing so point out to everyone else where the system is at fault. From then on, Kidson was going to do things his way.

Every bit as much of a pastoralist as he was an academic, he ploughed his own furrow so successfully that he ended up creating his own virtual house. There is no doubt that many of his pupils thought of him as their de facto housemaster and his study in The Corner House, then later his flat in the High Street, as their house.

Michael Meredith remembers that Kidson 'went around in his own bubble' and remained detached from school life. Eton is run by committees but, never a committee man, he did not serve on any of them and therefore missed out on contributing to the dramatic changes of policy in the late 1960s and early 1970s, when entry standards, the curriculum, and the emphasis on music and drama, all had a shake-up. In fact, he went out of his way to avoid staff meetings.

Andrew Gailey recalls that it was a tradition, on the morning of the meeting, that Kidson would telephone the Head Master's secretary from Gloucestershire: 'Car half-dead in the garage, I'm afraid. I'm sorry, I shan't be able to make it. Will you be so kind as to give my apologies,' until one year he got the date wrong and she was able to say, 'Actually, Michael, it's next Monday, so you will be able to make it, won't you!'

This was all long before the system of appraisals and Kidson would have been horrified at the idea of anyone sitting in on his lessons or overseeing his work. But what no beak could dispute was that Kidson was very good at what he did.

David Evans was Head of the History Department for much of Kidson's time: 'Year by year, Michael reported to colleagues in Chambers that he had yet again "lost his rag" with divisions which were surely the stupidest it had ever been his misfortune to teach. Amazingly, in view of the barren soil, the seeds sown by Michael again and again produced a bountiful crop of good A level results. Head Master McCrum used to send a note of congratulation to masters whose divisions had done particularly well, and Michael almost always received one of them.'

David himself had a great respect for Kidson. He 'never had any trouble with him', he was always very professional at meeting deadlines and getting things done. Evans would ask Kidson to mark the Common Entrance papers with him each year and found him a shrewd judge, able to discern between bright boys who had been badly taught and their dimmer brethren who had been well coached for the exam.

Kidson's relations with housemasters varied enormously. Some were very appreciative of his work as a tutor and an excellent partnership ensued, much to the benefit of the boys.

James Cook continues: 'We were all aware, of course, of Michael's popularity as a modern tutor, of the queues of his pupils waiting at his door, of the time he took with them, of the affection in which he was held, of his loyalty towards them (for all the banter and invective) and of theirs towards him, a loyalty that far outlasted the two years or so of their time as his pupils.

'Later on, as housemasters, we appreciated as much as their parents did, the trenchant wisdom of his tutor's letters, especially on those pupils who were finding the challenges of A level History a little daunting, or who were having difficulty in adjusting their adolescent expectations to what the school required of them. He would champion their cause, though never irrationally, and at the same time tell them not to be such idiots. He was masterly at dealing with situations just outside the official awareness of those in authority, thereby saving a good many Eton careers. Boys loved him for it and repaid him with their friendship for the rest of his life.'

Another housemaster who was appreciative of Michael's qualities as a Modern Tutor was Archie Nicholson. He wrote Kidson a note in 1977:

Dear Michael,

This is just to thank you for bearing the, I'm afraid, considerable burden of tutoring Hugo Guinness and Lachlan Campbell. Their A levels were much as might have been predicted; Hugo never did enough work and Lachlan hadn't much to work with, but had some ability and enthusiasm for History of Art.

The fact that both of them requested you as their tutor must have had much the same effect on your arrangements as happened to mine when they came to my house. Throughout their time, they were two of the most difficult boys I have ever had. But, like most such, they had, I hope you'll agree, some redeeming features. Anyway, thank you very much for bearing with them.

Yours ever,
Archie

However, there were a number of housemasters with whom he was at permanent loggerheads. No respecter of rank, Kidson never kow-towed to housemasters as other beaks might have done.

Tom Birch Reynardson: 'I remember the look of horror when I told my housemaster that I had chosen Michael as my modern tutor. The fact was they could not have been more different. His father had been a housemaster at Eton, he had been to Eton, went briefly to Oxford (he rowed in the Oxford boat that sank in 1951) and returned to Eton shortly afterwards. Kidson did not think this much of an education in life and made it rather clear to anyone who was prepared to listen!'

Those of us who were his more unruly pupils somehow felt that we led a charmed life under Michael's protection. One ex-pupil, now an eminent banker, recalls being caught smoking by his dame:

'Having been recently elected to Pop, I had been caught by the dame in my house with a cigarette in my hand during Chambers in a mate's room. Not only did she see this as gross dereliction of a prefect's duty, but the mate concerned was also in a lower year and therefore my example was appalling. I was duly asked to follow her through the house to my housemaster's office, with her carrying the still-lit cigarette as evidence of my misdemeanour. I received a dressing down from my housemaster, who said that he would think about the consequences and possible punishment.

'I immediately went to see Michael to explain this rather awkward situation. Having returned to my housemaster to find out that he would not be taking the incident any further and thereby remaining as a member of Pop, I was a little confused. It became apparent at my next tutorial with Michael that he had called my housemaster and persuaded him not to pursue the matter. More than that, he also suggested that should I want to smoke that I would be very welcome at his flat whenever I wanted, whether he was there or not.'

It was only when I was doing my research thirty years later that I realised we really were under his protection: the rule was that a boy could not be put on the Bill to appear in front of the Head Master unless both his housemaster and his tutor signed the application. It is a good system that prevents the Head Master being inundated with disciplinary cases. It forces housemasters and tutors to confront problems, rather than simply passing them upstairs, and prevents victimisation. Frequently housemasters would try and get Kidson to sign a form to put us on the Bill and he would wave them away. I can imagine him saying, 'Don't be ridiculous, this is a very minor offence. The Head Master does not want to be bothered with this sort of trivia.' Presumably this was much to their frustration. They must at times have felt chained to an anarchist.

The only modernist, Kidson remained a little detached from the rest of the History Department. David Evans felt that he did not like people 'peering into his emotional life' and kept his distance. Andrew Gailey remembers that Kidson would sit at the back at their rare departmental meetings and did not contribute much. They were not so much a team – they did not need to be – as a cast of talented performers, all chiefs and no indians. There was John Peake, a hugely charismatic housemaster, known as Tusker. Minter Dial recalls him taking his division of lower boys onto a muddy football pitch to re-enact the breaking of a square of British infantry by the Zulus at Isandlwana. There was Tim Connor – tall and cerebral, with a hint of John Cleese about him, Andrew Gailey with his quiet Irish charm, and the brilliant David Evans, whose passionate expositions in class are still mimicked by middle-aged OEs today.

Looking back, the History Department was full of the school's largest characters and it was almost as though the only way to get on as a History Beak was to have a silly walk. Kidson himself had a very distinctive gait, but he was a complete amateur compared to some of the others. Paddy Croker went like a horse going lame in front – he had a pronounced 'nod' as he bustled down the street, rocking back and forth unevenly with one leg rigid owing to a faulty hip, the result of too many rugby injuries. But their walks paled into insignificance beside Robert Franklin. Franklin seemed to us to be Eton's answer to Stephen Hawking. A highly intelligent man, cruelly afflicted by polio, he shuffled through life with a withered arm and a partially paralysed leg that he dragged along behind him.

Keith Wilkinson, then a young chaplain, later to be the Conduct, was once astonished to see the trio pass him in the street: 'Kidson was striding on ahead and turned to Croker and Franklin and shouted, "Come along, you cripples, do keep up."

'I remember Franklin replying, "Bugger off, Kidson."

'In fact, I think Franklin would have been furious if Kidson had been any less rude to him than he was to everyone else. Not long after, I saw Franklin have a fall and roll into the road. I was terrified that he was going to be run over and I rushed to help him up. He was absolutely livid. "Fuck off," he said. "Fuck off, I get myself up."'

There was a mutual respect between Kidson and most of his colleagues in the department, but he did not hesitate to be rude about those he felt were below par. Maybe he felt there was room for only one eccentric in the History Department and Paddy Croker and Bill Winter were in danger of raining on his parade. Perhaps also, it was their military pasts that gave him good reasons for keeping them at a distance. Croker had been a National Service officer in the Royal Irish Fusiliers, Winter had taken part in the Berlin Airlift, which led to conjecture about how the Royal Air Force had managed to lift Bill.

Winter was a grinning giant with a large red face, known as the friendly hippopotamus or, more rudely, as Bourgeois Bill. In some ways, he was a similar character to Kidson. He was also an eccentric bachelor who dabbled in antiques. He portrayed himself as one of the gentlemen, rather than the players, and stories about him are of a slightly louche nature – turning up to teach early-morning school still in his dinner jacket, straight from a London party. Kidson was always rather dismissive of Bill, but he reserved his most disparaging rhetoric for Paddy Croker.

Croker lived below Kidson in the High Street and they were in a state of perpetual enmity – just like the two grannies in *Cider with Rosie*. It probably did not help that Croker was in some way connected to the Irish politician John Croker, the close friend and confidant of Kidson's great hero Sir Robert Peel. Paddy taught me for a year and he was in every respect Kidson's opposite: gentle, unworldly, hearty, kindly towards boys, with a limited, if cheerful sense of humour.

Croker went red and sweated profusely in hot weather, while Kidson always retained his cool. Where Kidson made complex historical issues simple, Croker often made quite simple things incomprehensible. While Kidson respected the school's ancient traditions, but somehow soared above them, Croker was indignant about them. Michael Meredith remembers him being affronted by Praeposters sweeping into his division room to summon boys to see the Head Master.

Whereas Kidson's flat was furnished like the library of a grand country house, Paddy Croker's was like a monk's cell. As well as his pronounced limp, he had a facial tic and seemed to be troubled by inner demons. It was said that he had been deeply affected by the death of one of the soldiers in his platoon in a training accident.

There are almost as many Croker stories[82] in Eton mythology as there

82 I have sourced several of them from Patrick Croker's obituary in the *2014/15 OEA Review*.

are Kidson stories. There is the one about Paddy demonstrating a tackle to the rugby team he was coaching by tackling a tree with such vigour that he sustained serious injuries. Or when he tripped and fell flat on his face and was heard to shout, 'Well tackled, that man!'

Other stories demonstrate his naivety and his propensity to get himself into trouble. As an officer in the Corps, he is remembered for berating his squad for finding their packs too heavy on a sweltering route march; with the result that, one by one, he ended up carrying them all himself. On another occasion, he is alleged to have led his platoon to the top of the wrong mountain in Norway. And then there was the time he organised a manoeuvre in the CCF Tattoo where his platoon swam across the river with their rifles – several of which sank to the bottom, swiftly followed by Paddy in bright red swimming trunks.

Perhaps the best illustration of all is when he drove a team of boys to London to compete in a schools' general-knowledge quiz in Westminster. The car juddered to a halt in the Cromwell Road as it ran out of petrol. 'Don't worry, boys, I was expecting that,' he intoned seriously. 'You see, I've been trying to find out how many miles I get to a tank of fuel, and now I have my answer.'

Where Kidson and Croker were similar was in the love they had for their dogs: Croker was as devoted to his golden retriever, Timber, as Kidson was to Dougal, and this was one of the fault lines in their relationship. Their two flats shared a staircase and opened out onto a garden at the back. Both dogs from time to time had the run of both spaces and sometimes they disgraced themselves on the stairs. This led to a furious neighbours' dispute over the faecal ownership. It is said that things got so heated once that boys had to pull them apart. On one occasion, there was a large mess on the lawn, they each blamed the other's dog and a row ensued, which rolled like thunder for days. On it went, until one night the turd disappeared. 'Or to be precise,' a former pupil recalled, 'half the turd did.'

Kidson, as you have already heard, tended to bath in the early evening, in darkness. Croker, by contrast, would rise early and pour himself a cold bath, then he would shout, 'What are you, Croker? Man or mouse? …

MAN!' and plunge into the icy waters. This ritual could be heard in the flat above. The story, which I fear is unverifiable and may possibly be apocryphal – let us hope so for Paddy's sake – is that Kidson sneaked down one morning and filled the bath with scalding hot water, with predictable results.

Kidson would lower his voice and growl about 'that man Croker' or 'Crokker, a pseudo-historian'. Boys soon learnt to feed him lines and listen for the withering responses:

'Sir, I think I'm actually related to Mr Croker.'

'Don't be so silly, nobody could possibly be related to Croker.'

His treatment of Croker was not one of Kidson's more creditable sides. No doubt he hoped that Croker would give as good as he got and that it would turn into a deliciously full-blown feud. But Paddy was not good at feuds by nature. He was too much of an innocent and too serious to retaliate. Croker looked down on Kidson as a less intellectual historian and simmered with resentment on occasions when the feuding was overt, but mostly he was oblivious to it.

An exchange of letters in Kidson's files show that even the Lower Master (the closest Eton gets to a Deputy Head) was not immune from his invective.

After Kidson talked during Chambers to a boy who was wearing denim jeans, when there was a strict rule against jeans, Jack Anderson, then the Lower Master, went up to him to remonstrate, 'Michael, how could you have let me down by talking to that boy in jeans, when you know jeans are strictly forbidden!'

Michael replied, in front of all the other beaks, 'I couldn't give a f*** what he was wearing!' and walked off.

The following day, Kidson received the following note:

From: The Lower Master *6.vii.77*

Dear Michael,

I appreciate that it is hot and that we are all tired, but I must insist on an immediate withdrawal of the ill-advised and frankly unhelpful remarks you made yesterday morning.

Yours,

John

Kidson kept his head down and the day after that another note arrived:

From: The Lower Master *7.vii.77*

Dear Michael,

I tried to find you at Chambers without success. In consequence, I must take it from your silence that you have no intention of changing your position. It only remains for you to explain how you feel to the Head Master & I must ask you to do just that.

Yours,

John

Copy to the Head Master

Kidson decided that the best form of defence is attack:

7 July 1977 *134–135 High Street*

Dear John,

Thank you for your several notes.

I am sorry: but I decline to be treated as though I were a recalcitrant lower boy – which has been very much your style in this matter. I don't know what you mean by 'changing your position'. I have assumed no position to change. I am not in fact, particularly tired – that I must have said in exasperation. I have never complained at Eton of overwork.

However, the colour or texture of a pupil's trousers seems to me – and will seem to me if I live to be 1,000 years old – of small moment compared with the problems of trials' marking or other far more important end-of-half business (which was occupying my mind when you attacked me so peremptorily).When the minutiae of school change[86] *are given the preponderance you require – then really I begin to feel that I would be better occupied patrolling the corridors of a state penitentiary.*

Nor is it fair of you to make an issue of this kind with me: only the day before I had sent back two boys from the golf course who were improperly dressed, I do not condone – much less encourage – shoddy dress or shoddy manners.

I repeat – I'm sorry: but I think you have done your best to make a mountain out of a molehill.

I have, as you asked, sent copies of our correspondence the Head Master,

Yours,
Michael

7 July 1977 *134–135 High Street*

Dear Head Master,

In accordance with the Lower Master's wishes, I send you copies of correspondence which has passed between us.

I feel very strongly that there was no need whatsoever to make an issue out of so relatively paltry a matter at this stage of the half. In the last few days I have had to write – in addition to normal business – eleven brief leaving letters to you, and twenty tutors' letters.

Was it really necessary to compound this number because Morgan-Grenville was wearing the wrong trousers?

Yours sincerely
Michael Kidson

86 Boys were allowed to wear a 'change' of clothes on certain occasions (typically a tweed coat and grey flannel trousers, or a suit) when not in School Dress.

From: THE HEAD MASTER
To: MGMK
7.7.1977

Please come and see me at 12 noon tomorrow to discuss the Lower Master's complaint.
MMcC.

But Kidson had already left for the holidays.

Nearly forty years later, when I contacted **Roger Morgan-Grenville** to find out a bit more about 'trousergate', I was amused to find that he had no idea what trouble he had caused. He wrote: 'MGMK protected my dress-sense more than once. Having said that, he thought my taste dubious, and felt that I probably committed the ultimate solecism of buying clothes at Austin Reed. He meant it to sting!'

Though never afraid to speak his mind to the Head Master of the day, Kidson did have great respect for all three. He liked Tony Chenevix-Trench and was very sad at his early departure. He was not close to Michael McCrum, few people were, but he admired him. And he had a much closer friendship and a mutual respect with Eric Anderson.

This memo from McCrum just after Kidson's dog had been run over gives an interesting view of McCrum's character:

From: THE HEAD MASTER
To: MGMK
27.4.1973

I was so sorry to hear of the sad fate of your dog in the holidays, a most upsetting occurrence.
MMcC.

When Michael McCrum was due to retire, the Fellows[87] canvassed the beaks for their views on a successor. Kidson was not shy about offering his opinions and his submission is characteristically blunt:

1st December 1979 *134–135 High Street*

Dear Mr Hirst,

May I write to you briefly about a new Head Master?

I personally have unstinting admiration for what Michael McCrum has done here, and I believe that he deserves far more appreciation than he generally receives. The critical voice seems to come down to nothing much more than a determination that he sheds a good deal of light – which no one can dispute – and not enough warmth. I have not found this; and, for me, he has been an ideal Head Master of Eton and an example, therefore, by which one hopes that his successor will be measured.

Under him the school's academic standards have risen tremendously, and I wish very much that the Fellows intend to try to maintain that momentum. I do not take seriously those who, for one specious reason or another, object to this progress. They are generally prospective parents with very dim-witted progeny – or, possibly, the less industrious among us.

Another of Michael McCrum's great virtues is that he is thoroughly straight and unpolitical, never a protagonist of cabals and private interests.

Several of the names now canvassed simply do not meet these standards. It is hard indeed to believe that there is an agreeable candidate among those who have recently left Eton. I confess to an aversion for devious and ambitious clerics, from Wolsey to Cosmo Gordon Lang and Dr Stockwood, and whomever else the cap may fit (particularly if their academic qualifications fall short of their aspirations). Elsewhere, a well-known Eton patronymic cannot disguise other more obvious and

87 The Fellows of Eton are like school governors.

practical shortcomings. I have also heard mentioned the name of another headmaster, a former cricketer: a very nice man, but certainly not an intellectual one.

If a schoolmaster of the right credentials proves too elusive, is there no Oxbridge don of the necessary standard and promise?

Yours sincerely,

Michael Kidson

Kidson's high regard for McCrum led to his campaigning for a knighthood for him. He wrote a number of letters trying to enlist the support of, among others, the Cabinet Secretary, Sir Robert Armstrong, and the Home Secretary, Douglas Hurd, both Fellows of Eton. And then finally:

To: The Rt. Hon. Mrs Margaret Thatcher, P.C., M.P.
10 Downing Street *3rd October 1987*

Dear Prime Minister,

Several years ago I wrote to the Chairman of the Honours Scrutiny Committee to suggest appropriate honours for two distinguished men: and predictably I received from your office only a casual and non-committal reply.

I put forward the names of Mr Michael McCrum, a sometime distinguished head master of Tonbridge and Eton, and Vice-Chancellor elect of the University of Cambridge; and Mr. James Lees-Milne, a much respected biographer, and for thirty years an indispensable senior servant of the National Trust.

Neither man has been recognised. Could your Office be persuaded to explain the esoteric means by which all kinds of less eminent persons are preferred to men of this distinction? The anomalies and shibboleths are very difficult to follow.

I am, Madam, your obedient servant,

Michael Kidson

(M.G.MacD. Kidson)

Kidson was also on good terms with the Provosts. He reminisced in old age about attending a supper party that Lord Charteris had given for the Queen Mother and later he was close to the Aclands – Angus McGougan, Lady Acland's son by her first marriage, had been a Kidson pupil.

Kidson was often at odds with beaks of his own age, but he was more avuncular with the younger beaks, though, as with boys, he would test their mettle before allowing them to become friends.

Andrew Gailey arrived fresh from Cambridge in 1981 and, much closer in age to the boys than he was to Kidson, had a similar take on some of his older colleagues to theirs.

Andrew Gailey: I remember the head of the department, David Evans, asking me if I would mind teaching an Oxbridge division. I was surprised at the way it was put and replied that I would be delighted. He seemed a little uneasy and then said, 'Look, I think I should level with you. It has girls in it.' Clearly some of the more misogynist beaks did not relish the idea of teaching girls!

Not long after I arrived, I had to see Michael. He and I were teaching two halves of the same History division. We had to agree which one of us was to set the third essay of the half. I thought I would catch him before the start of a div, but when I got there the classroom was already full of boys. I asked him if we could talk about the essay and Kidson made a show of pretending that he thought I was a boy:

'OK, go and sit at the back and come and see me at the end.'

I stood my ground and we resolved the issue – he made a great gesture of giving me the essay to set (and mark!). He then did not speak to me for the rest of the half.

Then a few months later, he invited me to Sunday drinks in his flat. It so happened that my girlfriend – now wife, Shauna – was staying that weekend, so I thought 'right, I'll fix the old misogynist' and accepted, saying that she would be with me without giving him any option. It did not turn out quite as I had expected. Michael monopolised Shauna for half an hour, they discovered mutual interests in hunting and sporting art, and she found him absolutely charming. The rest of us were wanting to get away for lunch while they were still talking!

Some time later, after we were married, Shauna was very seriously ill one summer. Suddenly Michael started to ask me to play golf with him at the Berkshire. We played regularly and, although we never discussed Shauna's illness, he showed a touching concern for my state of mind. Fortunately, Shauna recovered and, just as suddenly, the golfing invitations dried up.

I began to think that I had gained his acceptance when we were standing in School Hall one Chambers and he pointed to a group of beaks and pretended that he thought they were a bunch of tourists who had walked in off the street. He said to me, 'Look at them, what an absolute shower. How did they get in here? Don't you think someone should say something to the Head Master?'

'But Michael, those are your colleagues.'

'Really? Are you sure?'

He took off his spectacles and started polishing them.

Martin Humphreys, whom we met earlier as one of Kidson's pupils, was another young beak who has fond memories of Kidson as he neared retirement:

'He was still teaching when I returned briefly to Eton to teach in 1994. This was my first teaching job. Typically, Eton made no concessions to the fact that I had never taught before, that I was not qualified to teach, that my only preparation was three weeks' furious reading, having resigned from my investment banking employment.

'Michael was endlessly encouraging in his inimitable way. Six weeks into my first half, I had a major meltdown as I imagined my Lower Sixth div all failing their A level. Michael was reassurance itself, "The thing to remember, Martin, is that we beaks really make very little difference."

'How right and how wrong!'

CHAPTER NINE

A Sheeted Tombstone

Kidson the report writer

> ***Praise is the best diet for us, after all.***
> *and*
> ***Praise like gold and diamonds owes its value only to its scarcity.***

Two seemingly contradictory statements from Kidson's commonplace book

Report writing is no longer the art form that it was. In these politically correct days in the twenty-first century, one suspects that few teachers feel they can be completely frank about their students. The word-processing revolution has not helped matters – the temptation is for them to write a generic report on the work that has been covered, which can be tailored to suit the whole class, with just one or two sentences at the end for individual pupils. Although I am relieved to hear from current Eton parents that they still get very perceptive and amusing reports on their sons.

Kidson's reports were carefully made to measure. He collected insults in his commonplace books and indulged in 'flyting' his pupils. Many of his reports are now treasured possessions of their subjects. They are, in their way and certainly to their owners, collectors' items as valuable as a first edition of Robert Burns's *To a Louse*.

Bertie Gore Browne's parents were left in no doubt about their son's performance in history that half.

> *History Report* *Lent Half, 1973*
>
> I cannot pretend that Gore Browne's presence in my division this half has filled me with fire and enthusiasm. As Sidney Herbert[88] once said in similar circumstances: 'It is like addressing a sheeted tombstone by moonlight.' Gore Browne is about as lively as an inanimate centenarian: no flicker of interest, no suggestion of reciprocal partnership in a lesson, not a sign of interest.
>
> It is all infinitely depressing for the wretched usher trying to keep him. And the sad thing is that he is by no means hopeless: on his best behaviour, he would achieve something above the bottom grades – but really he gives one no grounds for sustaining any kind of optimism.

Bertie himself bore Kidson no ill will and turned up at his memorial service forty years later.

Guy Morrison no longer has the report he received from Kidson one half, but he remembers it vividly: 'What can one say of Morrison? Immured like a drug addict in idleness, he hunts down the obvious with the enthusiasm of a short-sighted detective; abstracted one minute, bored the next. As Mr Gladstone once said, "When we were at Eton we knew little, but we knew it well." In Morrison's case, I fear the former is as true as the latter is remote.'

He described another boy as 'a truculent navvy'.

Whilst no insult was too ripe for those at the bottom of divs, despite the quotation at the start of the chapter, he could never quite bring himself to praise those at the top.

Charles Villiers came first in a class of twenty-three and received the following report: 'This is a very even division, and whoever finished

88 One of Kidson's favourite Victorian statesmen. Minister of War under Palmerston, friend of Florence Nightingale and chatelain of Wilton House. The quote refers to addressing the House of Lords.

top of it was probably going to be flattered by the honour. I can't quite see how he managed it: even very basic statistics like these can be misleading. Never mind – perhaps it's promise rather than performance that matters here. He might eventually make up into quite a competent historian.'

And **Maurice Fermoy** (then Roche) detected some faint praise in his report from Michaelmas 1983: 'After some grim and grisly early offerings, Roche began to improve a little. He was one of the few in this dismally weak bottom division who actually made an effort. He minded that his essays were desperate. And so more recently his essays have actually begun to shape a little and he looks to me, whatever happens in trials, nearly the most promising historian in the div, though heaven knows it is a wretched compliment.'

The convention was for modern tutors to write to housemasters about their pupils' academic progress. The housemaster was then supposed to forward it on to parents with his own letter and reports from each subject. Kidson's reports were sometimes so rude that housemasters suppressed them, rather than antagonising parents. Boys knew that they were not meant to be taken too seriously, and if they could not take a joke, they should not have chosen him as their tutor. Convincing parents that they should not be taken literally was not always easy, though. Most of his pupils would agree that whilst you could pull the wool over some beaks' eyes, there was no bluffing Kidson and he read their characters very well.

Perhaps that is why so many of his pupils have been happy to share them with us: they know they were fair depictions of their teenaged selves, and have respect for him for calling a spade a spade, and harbour no lasting grudge. I remember Kidson lamenting in one letter about me that I was 'a fairly indolent fellow' and there would be no point in my staying on after A levels unless I could 'develop some intellectual stamina', an uncharacteristically polite way of saying that I was doing the bare minimum to get by.[89] His reports, always very well meant, often made uncomfortable reading for their brutal honesty.

---

89 How I regret it now!

This letter about Hylton Murray-Philipson is typical of the genre:

Dear Payne,

If we are to accept Hylton Murray-Philipson's own estimate of his performance in A levels, then clearly he must have done pretty well. It goes without saying that his own estimate is a suitably high one. One can only hope that he's right.

Certainly the History papers were all very fair ones. He didn't revise the right things for English History Outlines – and that was entirely his own fault: he usually knows better than I do.

This is certainly not the moment when one would begin to wish that he should be deflated. He is by no means a powerful candidate for Oriel, and he very badly needs a platform of good A levels. I hope - and think - that he will achieve them.

I'm sorry that Hylton is still so loth to occasional self-examination. 'Every man has a right to be conceited until he's successful,' said the irrepressible Dizzy – but it becomes a bore if success is very elusive. Hylton has manifestly not been the meteoric prodigy that he would like to believe: he has only to look about him. Surely there must soon come a moment when he must wonder why this or that success or honour has not come his way. Might it be because one's bearing and behaviour – however well you may do things – does matter terribly. I'm often struck by the brand of 'charm' he exhibits – as though charm, instead of being natural and spontaneous, can be switched on and off like a tap.

Anyway, one puts it down to his growing up, which is harder for some than for others. But he mustn't think that I'm the only one who notices the unattractive side – as he affects to do – and, for that good reason, to dismiss it.

We shall very much hope for good news in August.

Yours sincerely,

Michael Kidson

Kidson wrote of **Napier Marten**:

Dear Spencer,

I am sorry to have to say it – but let us not dissimulate – Napier Marten is probably the laziest boy I have ever come across.

His Trials' results are not less than a complete disgrace: failure in two subjects, nearly bottom in all three. He seems to have absolutely no interest or commitment whatsoever.

Moreover – what is eminently worse – he is inclined to be less than frank about his frequent failures to produce this and that. I well remember from his being up to me in D that he would fail to produce an EW and pretend that it was mislaid – or smoother similar pathetic subterfuge. St Aubyn then advised me to watch him very carefully. There is in fact no need to do so: his laziness and utter incompetence couldn't be more obvious.

His main occupation seems to be going about the Eton streets being social and sociable – it's one protracted garden party.

And the result – disastrous failure. There really is no obvious reason why he should be here at all: and yet one has to try to convince the Head Master that he's worth keeping in the place. It's hard to find a convincing argument.

His – characteristic – panacea for his own shortcomings is to try to give up Economics. Why? – To give himself time to do well elsewhere? That is the story; but it cuts no ice, for we know that the real object is to give Marten more time to jettison. And no one jettisons time like Marten. I would strongly resist his being allowed to do any such thing: it is an open invitation to more incompetence and idleness.

What sympathy and support does this lazy, incompetent, unreliable boy deserve?

Enough of indulgence and pussy-footing with Marten: he needs firmly to be persuaded that the world doesn't exist as his private playground. Let him get on and begin – just begin – to earn his keep.

Yours sincerely

Michael Kidson

Napier, far from being cowed by this report, invited Kidson to shoot his father's pheasants and says, 'It still makes me laugh every time.'

Of **Henry Pitman**, he wrote:

Dear Faulkner,

I don't know what he'll achieve in Trials – one may be forgiven a certain nervousness – but at any rate Henry Pitman's reports this half are really rather encouraging.

Henry's powers of self-examination have never been strong: he is the eternal optimist who won't admit – whether he knows – that his work is rather scruffy, rather undisciplined, comprehensively illiterate. Perhaps, after all, this is a strength rather than a weakness – lack of confidence is a great handicap, & one from which Henry doesn't suffer.

And now, just modestly, he is beginning to shape. I believe that he might yet pleasantly surprise us in June if only he will work hard consistently, as Franklin enjoins.

Henry remains cheerful and good-natured as ever. I've no doubt said before that he would certainly be among my top several candidates for company in a slit trench.

Yours sincerely,
Michael Kidson

When the A level results came out Henry received the following postcard from Kidson:

18 August, Perthshire, Scotland.
Henry, I hope that you weren't disappointed by your results – probably they're as much as we had a right to expect: overall results this year were not as good as last (fewer than 20 'A's in History, for instance). We all want our geese to be swans, & you aren't a swan – & you really haven't done badly. Hope you're enjoying yourself.
Love Michael.

Of **Alex Bonsor**, Kidson remarked: 'He is undoubtedly an able fellow, but just a little too casual and cavalier, attractive though these qualities are. Better Rupert than Cromwell.'

Of **Jonathan Lloyd** he wrote: I confess that I shall await his A level results with some trepidation … I hope very much that he will contrive three modest grades: he has no right to expect anything better. There are worse sins than idleness. I have much enjoyed knowing him and wish him every possible success in the future.

Guy Butterwick: 'He wrote a letter to my parents when I got my A level results that to me says it all. It started, "Dear Mr and Mrs Butterwick, A major miracle has taken place. Your son has passed his A levels. An extraordinary achievement for a great thickhead like Guy."'

Whilst happy to use his wit to excoriate his pupils he did not like it when a colleague muscled in on the act and was trenchant in support of his boys.

Jeremy Harbord: 'When he was my Modern Tutor in December 1968, in his report to my housemaster Ken Spencer, Kidson refers to Alastair Graham's French report, which was indeed extremely convoluted: "I always find it a little difficult to unravel the tortuous anfranctuosities of ACG's style, but one gathers it was a bad division, and that Jeremy tried, but still has far to go."'

Edward Harley recalls that his reports read:

> *December 1976:* I like very much what I have seen of Edward Harley. Not everyone comes to mind as an improving sort – but Edward does; at the moment he is untidy and a slapdash performer – fairly comprehensively illiterate – but I believe has got a bit of an 'ear', and is a learner: he won't stand still.
>
> *March 1977:* There is also, I think, a bit of the un-Philistine about him.
>
> *July 1977:* He is an observant and intelligent fellow, by no means as lost and abstracted as he sometimes appears.

> *March 1978:* Connor says that Edward writes well, which simply isn't true; he can't spell, his basic syntax is invariably shaky, his vocabulary jejune, the style generally prosaic. I know it well; I've been trying to read his project; I was never able to go more than about two lines without finding something execrable. I think that Connor must have been thinking of someone else.

Harley says, 'This ringing endorsement includes two of his favourite words, jejune and execrable – neither of which I can ever see without thinking of MGMK. When I fluked a scholarship to Cambridge, he wrote with the opening line, "Of course, the whole thing is a complete joke …"'

While **Roger Morgan Grenville's** reports read:

> *1975 December:* His reports are predictably uncommitted, but everyone has something reasonably cheerful to say. He seems to me generally good value.
> *1976 July:* He seems wholly unable to criticise his own work. He is a bulldozer, who rushes in pachydermatously unaware that one might be talking to someone else. Perhaps, if we don't stop him, he will become an embryonic and ultimate club bore.
> *1976 December:* Roger wouldn't be my ideal companion if I wanted a quiet doze in the club, or a languid walk in the hills. He might pleasantly surprise us in the summer if he concentrates on channelling his energies and not wasting them in the desert air.
> *1977 March:* He is a cheerful and likeable character, whom one is especially anxious to see do really well.

Simon Broackes: 'In the full page available for his tutor's report in 1983, Kidson wrote the sentence, "Amongst the also-rans." It is a shame I don't still have that!'

Matthew Gordon Clark: 'What I thought of at the time as being one of my proudest achievements as far as he was concerned was my treasured report at the end of a summer half, which read:

Dear Roynon,

It is possible that Gordon Clark [the one and only time he used my proper surname – he usually called me Gordon-Lennox!] may become a half-tolerable historian. Or not. I have no way of telling as I have barely seen him this half.

MGMK.

P.S. Good luck at Henley.

'I think I was more proud of the PS than anything else!'

Sometimes in a lesson, Kidson felt that the circumstances required an emergency report and he scribbled this one on the spot and gave it to **Ben Weatherall** to take it to his housemaster, David Evans, to be signed:

To: DAE
Weatherall thinks it amusing to sit in my division and emit noxious fumes – noisily and thoroughly unpleasantly. These things are not, I know, always controllable. It is particularly objectionable when he advertises his weakness, and thinks it generally rather funny.
MGMK
10 March 1983

Ben did not get it signed, he got it framed to hang on his wall.

Forty years after the event, **Andrew Joicey** remembers being given this ticket for his housemaster: 'CWW. I am fed up with Joicey's clever remarks. He will write me an essay, "How important is dramatic irony in Macbeth?" MGMK.'

And **Ed Lennox** was given this one to give to his housemaster, Jeremy Nichols: 'JGLN. I will not have Lennox in my division. His behaviour is steadily impertinent, & I have had constant trouble with him. As we have just begun a new subject, it should be quite simple to make other arrangements for him. MGMK.'

Ed was soon reinstated and appended the report to his leaver to Kidson as a reminder.

There must be many more collecting dust in attics.

Once Kidson had accepted a pupil, he saw it as his mission to ensure that the boy made it through to the end. As well as the ever-present threat of expulsion for rule-breaking, there was a risk that if you failed Trials – the exams at the end of each half – you would be asked to leave. This letter about **Hugh Roche**, now a successful entrepreneur, was a pre-emptive device:

Dear Head Master,

I take a risk in defending him before the event – but, as there is some danger of Hugh Roche's failing Trials this half, will you allow me to make a special appeal for him?

He is, in my view, a thoroughly good man. We took him when he passed CE; subsequently he qualified to specialise through O Level and GCSE, although manifestly unacademic. Since then, predictably, he has struggled.

Don't we have a duty, occasionally, to try to make the best of these boys, even if specialist work is going to be uphill?

He is kind, cheerful, honest, thoroughly well-liked: frequent peccadillos can't damage the good side. If there were a conventional war tomorrow, you couldn't wish for a better companion in a slit trench, & he would win an MC straight away.

To send him away would do him no good, & only put a great load onto his mother's shoulders.

Yours sincerely,
Michel Kidson

Other pupils who seemed in danger of failing their A levels say that their bacon was saved by a miraculous result in History of Art, particularly in the project, which contained rather more of Kidson's original thoughts than their own.

Benjy Mancroft was another pupil who courted expulsion and attracted the attention of the Head Master, Michael McCrum:

From: THE HEAD MASTER
To: RDB
13 December 1973

Thank you for sending Mancroft with his reports. They are indeed dismal, and I hope he takes good notice of what MGMK has written. But he is pretty impervious to adverse criticism.

I think that at this stage, more important than threatening him with Superannuation in July 1974, will be very close supervision of his work by MGMK and yourself, with weekly reports for the next two Halves. If necessary, I am prepared to come in too.

I think that any bad piece of work should involve his suffering a certain amount of discomfort, e.g. detention on Saturday evenings, until the penny finally drops.

MMcC

Benjy Mancroft: 'I found education paralysingly boring and I rather gave up on school. I was on the Bill more than anybody else, usually for minor things. Kidson realised that I was not responding to the conventional way of teaching and he just threw books at me to read – history and particularly political history, which I found really interesting, an interest that has stayed with me. We would sit up arguing late into the night about them. I remember once talking about Charles II and saying that he had behaved in a rather underhand way over the Secret Treaty of Dover and Kidson saying, "Well, he was only behaving like you do towards your beaks."

'He succeeded in dealing with difficult boys, because he treated everyone as equals and did not put up with any bullshit. I did go off the rails after Eton and many years later he wrote to me saying, "Of course, you had your difficulties, but there was never any doubt that you would come through them."'

Henry Hood was worried about his work as A levels loomed. He was a good cricketer and scored a century against Winchester. Later he found a note from Kidson in his pigeon-hole in the house. He had written

H.L.A. Hammond and crossed out the Hammond and inserted Hood.[90] Then he had written, 'Other things are more important than A levels and your century is always something you can be very proud of.'

Michael kept a watchful eye on his pupils as they neared their A levels. Frequently, though, his mentoring could not make up for too much play and too little work and the revision was too little and too late. One of them asked him for an opinion on his exam prospects. He looked over his spectacles in that mock magisterial way of his and said, 'Lady Nemesis has laid her frosty hand on your shoulder, and you must pay the cost.'

And once the results were in he was on hand to lend support. Radio journalist **Cornelius Lysaght** received the following letter:

16 Rue Lauriston,
1st September 1982 *75116 Paris*

My Dear Cornelius,

As I'm away, I'm only now getting abreast of A level results. Yours were undistinguished, certainly, and I hope that you aren't too disappointed. You aren't a very clever old thing, so you mustn't think it's the end of the world (as you fiddle away with your super-sensory wireless buttons in the attic). Soon you might be a great tycoon owning 20 new dynamic radio stations. That's as may be, but the world certainly doesn't hinge on A level results, so don't be depressed (& don't let your parents creep quietly off to the barn to blow their brains out).

I don't know what your immediate plans are – let me know if I can help – & stay cheerful & philosophic – & thank your lucky stars that, unlike me, you don't have to start back in a few days' time.

Best wishes,

Michael K

90 This is a reference to Wally Hammond, one of Kidson's cricketing heroes (whose initials were in fact W.R.).

CHAPTER TEN

The Heartless Ramparts

Kidson on pronunciation and style

Look at her, a prisoner of the gutter,
Condemned by every syllable she utters
By right she should be taken out and hung,
For the cold-blooded murder of the English tongue.

Alan Jay Lerner, ***My Fair Lady***

A gentleman never looks as if he has just had his hair cut.

Anon, from Kidson's commonplace book

Anyone who was taught by Kidson will remember that he was a stickler for correct pronunciation. If I am honest about it, he was rather pedantic and in many people this might have become a bore, but it was always a game with him. I suspect he hit upon it as a way of keeping pupils on the ball and of keeping the banter going – in such a way that he kept the upper hand.

We would greet him by saying, 'You're looking very "swarve" today, sir.' (And he usually did, from the neck down, anyway). He would give us an arch look and say, 'The word is suave,' rhyming with wave. On other occasions, he would talk about someone having committed a heinous crime and someone would ask, 'Do you mean "heenious", sir?' And he would look over his spectacles and say, 'Of course not, I mean heinous,' with a long 'a'. Then some wag would say, 'Ah, but you're wrong, sir. I'm sure the "h" is silent.' And this would be rewarded by a Captain Mainwaring-like, 'You stupid boy.'

It was also another way of expanding our vocabularies with a mouthful of useful and near-extinct words. His History of Art pupils were able to dazzle examiners with their employment of the word chiaroscuro.

He would tell us, 'Don't say "Edwawrdian", but "Edwardian" – as in guardian' and 'Westcut, boy, not waistcoat.' Someone from Scotland was not Scottish, he was 'Scotch'. Boys from Hertfordshire were a favourite target, especially if they committed the solecism of sounding the silent 't'. He threatened to send us to 'Cuventry' and talked about shops in the 'Crumwell Road'. He was particularly vehement against genteelisms, muttering about colleagues who talked about someone having 'passed away', rather than died.

He would have expired at the thought of being described as a teacher, he was always a schoolmaster, and this (unpublished) letter to *The Times* from his desk makes his views trenchantly clear:

> *From Michael Kidson*
>
> *Sir, It must say something about the changed character of your newspaper that on September 17 it contained among its Latest Wills notice of the estate of a recent distinguished Head Master of Eton, describing him as 'headteacher of Eton', and more correctly Master of Corpus Christi College, Cambridge. I wonder if you have further plans to revise the nomenclature of other significant offices, and, if so, what is the purpose?*
>
> *Yours faithfully,*
> *Michael Kidson*
> *Ivy Cottage, Westonbirt, Gloucestershire GL8 8QT*

A favourite word was 'soddering' – the correct way of pronouncing soldering.[91] He would look at pupils and say, 'I shall have to cut this short as

91 Fowler says: 'The only pronunciation I have ever heard, except from the half-educated to whom spelling is a final court of appeal, is soder, which is accordingly here recommended.' So there.

I have some soddering to do this afternoon.' When the mirth subsided, he would affect to look perplexed by our humour and say, 'What is so funny? My toaster is broken and I need to stick the handle back on.'

Actually, the thought of him soldering was funny, as he was so impractical he would have ended up sticking his fingers together. This particular pronunciation entered Eton mythology – as he surely intended it to – when he went into the ironmongers in the High Street and asked for a 'soddering iron'. After several minutes of confusion, the shop assistant replied, 'Do you mean a soldering iron, sir?' Kidson answered, 'I will not prostitute myself in your shop!' and stormed out.

The Bible on these occasions was 'Fowler' and to this day I have a copy of *A Dictionary of Modern English Usage* by H.W. Fowler by my desk, as, I suspect, do many other pupils of his.

Fowler himself says of pronunciation: 'The ambition to do better than one's neighbours is in many departments of life a virtue; in pronunciation, it is a vice … the moral of which is that, while we are entitled to display a certain fastidious precision in our saying of words that only the educated use, we deserve not praise but censure if we decline to accept the popular pronunciation of popular words.' I vaguely remember Kidson paying lip service to this once in a tutorial, before reverting to fastidious precision.

Kidson's old-fashioned way of speaking was maybe partly because he was brought up by Victorians. Perhaps also, he believed that one of the greatest favours you can do an Englishman, as George Bernard Shaw and Alan Jay Lerner knew, is ensure that he is not going to be 'condemned to the gutter by every syllable he utters'. As someone who was in some ways an outsider, he would have been acutely aware of this. The boy from the orphanage, despite his respectable origins, probably made his way through the Army and Cambridge modifying his speech a little as he went.

Like many writers and public speakers, Kidson sharpened his wit by writing down anything that interested or amused him that he had read, or heard, in a commonplace book. Two volumes survive. They are smart, leather-bound notebooks with NOTEBOOK M.G.MACD.K. in gold lettering down the spines and on the front. Inside, on lined notepaper, he has copied down quotes from a wide range of sources, often from his heroes: Dr Johnson, Jane Austen, Gladstone and others.

It is possible to trace the development of his handwriting from the neat hand of a recent Cambridge graduate to the random hieroglyphics of middle age, which I remember so well from the bottom of my essays. One can discern traits of behaviour or style of communication that he admired, or deprecated, and sound advice that he sought to pass on to his pupils. The extracts in his notebooks would sometimes find their way into his insults, his damning reports and his letters. I have included a number of them in this book.

They form a revealing picture of Kidson, his sense of humour and his creed, a road map of the Kidsonian hinterland. They are a reminder of the richness and subtlety of our language, when it is not mangled by bureaucrats, or reduced to the words-of-one-syllable directness of the soundbite.

One of them inspired the title of this chapter, 'The Heartless Ramparts'. The quotation comes from Leo Rosten's comic book *The Return of Hyman Kaplin*, published in 1959, the sequel to *The Education of Hyman Kaplin* of 1937 – both being based on short stories from *The New Yorker*. The books are set in a New York adult night-class for immigrants learning English, and the Jewish Hyman Kaplin is a very well-intentioned, but hopelessly unteachable, man, who always fails to understand the meaning of a sentence, or the drift of an argument. In his class are many other extraordinary men and women, including the fat Mrs Moskowitz, described as 'massive and doleful as ever, heaving her double chins and ample bosom, which always accompanied her efforts to scale *the heartless ramparts of English*.'[92]

The phrase sums up nicely the way that the English educated classes have – more so in those days – of repelling intruders and tripping up imposters by an invisible barrier of vowels and consonants. There is a confidence that

92 I am indebted to Michael Meredith for finding the source.

comes from knowing how to say things correctly and Kidson did his best to ensure that his boys went out into the world properly equipped. It is thanks to him that if I ever come across someone with the misfortune to be called Cholmondley-Marjoribanks, I will know to say, 'How do you do, Mr Chumley-Marchbanks?'[93]

In his desk, he kept a list of commonly mispronounced words, which I have reproduced below. I am sure that readers will have no difficulty in pronouncing them, but if there is any doubt, they need to refer to Fowler; then they can discuss their eleemosynary lucubrations with confidence:

> Abdomen, apartheid, applicable, ate, bathos, charleton, chastisement, chiaruscoro, chiropodist, cinema, combat, communal, consummate, controversial, culinary, decade, denigrate, eleemosynary, envelope, expletive, forebade, forehead, formidable, genie, genii, golf, gratis, heinous, incomparable, integral, invalid, inveigle, lamentable, lather, leeward, loth, lucubrations, machinations, momentary, negotiate, negotiation, niche, often, omen, ominous, orangutan, patron, patronage, plastic, prescience, privacy, pronunciation, respite, sheikh, sinecure, sojourn, solder, stance, trajectory, traverse, trough, urinal (*this was a particular favourite of his, short 'i'*).

Another one of Kidson's favourite words was Trafalgar – he missed out the middle 'a', but goodness knows what the authority for that one is!

To us, of course, it was all great fun and had the advantage of novelty. Those beaks with whom he enjoyed a bit of banter also remember the hilarity of Michael's mock serious pedantry. Michael Meredith recalls a night of laughter in the colony in The Corner House, arguing about the 'coolinary' efforts of their latest cook. But some of his colleagues, who were less inclined to be corrected on their pronunciation, and could be

93 And never 'pleased to meet you'.

prickly as only academics can be, found it less amusing – particularly as some of them suffered his rudeness for decades.

It was another way he found of keeping them at a distance. The ramparts were erected by him to keep the other beaks on the outside, and in doing so, some of them found him heartless. They dismissed him as a pompous pedant and felt that it was obsessive behaviour, which indeed it became. Michael Meredith says that Kidson kept up to date by buying each new reprint of Fowler as it came out. And he waged a solitary campaign against the BBC over the 'ghastly' pronunciation of their newsreaders, which intensified as he aged.

Just as correct pronunciation was drilled into us, so we were also corrected on our grammar and syntax and, again, the great H.W. Fowler had the last word. Where other beaks might have let some minor error pass, Kidson was unswerving in his criticism. If I had a pound for every one of his ex-pupils who has told me that they cannot write however COMMA at the beginning of a sentence without thinking of Michael, I would be able to retire in style.

David Cameron remembers: 'He once made me write out one hundred times, "I will always use a comma after the adverbial however."'

And I am sure he does to this day.

The English-speaking world may be 'divided into those who neither know nor care what a split infinitive is, those who don't know, but care very much, those who know and approve, those who know and condemn, and those who know and distinguish'. But for Kidson, the issue was binary. Recent edicts from the style gurus allowing the splitting of infinitives would have poor Michael spinning in his grave. Incidentally, Fowler concludes that split infinitives should not attract as much attention as they do, and says that they are indeed sometimes the best way to express one's meaning.

Essays often ended up with a labyrinthine network of arrows restructuring sentences in red ink, so that anyone who dangled participles, or left prepositions hanging, was left in no doubt about the error of his ways. Starting a paragraph with the word 'firstly' (as opposed to first) was always guaranteed to get a rise. I remember once being excoriated for writing 'due to' when 'owing to' was more appropriate.

Tom Parker Bowles, who now lives by his pen, has never forgotten a particular Kidson story: 'He once told us a tale of a handwritten sign he saw, hastily posted in the window of the chemist on the High Street. It read, "We will not be open today due to a death in the family."

'Kidson said: "So, I tapped firmly upon the door with my umbrella. And it was opened by some tear-stained chap. 'Now look here,' I said, 'your sign is all wrong. You must always start with "due to", not let it hang uselessly mid-sentence. It should read, "Due to a death in the family, we will not be open today".'

'The thing is, it could well have been true. In the gruff persona of "Mr Kidson". But in reality, he was far too kind a man ever to dream of such insensitive intrusion.'

It was not only grammar. Kidson was equally punctilious about the use of correct spelling in essays. **Justin Welby** can still recall 'being yelled at for not spelling particularly properly.'

But whilst he was scathing about our prose styles, it was very rare indeed that he criticised a boy for his handwriting, and that was undoubtedly because his own was usually indecipherable, until one had been up to him for several weeks. Although he had firm views on the use of biros – as in this note at the bottom of an essay: 'Why are you writing in biro when you can buy a perfectly respectable fountain pen for sixty or seventy pounds.' (This was in 1972!)

He also set high standards of dress and liked to keep at least two generations behind on questions of sartorial etiquette. This gave him more freedom to pick us up on any lapse. He hated 'jacket and tie,' it always had to be 'coat and tie'. Only potatoes wear jackets. He wore a 'top coat' in cold weather, not an overcoat. And he paraded his views on the matter to readers of the *Daily Telegraph* letters page:

> SIR – Lord Deedes is wide of the mark
> (Notebook, Jan 23) in claiming that 'there are
> no sartorial distinctions left'. On the whole

gentlemen (still) don't:

- Wear (or even possess) a blazer (except, possibly, on rare nautical occasions).
- Wear a Windsor knot in their neckties (I raised this matter recently with Mr Portillo).
- Wear signet rings (which is allied to fashion).
- Wear a recognisable club tie in public places.
- Wear ready-made suits in the mistaken belief that they are indistinguishable from the proper McCoy.

Michael Kidson
Westonbirt, Glos

A short time after, Douglas Sutherland, who wrote about being a gentleman for Debretts, wrote a letter contradicting some of Michael's points!

CHAPTER ELEVEN

Sport

You will never have a revolution in England as long as you keep up your racing.

Bismarck to Disraeli, from Kidson's commonplace book

Although a good games player himself, Kidson did not throw himself into umpiring the mainstream sports as other beaks did.

Michael Meredith: 'The rest of us (beaks) would be running ourselves ragged, refereeing football matches on Dutchman's every afternoon and there would be Michael wandering around with his spaniel and an upturned golf club making facetious comments on the touchline, which caused a certain amount of resentment. What none of us realised was the time he devoted to looking after his pupils.'

James Cook: 'He was a keen cricketer, though he never coached a team, and a regular observer of boys' sides practising in the nets, where he might be joined by other sages or a group of his pupils; he propped himself up on his shooting stick, while his dog would be scrabbling around in the bushes by Upper Club pavilion. He would then hobble off, calling for his dog, who would follow at a respectful distance, but woe betide him if he crossed Pocock's Lane without permission.

'He was a big fan of Tom Graveney. His admiration was well-deserved, for Tom was one of the most elegant batsmen ever to play for England and it was a great sadness to Michael and many others that he was not selected to play more often. I wonder whether Michael wrote to the England selectors as often as he wrote to Margaret Thatcher!'

Henry Wyndham recalls Kidson being a useful cricketer: 'Our housemaster, Jack Anderson, put together a beaks' team to play against our house side. Kidson bowled a few overs of rather indifferent off-spin, then he took to the crease and made about forty. I remember trying very hard to get him out, but there was no shifting him.'

Kidson was a dedicated proponent of the game. He was generous in lending his MCC pass to Lord's Cricket Ground to his pupils and several of them reminisce about going to watch Test matches masquerading as M.G.MacD. Kidson. He also acted as a referee for a number of them to become MCC members when they left Eton. I remember Kidson being a good judge of cricketing talent. He would enthuse about a boy in my year, **Matthew Fleming**, saying that he was the 'finest schoolboy batsman he had ever seen' and Matthew did indeed go on to play for England. When I relate this story to Matt, he is surprised:

'He was definitely ahead of his time on that score. I was in the XI for two years and might have been the Captain of Cricket if I hadn't been caught smoking, but I was not exceptional and no one would ever have guessed that I had a career in first-class cricket ahead of me. I was a late developer, and in fact, when I tried to join Kent straight from school, they turned me down. I then spent five years in the Green Jackets, where I did play quite a lot of cricket, captaining the Army and Combined Services teams. It was only afterwards that things took off. I tried to sign for Worcester, but they signed Kapil Dev instead (a no-brainer for them really!), although then I did go to Kent and never looked back.

'I had been up to Kidson and he despaired of me academically. I remember him laying into me because I pronounced Kabul as "Kar-bull" and not "Korball", and I said "Trafalgar" not "Traffle-gar". But he always seemed to like me because I played cricket. I was captivated by the sight of these two great eccentrics, Kidson and Patrick Croker, watching on the boundary with Dougal and Timber and showing a genuine interest. I think Michael liked my batting style because it was quite attacking and he was really a 'two-up and bags of smoke' man. I always thought Kidson and Croker quite liked each other behind all the bickering about their dogs. I kept up with Patrick and used to have dinner with him and my dame, Anne

Pease, every year when I went to Sussex until quite recently.'

Though he took a keen interest in cricket and football, Kidson was never very interested in the aquatic side of life.

Matt Pinsent: 'I regularly had to ask him for Saturday morning off his class to go to rowing regattas in the summer half and the answer was always the same. He would fix me with a beady eye and ask, "Are we bottom of the river again?" We weren't and had not been for quite some time, but he never let on that he knew that perfectly well. The Captain of Boats and I sent him a pair of tickets to Henley in our leaving year, but though I like the image of him cheering us on from the Stewards' Enclosure that summer, it was a dream surely never to be fulfilled. He was much more of a dry bob than a wet bob.'

The Captain of Boats was **Matthew Gordon Clark**, and he takes up the story: 'Matt Pinsent and I were somewhat affronted when Kidson announced that Matt and I were "exactly like Mussolini". This predictably caused some uproar and ribbing from the rest of the div. "Why, sir, are they fascists?" "Is it because rowers always finish all the pasta at Bekynton?"[94] Other imagined comparisons involved Italian parentage, or thuggish and loutish behaviour, of which oarsmen at Eton were always being accused (unfairly, obviously), before Kidson held up his hand and announced that the reason we were "exactly" like Mussolini was because we had failed to grasp the concept of futility.

'He explained that Mussolini had failed to understand that thinking he could negotiate with Hitler was utterly futile, just as we were failing to understand the futility of sitting the wrong way around in a boat trying to propel it up and down stream endlessly. "Rowing," he said on a number of occasions, "barely qualifies as a sport. It's merely exercise." We had a long-running but always humorous battle to convince him otherwise.'

In the end, Kidson carved himself out a unique role as the Master in Charge of Rackets. This suited him perfectly, as there were no other beaks

94 Bekynton is the school's central dining-room, where about half the houses eat.

involved and there was a professional – first Jim Dear (a former world champion) and later Norwood Cripps – to do the coaching. He ran it on a 'Carry on, Sergeant Major' basis, allowing the professionals to get on with their work without too much interference.

According to Michael Meredith, Kidson was thought to have made a success of rackets. Previously it had endured a poor reputation amongst the beaks, because it was 'thought to attract some of the most arrogant and difficult boys.' He is credited with gripping it and 'ridding the sport of the raffishness that had characterised it in the past.'

Kidson delegated as much responsibility as he could to the boy who was Keeper of Rackets. This *laissez-faire* policy backfired once, when he asked the Keeper why there appeared to be fewer fixtures than normal. The boy replied insouciantly that he had 'arranged matches against Winchester and Harrow, but not against any of the others, as they were not gentlemen!'

He did not play rackets himself. He probably discovered he was too old and short-sighted to compete safely in the fastest ball game of all and wisely confined himself to refereeing matches from the balcony.

The professionals were fond of him and became used to his idiosyncrasies, sometimes being sacked and then reinstated, although on occasions they complained about his dogs eating the rackets balls. They knew that he stood up for them and for the sport, which was always in danger of being muscled out of the way by the major sports, and were as intensely loyal to him as he was to them.

Two of his former players, Richard Graham and Alan Giddins, share their memories of what it was like being a member of Kidson's rackets team:

Richard Graham: Michael was Master in Charge, not because he had ever played the game (he hadn't) or knew much about the game (he didn't), but because the nature of the game – elitist, quirky and unchanged in technology, courts, rackets or clothes (give or take the odd tracksuit, which he deplored) – suited his sense of potential for life as an Edwardian drama.

The structure of the game in the mid-1970s helped him. The school 'professionals' or 'pros', like our own Jim Dear MBE, pre-war world champion of three sports,[95] were from an era of gents and players – eking out a modest retirement by working for public schools: wrapping cloth around rackets balls, re-stringing rackets and marking games. Jim was a far cry from today's articulate, media-star millionaires, and we had the unique chance to be coached by someone who had been the best in the world. Michael rightly did not interfere or second-guess this at all.

Masters in Charge accompanied teams to games and drove the ancient Ford Transit to away matches. In Michael's case, he had Dougal, his spaniel, in the adjacent front seat, raised his felt hat to mothers outside the court, and boomed 'serve up' and 'have him out' from the gallery.

Technical, tactical, eating, health, warm-up exercise, or any other pre-match advice relevant to rackets, came there never from Michael. He thought the habit of other Masters in Charge to come downstairs and offer thoughts or encouragement in-between games was very infra dig, if not slightly vulgar.

But acid post-match commentary was his unrivalled forte.

'Come along, Dougal, let us flee from this scene of disastrous humiliation,' he cried, leaping into the driving seat at somewhere like Rugby, after Hylton Murray-Philipson and I had somehow – not for the first time – snatched defeat out of the gaping certainty of victory.

There was no question of staying for tea in these circumstances, where he would have had to make polite conversation with the victorious host Master in Charge. This was not Michael's idea of fun, with one or two favoured exceptions.

Winchester's Master in Charge was known as Podge, who once described me (after a game I think we did win) as 'a bit of a flaneur'. I

95 Jim Dear started his career as an apprentice ball boy at Queen's with Dan Maskell, later to be the voice of tennis. He went on to be world squash champion (at that time synonymous with the British Open) in 1939, world rackets champion 1947–54, and world real tennis champion 1955–7. Sports writers speculate that if it had not been for the Second World War taking him away in the RAF during his prime, Jim Dear would be thought of as one of the all-time greats and that, had he focused on lawn tennis instead, he could have been another Fred Perry.

had no idea what he was talking about, but Michael approved of the word. Few rackets masters, though, could rise to his expectations of occasion or language.

No, it was into the van. 'Immediately, do you see? No, no, there's no time for that sort of nonsense, get in man, do you hear me, oh, do get a move on, Pease. You're moving so slowly, we won't be back for breakfast. What? Barham? Left your jersey behind? Well, that's bad luck, isn't it. What? Of course, we're not going back. No other jersey? Well, I'm sorry. Write them a nice letter and they can post the damn thing …'

And off we would charge, for a long and sick-making drive back, on now very empty stomachs. MGMK would ram the rusty chariot into reverse gear and almost into a brick wall ('idiotic place for such a thing'), a passing boy ('fool – has he never seen a vehicle reversing?') and even the waving host Master in Charge ('no wonder he's got an idiotic grin on his face, after that unbelievably inept performance by our own brace of pocket Hercules …').

On at least one occasion, said Master in Charge had to leap out of the way to avoid being run over, as we roared off, in the wrong gear, handbrake still on, with as much remaining *amour propre* as Michael, Dougal and the ancient Ford Transit could muster.

Over-sensitive souls like me would sometimes wonder what this did for the school's reputation, or even whether the result of a rackets match was really the end of the world, but Michael was passionate about winning.

So the journey back after a loss of this kind invariably prompted comparisons with England, or Britain's battlefield disasters – the American War of Independence, North Africa in the Second World War, Bannockburn and Isandlwana were frequent points of reference.

The conclusion was inevitable: 'Never in the field of human sport has so little been done by so many for their school.'

And then Michael would bring us back to rackets: 'Do you think Norman and Leonard, or Boone and Faber would have managed to lose a game like that, against the feeblest possible opponents? Of course not.'

Nor was it wise to laugh at the neo-Churchillian rhetoric. My partner once got into the driving seat before Kidson to deliver the anticipated assessment of our bungling incompetence. Michael appeared as Hylton reached a rhetorical climax that included the surrenders at Singapore and Stalingrad. 'It is not funny, Murray-Philipson, but if you think it is, we can find someone else to play who does not think serving thirty double-faults and losing to a pair of donkeys is particularly funny.'

Michael Kidson was a one-off, even in the 1970s. Masters making fun of boys is probably banned now, but boys do not want to be told they did their best, when they palpably did not.

The long-lasting benefit of going to rackets matches with Michael Kidson was part learning how to laugh at yourself, a great lesson for life, while understanding the comic power of vocabulary and analogy. Most of all, perhaps, we learned that if a master and his dog could volunteer to spend a day driving you around the country to play games, then you could jolly well pull your finger out when you got on court.

When victory did happen, miraculously, Michael rose to the occasion in his own way: 'That was not a bad effort today, not a bad effort at all.' And really, in life, that remains the bar. Michael set it.

Alan Giddins: 'Michael had a somewhat unorthodox approach to refereeing rackets matches. While fully versed in the laws of the game, he would occasionally see a decision on whether or not to give a "let" to an Eton player as a way to communicate clearly the level of his displeasure at the Eton pair on the court. As such, he would use it as an opportunity to glare down and declare "no let", with limited regard to the justification for the decision, so there was no doubting that, as far as Michael was concerned, the Eton pair needed to buck up their ideas before he would agree to give them anything. By contrast, Michael would shamelessly give the Eton pair a "let" where he felt it was "fully deserved" in the context of the previous few rallies.

'Michael also had a loathing of Etonians who started playing a match still wearing several "colours" sweaters. As far as he was concerned, irrespective of the often near-freezing temperatures in the rackets courts, it was important to demonstrate clearly to the opposition that you were hungry and ready to play. He would remind us that you never saw May or Cowdrey start a match wearing their tracksuit, so nor should an Etonian.'

Kidson flew top-cover fearlessly for his rackets players against the rival claims of other commitments. He had a number of tussles with the beaks in charge of other sports, but his fiercest foe was Roddy Forman, the Master in Charge of the Field Game. The exchange of letters below is typical of the skirmishing between them:

6th February 1989 *Common Lane House*

Dear Michael,

As you will doubtless remember, the Public Schools Racquets Championships clash with the finals of the House Field Game competitions, and the Head Master has ruled that the championships should take priority over the finals (he did not, incidentally, make the far stronger ruling that all boys required for the championships must be made available to compete in them, which would of course have been unsound, since no boy can be required to engage in a Minor Sport against his will).

As the Field Game is quintessentially a team game, I think it reasonable to establish at this point exactly which boys have opted for Racquets and may consequently be unavailable for Field Game finals. Would you therefore very kindly furnish me with a list of the boys who have so opted, together with an assurance that you have explained to them the possible consequences of their option. I will then be able to warn the House Masters of the boys involved. Very many thanks.

Yours ever,

Roddy

Kidson was not going to take this lying down:

6th February 1989 *134–135 High Street*

Dear Roddy,

I think that your judgement has gone seriously astray.

The import of your letter is that you are doing your best, by sinister means, to dismantle the Head Master's ruling (in my view an entirely right one) that the Fives & Rackets Championships should have priority over House Field Game finals.

Your casuistry aside – it was the Head Master's ruling that the onus of the choice should not be put upon the boys (to spare them the pressures you want to apply): and now here you are – in defiance of his decision – trying to do precisely that in your determination to have your own way.

'The possible consequences of their option' is a phrase that can only be construed as intimidatory; and you should not have used it. Indeed, your letter would have been better not written at all.

It is very unlikely that boys playing in School rackets teams – and they, too, are teams – would be doing so 'against their wills'; but you seem very anxious to try to establish and encourage that situation.

I'm sorry, but I think that you have not done well.

Yours,

Michael

Kidson was also not above fighting a turf war against the Master in Charge of Squash when it suited him.

Alan Giddins: 'Clashes with squash matches were inevitable at Eton, particularly in the Lent half. It was rare that at least one member of the first pair was not either number one in the squash team, or Keeper of Squash. As far as Michael was concerned, no accommodation should be made. Rackets should always be the priority, it was simply the better game. He could not understand the frustration of successive Masters in Charge of Squash, as their best players either could not play, or went on court having already played for two hours on the rackets court.'

Kidson would persuade boys who had been overlooked by all Eton's other sports to take up rackets purely for pleasure. **Jamie Sainsbury** was one of his pupils who, despite having little natural ability, enjoyed having rackets lessons with Jim Dear as a result of Kidson's encouragement.

Rackets provided another bond between Michael and the boys, many of whom he kept up with in later years. David Pease, whose partnership with David Faber was perhaps the most successful of his time in charge (Junior Public Schools Champions, then runners-up in the Senior Championships), remained a good friend of Kidson's to the end.

David Pease: 'Rackets for me at Eton was my complete *raison d'être*. I was totally obsessed with it. It was the one thing that I could do to a reasonable standard and so it gave me my identity amongst contemporaries – and gave me my self-esteem. The reality, of course, is that rackets is a tiny world – and there were only two of us in our year who played the game. But never mind, for me it was the one area where I could really hold my head up high. I was not that talented and I was terribly lanky and weak. But by practising every day, I could make up for the lack of natural ability. Faber by contrast was hugely talented.

'Kidson, of course, was part of this little journey I was on, lacking confidence, trying so hard to achieve something worthwhile. He would nurture me along the route. I remember him being nonchalant on the surface – but caring so much underneath. He would share in the excitement of victory and the disappointment of loss – but not really show his emotions. But one knew that he really cared. The away matches were fun, as Richard Graham has described so well. They were a big commitment for him. Driving to Malvern and back must have been quite a hike.'

Unfortunately, Kidson's era as Master in Charge was not a golden one for Eton rackets. Eton were the runners-up in the Public Schools Championships in 1974, 1979, 1983, 1985 and 1990–1, but never the champions; though they did win the Junior Championships six times over this period.

With his love of hunting, it was natural that Kidson should also take an interest in the Beagles. **Andrew Joicey** remembers Kidson often driving the minibus to take them to weekday meets. The form was that the boys had to approach beaks and ask them to do this as a favour. Kidson was as fond of the social side as of the venery and would ask whether there was going to be a good tea afterwards,[96] or a good pub, before accepting the job.

The boys would gather at the Burning Bush,[97] in the expectation of seeing Kidson there with the transport and Andrew recalls their astonishment at Kidson arriving on foot and throwing the keys to one of the boys, saying, 'Just go and pick up the minibus from outside the Fives Courts, will you. I can't be bothered to walk all that way.'[98]

Later Kidson also found himself suddenly thrust into the role of Master in Charge of Riding. The previous beak was Martin Whiteley, legendary housemaster and Master in Charge of the Gymnasium.

Johnnie Boden: 'The gym. How can one forget Martin Whiteley's three blows of the whistle, followed by, "Hands out of pockets, Money-Kyrle, quickly and quietly into your three groups, fall in." I am embarrassed to admit that if I ever play the hat game with an Etonian, I will always throw MFW into the hat and one of us will always say "quickly and quietly". And the other will get it immediately.'

A retired Rifle Brigade officer, Whiteley was a very distinguished equestrian. He had won Little Badminton twice[99] and the silver medal in the 1967 European Championships when in the British Team. Martin had a heart attack and died suddenly one afternoon in 1984 while umpiring the Field Game. It was a hard act to follow, but Kidson – a great enthusiast for anything to do with horses – was the obvious choice to take over.

---

96 Landowners across the home counties (and further afield in the holidays) were very generous with their hospitality. The author remembers a very good lawn meet at Royal Lodge in Windsor Great Park hosted by the Queen Mother.

97 A Victorian lamppost in the centre of Eton, which is the rendezvous point for almost any activity.

98 This entailed a probably unlicensed teenager driving a minibus on the public highway!

99 To add to the distinction, on two different horses, Peggoty in 1960 and The Poacher in 1965.

William Fox-Pitt: 'Riding was a very minor sport, barely recognised by the school then, it did not have a Keeper, or colours, or anything like that. I remember the Lower Master, Jack Anderson, saying to me, "We think of horses as a hobby, and we like to keep it that way." I loved riding, although I never dreamt at that stage that it would be what I do now. My Mum kept the horse going during term time and I was always asking for extra time off at weekends to go and compete (there were not many exeats in those days!). My housemaster Michael Meredith used bribery on me – I was not allowed out to ride unless I worked hard. As a consequence, I did work hard and was a real goody-goody; Mum would have been so livid with me if I could not come out and compete after all her hard work. So Meredith's strategy was successful![100] Riding was not something you talked about, we just did it quietly.

'Mr Kidson was a real support and enthusiast. He made us feel that what we were doing was important and made us feel proud of what we achieved. I have to say that Eton never came anywhere in the Inter Schools Competition at Hickstead, we were very much bottom of the pile, and my personal contribution to the team's performance was minimal! It was a great thing to do, though.'

Riding was quietly watched over with a benevolent eye by the Head Master, Eric Anderson, who wrote:

From: THE HEAD MASTER
To: M.G.M.K. *12 July 1984*

Dear Michael,

I cannot tell you how grateful I am to you for your good efforts on behalf of the horsemen. I very much hope I can find a new Beak this coming year to take an interest, so that you will not be landed with this for life,[101] *but it is excellent news that the Equestrian Society is to*

100 In fact, Meredith was also needing to show Anderson that Fox-Pitt could afford to take time off.

101 Despite this hope, Kidson did carry on running all things equestrian for many years.

continue and that you have raised two teams for Hickstead.

Have a very good holiday.

Yours sincerely,

Eric Anderson

Kidson also kept a benevolent eye on the school's racing community. **George Baker** would sit in the back row of Kidson's history div with Piers Inkin, with the *Sporting Life* spread open on their desks: 'He would know and approve, but there would be a lot of faux outrage and we would be told to stay behind and see him at the end of the div. Then we would spend a few minutes with him reviewing the day's racing and discussing what was likely to win. He would show a particular interest if one of the Greenall brothers was riding. Sometimes we would be invited to spend the afternoon watching the racing and chatting in his flat.'

Tim Thomson Jones was another future trainer who remembers spending time discussing racing in Kidson's flat.

'I was up to him for History and felt confident about my chances in the A Level as he had taught us well; so confident in fact that I started missing his divs to concentrate on my Maths. Kidson didn't make a fuss about that, but quietly got his own back. He knew that I was looking forward to going to the Oaks at Epsom and a few weeks before I was astonished to find that I had been entered for the S Level exam by Kidson. Missing it would have been a hanging offence, so I had to sit it and it so happened that it coincided exactly with the Oaks, so that I couldn't even watch it on television! It ended well, as by sheer fluke I got the highest grade in the S Level and Kidson was sent for by the Head Man for a pat on the back. He said he told the Head Master, "It's amazing what a moderate talent can achieve with the co-operation of the examiner!"'

But perhaps Kidson's most important contribution in the sporting arena was the time he devoted to playing sport with his pupils. Sometimes he played tennis with us and his mastery of the psychological game made up for the handicap of age.

This leaver from **Rupert Uloth** gives us a flavour of his tactics:

Michael,

A very perfunctory little note which can hardly begin to thank you for all your kindness to 'Ukridge' … The only thing I regret is not thrashing you soundly at tennis. I had so many opportunities, but my charitable character was overcome with pity when I saw this aged, doddery creature staggering around in the opposite court, looking as if he was about to pass-out, that was one of your more underhand tricks; next time there will be no mercy …

Love ~~Peregrine~~ Rupert

Rupert writes to say, "He was so funny on the tennis court, he also got me into serious trouble when he agreed to be beak in charge of croquet knowing perfectly well (which I didn't) that there was already a beak in charge. The proper incumbent predictably went berserk when he saw the announcement sent to the house notice boards".

Michael understood instinctively that teenage boys were bound to get themselves in trouble and he did his best to get us through our last two years without being expelled. He helped to keep us on the rails by playing golf with us in the afternoons and it was an experience to charge round the school course with him – and of course, Dougal – relishing a torrent of invective from him on any slow play in front. It meant withstanding continuous sledging from Michael that would have made the Australian cricket team blanch.

Playing off about 16, he never used a wood and had a very short backswing, but his game was generally steadier than his younger opponents' and he was very hard to beat.

He once piled several of us into his Ford Escort, with its racehorse mascot on the bonnet, and took us to see a golf tournament at Wentworth. We followed the great Gary Player round, one of Michael's heroes, with Dougal sauntering around the hallowed fairways as if they belonged to him.

Richard Cormack: 'On many weekends, Michael would take me and some friends to the Berkshire for a round of golf – lots of great memories of Boodie running off on the first and not to be seen until mid-round, when a deer would shoot across the fairway with dog in rapid pursuit. It also used to amuse me that he would send me up to the bar to sign-in for green fees, with the instruction, "Bend your knees a bit, so you look smaller – it is cheaper if I sign you in as an under-sixteen – oh, and while you are there, do order yourself a pint of beer!"'

Guy Butterwick: 'We played golf at the Berkshire together quite often and on one occasion I was seven up with eight to play. From that moment onwards, he would play little tricks on me to try and distract. A cough, a splutter, Dougal running on my line, pretending to trip over, and so on … I lost on the 18th.

'We also went to the Suntory World Matchplay Championship together at Wentworth. In a very tense final, Dougal decided to slip the lead on the 11th and run onto the tee, right in Gary Player's backswing. Thank goodness he was a man of good humour. Exit stage left.'

Tom Goff recalls Kidson's enthusiasm for the game: 'He loved to watch golf on the TV and would often call by our house, Warre, on the way out to the rather mediocre Eton nine-hole track at around five p.m. on a summer's evening, and shout: "Who's for golf?"

'He would then tee-off first, with that magnificent thrash of his that had no back swing or follow through, but contained a hungry look as to where his ball had ended up. It was such fun. He took us to the Berkshire often and sometimes to Swinley, which was a joy, and insisted on us all having eggs and bacon after a round. He said: "All good Englishmen should enjoy good food and a drink after a round of golf, however moderately they've played."'

Kidson's encouragement to his pupils on the golf course was not entirely altruistic. Each year, Kidson was on the lookout for golfing talent amongst his pupils. The best of them would be selected to play with him in the 'Tutorial Beakers' – a pairs competition where tutors played with their pupils.

Rupert Hancock: 'This was my clearest view of his famous rivalry with Paddy Croker. Regrettably we never won the competition, but as the main objective was to beat Croker, my recollection is that we were successful in this limited aim, to be rewarded by toasted crumpets, buttered and cut in half (no other presentation is acceptable).

'Our visits to Berkshire, Swinley Forest and North Hants golf courses were an enormous privilege, most entertaining and unforgettable.'

Mark Burnyeat: 'Not only did I play with him, I think we WON the golfing Tutorial Beakers. I remember Jerry Nichols drove us to the (away) course, sticking religiously to the speed limit all the way. "Why do we keep going so slowly?" Kidson kept fuming. When we got there, Kidson and I were obviously doing quite well, but Jerry had the temerity to point out something about MGMK's swing. "What do you mean?" said the Great Man. "You're not even in contention!" It was a very hot day and my final memory is of Dougal disappearing into the Gents' loo after the round for a drink ...'

CHAPTER TWELVE

Parents

A fond mother … in pursuit of praise for her children, the most rapacious of human beings, is likewise the most credulous; her demands are exorbitant; but she will swallow anything.

From Kidson's commonplace book

I daresay quite a few parents had helicopters – regrettably, mine did not[102] – but the expression 'helicopter parents' did not exist in Kidson's day. This is for the simple reason that it would never have occurred to parents to hover above their offspring and swoop down at the first sign of adversity. Nor did it occur either to the school or to the parents that there was a need for parent–teacher meetings. My parents did not queue for hours to exchange a few platitudes with my teachers about my disinterest and lack of prospects in their subjects.

Mothers were not pushy, at least, if they were, the pushing was more a gentle shove in the direction of the right sort of debutante, than a prod in the hope of academic success. In fact, as far as I know, neither of my parents ever met Kidson, an arrangement that probably suited both parties. He would have loathed the modern culture of parent involvement in the minutiae of exam grades and UCAS applications.

He was quite shy with parents. **Hugo Guinness** remembers Kidson dropping him off at his parents' house in London and when Hugo invited him in for a drink, eager for him to meet them, Michael would not come in. Instead, he quickly made his excuses and drove off. Others used to go

---

102 Far from it!

looking for Kidson on the Fourth of June or St Andrew's Day, so that he could meet their families, but invariably he would hide himself away to avoid contact. One ex-pupil arrived at Eton for the Fourth of June to see his old tutor driving fast in the opposite direction.

Hylton Murray-Philipson was one of the few of Michael's pupils who managed to get him to lunch with his parents one holidays. It was a slightly awkward encounter:

'My parents did not altogether "get" Kidson and he, in turn, was ill at ease. My American mother started questioning Kidson about universities, suggesting that I should go to Harvard or Yale. Kidson replied dryly, "What, you mean then go to a proper university after that?"

'Kidson had arrived wearing an immaculate tweed suit, which had been made by Mr Boddy only weeks before. To everyone's mortification, I managed to trip while passing the soup around and spill it down Kidson's front. There was a pained silence, which Kidson then broke by saying, "Well, Hylton doesn't seem to mind, so why should I?"'

The correspondence Kidson had with parents indicates a shift in the culture of parenting over the thirty years he was at Eton. In the early days, letters were more to seek help in dealing with difficult boys, or to express gratitude for his dedication in helping to turn their delinquent sons into adults with prospects. This mother spoke for a number of our mothers, when she wrote:

Dear Michael,

Just a belated thank you from the bottom of my heart, for everything you have done for Rupert. There is no doubt that, but for you, he would never have stayed at Eton, nor would he have achieved those grades.

You really put up with a silly spoilt boy in a way which I believe to be unique.

Thank you more than I can say.

Yours,

Sally

P.S. Where do we go from here??

And Charlie Mortimer's father, Roger, while writing his son the famous 'Dear Lupin' letters exhorting him to mend his ways, wrote to Kidson regularly to share his anxieties, not only while Charlie was still at Eton, but also after he left:

26 February

Dear Michael,

I need your advice, please. I have come to the conclusion, reluctantly, that Charles would derive little benefit from Eton – and Eton from Charles – if he stayed on after the termination of the Summer Half. Addison agrees on that point. Charles himself is unhelpful; one day he wants to leave, the next to stay. His mother wants him to stay on, in the faint hope that he will be called upon to exercise some authority and responsibility.

In July, Charles will be seventeen and three months, and it is essential to have a definite course of action planned for him. I am not enthusiastic about crammers; in my days, most boys at crammers tended to be loutish, but of course, that may not apply today. Is it really important for Charles's future to get a couple of A levels? If it is, is he more likely to obtain them by remaining at Eton – Addison says he is not 'specialist material' – or by having special tuition elsewhere? Charles, of course, prefers to live from day to day and declines to discuss the future, except in the vaguest and most immature terms. I still think it would do him good to go into the army for three years. It might help him to grow up.

Please do not bother to write in reply. Just ring up one evening if you can spare the time.

Yours sincerely,
Roger Mortimer

Then matters came to a head.

Dear Michael,

I'm sorry I have not been to see you, but first of all I had a nasty go of influenza, and as soon as I could crawl out of bed I had to go to Cheltenham. As soon as I got back home, I was rung up by Norman Addison who wanted to see me.[103] *After hearing what he had to say, and after learning the opinion of Dr Clayton, I have decided to take Charles away at the end of this half. He seems in a very confused mental state and Clayton wants him to see a London consultant.*

I don't quite know what has gone wrong. Charles has been very restless and has expressed a desire to leave more than once. He seems very closely tied-up with another boy, who is also leaving. Perhaps I am doing Charles an injustice, but there are times when I think he has formed a romantic attachment for him; there are times, too, when I wonder if they have both been experimenting with soft drugs. Charles was determined to leave Eton when the other boy left and I think hoped to end up at a crammer with him.

You have been a very good friend to Charles and I am most grateful for what you have done. I only wish you had had a more rewarding response. I don't honestly know what to do with Charles now, but will wait and see what the consultant says.

Yours sincerely,

Roger Mortimer

Charlie Mortimer left, but kept in touch with his friends at school.

Dear Michael,

It was good of you to take the trouble to write. I think Charles has been tactless, to say the least, about visiting Eton and I have given him my views on the subject. In fact, I have asked him not to go there, yet I happen to know he was there again yesterday. Knowing what I do now, I

103 Charlie had attempted suicide by overdosing on paracetamol.

cannot blame Norman Addison at all for the view he has taken. In many ways, I think he has been remarkably tolerant.

*Charles is working hard, but is still rather an ass; for instance, he now owns an ancient car, which he has painted orange and violet with flowers on it. Naturally it is stopped at every opportunity by the police; hardly a wise policy for Charles in view of his unfortunate record. I fear, too, that Charles's affection for ***** ****** and ***** **********, both of whom I dislike and distrust, remains undiminished.*

Thanking you again.

Yours ever,

Roger

Then Charlie joined the Army.

Dear Michael,

The Gods themselves cannot battle against stupidity and Charles has made a complete ass of himself – not for the first time. Without a word to his parents, or to anyone else as far as I know, he marched into the Commandant at Mons and said he wanted to leave at once to do some form of social service. The Commandant at once rang me up and said he was mystified, as Charles was doing extremely well and was certain to get a commission. He urged me to persuade Charles to return. I tried, but failed utterly, and could not even obtain a remote sort of contact. His mother failed and so did his uncle, a very distinguished but very human general, who is extremely fond of Charles. Charles told me some balls about wanting to help mentally retarded persons, and he eventually told his mother an equally puerile story of feeling it was unfair that upper-middle-class boys should be officers commanding soldiers, who were their superiors in every respect.

I had asked Charles three days before the debacle if he was happy and if everything was going well, and he assured me that it was. The whole business was a great shock to me and it is really heartbreaking to see him opting out, when just for once he was doing well. He now has no job, no qualifications and a poor record. He has no feelings towards those who took a lot of trouble to get him into the army at all – no easy matter in view of his record – or towards those who have shown immense kindness during his brief military career. He cannot understand the disappointment he has caused his parents and complains, most untruly, they did not appreciate the effort he was making. He is, in fact, rather pleased with himself and thinks he has done very well. It is like the owner of a horse that ran out at the Canal Turn claiming he won the Grand National.

I suppose elderly parents are the last people to know the truth. I expect you will find out why Charles kicked the ball through his own goal long before I shall.

I am off to France for a week to try and forget about it all. Meanwhile Jane wants to get married to a young man of whom I approve, but in a thoroughly eccentric manner!

Thanks for all you did for Charles; you have been a better friend than he deserves.

Yours ever,

Roger

Parents were often particularly grateful for Michael's continuing support after their sons' expulsion. One father of a boy who had just been expelled for growing cannabis wrote: 'Thanks for your telephone call at our darkest hour. You were the only one, though I thought we had other friends at Eton.'

Lady Mancroft was worried about her son Benjy, and Kidson's reply is typical of his genre of reassurance:

10.1.74

Dear Lady Mancroft,

I am very sorry to be late with an answer to your letter, written before Christmas. I don't stay here in the holidays, & there is usually no one to send on letters, so I only saw yours yesterday.

Benjamin is by no means uniquely awful. It would be odd if he hadn't got much to learn at this stage, & it is extraordinary how successfully boys do shake out of their difficulties.

I would say – give it a bit longer, & let's hope for better things. It is trite to remind you of what, say, Robert Clive's mother must have thought, or Winston's (when she thought) – by comparison B's situation is tame! (I'm not putting B in this category: merely saying that we can't possibly tell).

This first specialist year is quite important. My own guess is that he will improve, & grow up, & that it's best not to be too sombre about him. I have a feel slightly that it might help if we pursued him less obviously: that he's beginning almost to enjoy the prestige of a victim.

And time is still on our side. I'm sorry: this isn't very positive or helpful; but I do feel rather strongly that we should try to be positive and not write him off! Certainly I don't feel that this is a complicated problem: lazy, tiresome boys are two a penny.

At least Benjamin's modest and immediate ambitions are straightforward ones, although, certainly, Mastership of the Beagles looks at the moment more plausible than a better distinction. Frankly, I don't think that Benjamin has any great talent, in general terms; but if he grows up into an honest, straightforward & reasonably conscientious young man, this would do very well (this sounds like Squire Brown, I'm afraid). Anything's possible from there.

Yes: He'll improve.

Yours sincerely,

Michael Kidson

A year later Benjy Mancroft's father felt that Kidson's characteristically blunt report about his son half-struck a chord and he wrote to the housemaster, Bobby Baird:

From: The Rt Hon Lord Mancroft KBE TD

31st December 1974

Dear Bobby,

Benjamin's report reached me undiverted. I myself was not, of course, diverted by what I read. It is beginning to have an all-too-familiar ring.

Mr Kidson compares Benjamin to Uriah Heep. A comparison with the Artful Dodger I would have understood, but Uriah Heep, if memory serves me right, got a life sentence for fraud and theft.

What an amateur parent can achieve that professional school teachers have not yet achieved I do not know, but if there is anything further I can do to push him in a straighter direction, for God's sake, let me know.

Yours sincerely,
Stormont Mancroft

Kidson wrote back in robust fashion:

Dear Lord Mancroft,

Bob Baird has passed on to me your letter.

I'm sure I don't need to point out that my Heep analogy was in no sense a prediction of Benjamin's ultimate prospects – merely a comment on his occasional style – reserved, perhaps for school.[104] *Was Uriah really consigned for life? It seems harsh.*

You talk of an 'amateur parent'. What, I wonder, is a professional one? As for us schoolmasters, few of us would claim to be more than very amateur indeed. I, personally, wouldn't remain in the profession for ten minutes more if I thought that my influence (for instance) vis-a-vis yours was more than minimal. Why should a wretched schoolmaster know a boy better than his own father does?

---

104 Frustratingly Benjy cannot find other letters, but apparently the correspondence continued and his father and Kidson compromised on Flurry Knox (from *The Irish RM*) as a suitable analogy for him.

The reports you receive on Benjamin three times a year reflect his current performance. They do not consign him to perdition for ever: they are staging posts – one hopes – and eventually he may get there. But I don't think that the principal coachman – the parent – should expect miracles from his lackeys.

Please don't bother to answer this.

Yours sincerely,
Michael Kidson

Charles Burrell was another father who was in no doubt about the important role Kidson had played in mentoring his son, Duff. Filled with paternal pride, he wrote to thank him three years after Duff left Eton, and after he had won the Sword of Honour at Sandhurst:

Broome Park,
Alnwick,
Northumberland

14th April 1972

Dear Michael,

We have just returned from Duff's passing out parade & seeing him get the 'Sword'. I thought I would write to you, principally to thank you for all you did for Duff when he was at Eton. There was a time, if you remember, when he got into his difficulties & I for one had an anxious time wondering if his good sense would prevail. It was at this particular time that you were his sheet anchor & I know that your advice & help that you gave him pulled him out of what could have developed into a major disaster.

So perhaps you will understand how deep and genuine are my feelings of gratitude to you because I know, without any doubt, that none of this would have come about, but for your friendship & wise counsel.

He has had a long hard slog and I'm so pleased for his sake his efforts have been crowned with success …

Do come in anytime you are passing, no need to give any warning. It's been beastly cold & wet up here & really no signs of any spring yet.

Yours ever,

Charles

Towards the end of his teaching career, in the late eighties and early nineties, there was a shift, perhaps reflecting the wider changes as society – and Eton parents – became more plutocratic. The letters show a tendency for parents to want to coerce him into furthering their ambitions for their sons; and the focus is on finding an edge to get their sons to Oxbridge. His replies to these three mothers left them in no doubt about their sons' prospects:

*Dear Mrs ********,*

Many thanks for your letter.

I personally can't see the advantage of Johnny's staying on for Oxbridge, now that we have last half's results and experience to use as further evidence. Admittedly, it remains quite a lottery: good boys are sometimes rejected, inexplicably; moderate candidates still occasionally get in.

But Johnny isn't, I fear, strong enough. I don't agree with you that there is virtue in courting failure: we have disappointments enough in life without compounding them gratuitously. To come back for a long Michaelmas half on a forlorn venture, among a whole lot of boys who will have real prospects, seems to me unwise.

There is a slightly pessimistic climate to your letter! Single-sex schools like this are not quite as perverting and atrophying as you seem to think: Johnny is growing up quite normally and steadily, and I should be careful neither to over- nor under-estimate him.

As for his literary shortcomings, I hope it won't shock you if I tell you that he is by no means the worst here: we don't have special facilities for transforming bad spellers into good ones, and poor stylists into elegant ones. With a reasonably intelligent boy like Johnny, we expect steady progress, and usually get it. I can assure you that Etonians are worked very hard indeed – inestimably harder than their American counterparts, if my friends who have taught in America are to be believed.

When I came to Eton seventeen years ago, we used to think that 20 Awards[105] *a year at Oxford and Cambridge was about par. Last year we had 48 – 16 more than the next school – and we have had over 30 six years running. It is a very different school from the old one.*

I don't believe that you need be anxious about Johnny. Distance seems to be lending you a certain disenchantment, and I don't think it need.

Yours sincerely,

Michael Kidson

P.S. There is no axe to grind, except the boy's interests.

5th December 1991

*Dear Mrs ********,*

Damien's housemaster has passed on to me your letter to him about Damien and Oxford.

I think you are rather hard on us.

I agree entirely with him, and other colleagues whom we have consulted, that Damien is manifestly not Oxbridge material. I personally am always in favour of hitching wagons to stars; but tilting at windmills is another matter. It may sound brutal to say that I don't believe Damien is an Oxford runner by any stretch of the imagination.

We do know something about the game. On the contrary we always put boys first. We aim to be realistic.

I gather that you are placing some reliance on inside help of some kind: in my experience, these days it needs to be very formidable indeed, unless St Edmund Hall is a very venal organisation (which I'm sure it's not).

We should love to be proved wrong about Damien: but you cannot

105 By this he means scholarships and exhibitions.

want us to dissimulate or to encourage false hopes. I have just spoken to Henry Proctor, a colleague who has been teaching History to Damien this half: he was incredulous at the idea of Oxford, putting Damien among the bottom two or three in a very low division.

The 'N' mode entry at Oxford was never designed for schools like this, but primarily as help and encouragement for state schoolboys who don't have Eton's advantages.

Incidentally, Damien himself has shown scarcely any initiative in the matter. All I recall is a perfunctory reference some months ago. Lectures are given here in April about university entrance; datelines made clear, &c. Any serious candidates can hardly expect to be spoonfed day in and day out.

Yours sincerely,
Michael Kidson

7th February 1993

*Dear Mrs *******,*

Thank you for your letter.

It was a brave maternal gesture to write to these colleges, but I fear that you will already have received courteous rebuffs.

In my experience, this kind of approach hardly ever works …

CHAPTER THIRTEEN

Hold on, Jack!

Kidson on the road and on holidays

The poetry of motion! The real way to travel! The only way to travel! Here today – in next week tomorrow! Villages skipped, towns and cities jumped – always somebody else's horizon! O bliss! O poop-poop! O my! O my!

Kenneth Grahame, *The Wind in the Willows*

Kidson drove like Jehu. **Johnnie Boden** remembers being taken on trips to Hughenden and Waddesdon: 'It was absolutely hair-raising and we all flinched as Kidson's minivan screeched round roundabouts without pausing. He called all the other drivers on the road "Jack" and would shout "Hold on, Jack!" as he cut them up.'

The green minivan had the number plate CAD and **Tim Thomson Jones** remembers Kidson being very pleased at this accoutrement to his caddish persona.

This cutting from a local newspaper in Berkshire was in his desk:

> **Eton Schoolmaster escapes speed charge**
> Eton Schoolmaster Michael Kidson was cleared of driving at a dangerous speed by the Chertsey magistrates on Wednesday after the police alleged that he drove at 70 miles an hour in a car which Mr Kidson said he was still running in.

The police motorcycle patrolman who chased and stopped Mr Kidson said that he overtook two cars as he came up Egham Hill and accelerated from 47 to 73 mph in half a mile. When he left the 30 mph restricted area, he was still accelerating.

The officer said that at one point his motorcycle was almost travelling at its maximum speed and said that he would not have caught Kidson if the road had not begun to slope down. Mr Kidson also jumped the traffic lights while driving at about 70 mph. When stopped, he told the officer: 'I am alright as I have got disc brakes.'

Mr Kidson said that he had wanted to run the car in over 1,000 miles although the running-in distance of the car was 500 miles. He said he wanted to run it in for a bit longer because he was reasonably cautious and added that he did not ever exceed 50 mph in the car.

When cross-examined he agreed that the car, an Austin Mini Cooper, was a 'hotted up' version of the Mini. Its maximum speed claimed by the makers was 85 mph. He was not conscious that he was driving in a restricted area.

After being found not guilty of driving at a dangerous speed, he pleaded guilty to speeding and was fined £10.

Alex Sherbrooke: 'Michael had an innate recklessness and courage. Once Peter Daresbury had lent him his BMW and Michael took me out for a drink in a pub. He drove through Windsor Great Park like a madman, overtaking on bends and cornering as if he was dancing with death.'

Charlie Arkwright: 'He never drove anywhere, he always "motored" and he was always very particular about his cars and he would complain bitterly if they were dented. "Look, it's been stove in!" And the "wireless" was never on.'

John Benson: 'My favourite anecdote about MGMK was a conversation I had with him around 1978, just after he had bought a new car. He said he had not been at all sure whether or not he would buy it, because it was a Ford (a little bit common), and this particular model was called the "Popular". However, in the end he did go ahead and buy it. "Of course, I paid £300 to have the word 'Popular' removed from the back of the car."'

The other thing everyone remembers about Kidson's driving is that he never wore a seatbelt; he had somehow contrived to have been issued with a doctor's note excusing him on health grounds – the note was kept in the glove box.

He loved cars for their speed and glamour, but he was not a conventional petrol-head. Whatever went on under the bonnet was best left to men in overalls. Sometimes ex-pupils would lend their cars to Michael in return for him driving them to and from Heathrow. On one occasion, he was driving a state-of-the-art BMW, when he was startled to hear the voice of the on-board computer: 'Please fasten your seatbelt.'

A long argument ensued.

He took an avuncular interest in his pupils' driving. Most of us started having lessons as soon as we were seventeen and would meet our driving instructors at the Burning Bush on a Tuesday afternoon and head off like friendly bombs towards the unsuspecting streets of Slough.

Kidson allowed **Hugo Guinness** to take his test in his green minivan: 'Except that when we reached the Test Centre together, Kidson went off to the loo and put the keys down next to the sink and forgot about them

... I never actually took the test, because by the time we found them again, we had missed the slot.'

On one memorable journey, David Gerard Leigh[106] had not long before passed his driving test and was still of a somewhat nervous disposition when it came to driving:

David Gerard Leigh: It would be my habit from time to time to go and see Michael after lunch, as occasionally one might benefit from a cold glass of beer!

So, I am at his flat.

MGMK: 'Right, off we go.'

Me: 'Ya, where to?'

MGMK: 'You'll see soon enough – there are the keys, you're driving.'

So we go down the fire escape and into his green Mini with the dog on the back seat. We set off. Somewhere in Windsor, we come to a traffic light, which is turning to red.

MGMK: 'Don't, don't slow down ... go through the light. You mustn't stop!'

Me: 'What – are you mad?'

MGMK: 'No, but if a policeman decides to cross the road here, I'll be in trouble, as the car isn't taxed.'

Me, silently to myself, 'Great, just run a light and the car's not taxed.'

At the next light, there is a policeman.

MGMK: 'For Christ's sake, drive faster, then he won't see the tax disc is out of date!'

The rest of the journey remains fairly peaceful, in as much as there is a constant flow of criticism and abuse at my nascent driving skills. So, we are now in Crowthorne and we proceed up this drive to a very imposing façade.

---

106 Though it was still secret at the time, Kidson would have been fascinated by the unique role David's mother, Jean, had played in MI5 in the Second World War. In Operation Mincemeat, she was the fictional girlfriend of 'Major Martin – the man who never was' and her photograph and letters were washed up with the body on the beach and helped to deceive the Germans into thinking that the invasion of Italy was going to be through Sardinia rather than Sicily.

Me: 'Where are we? It's obviously a school, as there are boys playing on the games field.'

MGMK: 'Wellington, don't you recognise it? You're just so ignorant.'

Me: 'So why have you brought me here?'

MGMK: 'Just thought I would let you see what could have been … Turn around, we are going now.'

The return journey through Windsor was again embellished with much gesticulation and firing off of instructions.

Got back in one piece, thankfully … and it was off to Tap for me to calm the nerves.

Sometime in the late 1970s, Kidson bought himself a house in Gloucestershire, Ivy Cottage in the hamlet of Westonbirt, between Tebury and Malmesbury, (which typically he always pronounced Mawmsbury). And this became his retreat in the holidays. It is a Victorian estate cottage on the edge of the park of Westonbirt House, the great neo-Elizabethan pile with its famous arboretum. The house has been a girls' school since 1928 and the village now owes some of its character to the community of the school.

The immediate neighbours, John and Marion James and Andy and Kathy Clarke, have vivid memories of their first meetings with him. The Jameses remember going across to greet their new neighbour and seeing an educated man, surrounded by piles of books and pictures, looking at a pot of paint and a paintbrush with clearly no idea of even how to open the pot. When the Clarkes pulled up in their drive with Kathy at the wheel, Michael looked over the fence and greeted them with the words, 'I don't much hold with women drivers.'

He soon became one of the characters of the village and the inhabitants grew either very fond of him or incensed by him, or both, according to taste. Andy is a former RAF officer and Michael soon detected his technical ability and, never remotely practical himself, asked him to change light bulbs, or give advice about his car. On one occasion, he was asked to examine a strange vibrating noise every time Michael reached a certain speed; he recommended closing the rear windows before setting off!

Michael became firm friends with June Goatley and her husband Geoffrey, a retired gunner officer, and fitted into village life in Westonbirt's one street. Stories began to circulate about the eccentric schoolmaster in Ivy Cottage. One young family recalls him turning up on their doorstep one Christmas with a cake for the children, only for him to return half an hour later with another, much smaller one, and swap them over. 'I'm awfully sorry, I have given you the wrong cake …'

Away from Eton's suburban environment, Michael – and his dog – relished the opportunity to walk in the Arboretum, until:

H. Angus Esq.	*134–135 High Street,*
Westonbirt Arboretum,	*Eton*
Gloucestershire	*7th September 1990*

Dear Sir,

I'm afraid I think that the decision to ban dogs from the Arboretum is one of the silliest I have come across in years.

It is incredible to me that a countryman – for such you presumably are – is prepared to endorse the daft decisions of Forestry Commission bureaucrats (or am I being unfair in blaming them?).

I think it wretched that you should so willingly give way to the thoroughly unattractive anti-canine lobby, a minority of suburban-minded people who should be opposed strenuously, not pandered to in this way.

I should tell you that I have a cottage in Westonbirt, and have walked my Springer in the Arboretum for years in the holidays. When this news reached me, I was about to convert my subscription into a Banker's Order: I have terminated all interest in the Friends of the Arboretum (I attended the very first meeting).

It seems to me thoroughly crass and myopic.

Yours faithfully,

Michael Kidson

Dave Ker, one of Kidson's closest friends and his executor

'To be born a gentleman is an accident – to die one is an achievement. Will you?'

Justin Welby, later Archbishop of Canterbury

Oliver Letwin, later to become a Cabinet Minister

'Mr Kidson, I have always thought of you as a romantic figure posing as a romantic figure. The only blot on the landscape is your view of constitutional questions. Oliver.'

Mungo Stormont (now The Earl of Mansfield) was told 'Don't touch my dog, you'll give it fleas'

Alexander Sherbrooke, later to be a Roman Catholic priest

'I don't know where to begin in thanking you for all the work you have done on my behalf. I am sure I would never have been taking University Entrance or have a place at Edinburgh if it had not been for you. For all your help not only on the academic side but in many negotiations on my behalf I am enormously grateful. When I look back at my days at Eton in ten years time you will always be one of my fondest memories. Private business and history divs were a source of constant amusement and entertainment. I will be coming back in due course but just for now, goodbye and thank you very much for all your hard work on my behalf.'

MCMK,

I know you think that I know less History than you do but all the same I greatly enjoyed being taught by you for the two years of specialisation. As you once said, I fear the oxbridge dons may well be more perceptive than the A'level markers but the strangest things can always happen.

Thank you once again for everything – best of luck with "HC" –

Love

DAVID

David Cameron, Prime Minister, 2010-2016

Rupert Soames, later to be a captain of industry

Matthew Fleming, now President of the MCC

David Pease, later to repay Kidson's kindness in his old age and become his executor

Mr Kidston,
It has been an "experience" being up to you – and one which has been truly ejoyable. I am not sure that I will be able to fulfil any prophecies/predictions above a 'C'!!
You're a great man ...for an Englishman.

Minter Dial
Kidson fascinated Americans

'... and you would be very welcome to come to visit me in the States. If I return to England in the future, I shall get in touch with you. There were a lot of good times, though some bad worries and hitches arose during the exams. Keep working on the ground strokes – I'll give you some free lessons. The breakfast was also terrific. All in all, it was tremendous. Take good care of yourself and dodge those haphazard cars! Much love Minter.'

William Sitwell, later to be a writer and *MasterChef* judge

'Dear Sir, I have very much enjoyed knowing you. Thank you for all the help you gave on my history project on Edith, I still managed to get a "D". Thank you for all the amusement you have given me. I expect I'll bump into you sometime in the future. Yours ever, William.'

Johnnie Boden took an early interest in fashion and admired Kidson's style

Dominic West, later an acclaimed screen actor

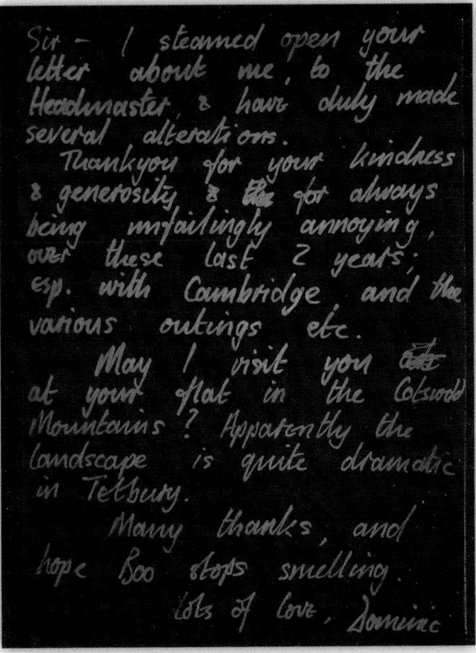

Sir – I steamed open your letter about me, to the Headmaster, & have duly made several alterations.
Thankyou for your kindness & generosity, & for always being unfailingly annoying, over these last 2 years, esp. with Cambridge and the various outings etc.
May I visit you at your flat in the Cotswold Mountains? Apparently the landscape is quite dramatic in Tetbury.
Many thanks, and hope Boo stops smelling.
Lots of Love, Dominic

Tom Parker-Bowles now a food writer remembers Kidson's insistence on grammar

'Dear Mr Kidson. You have injected life into my history, and managed to raise my essay standard from "E" to pretty much "B". If you are around us at any time, please come and have drink / dinner / stay. It's been a pleasure knowing you. Love Tom.'

Sir – just a note to
say goodbye and
many thanks and sorry
for letting you down
at Hickstead last year.
I won't this year I
hope.
Have a great holiday in
Scotland and I'll see you
at Hickstead
William J.87

William Fox-Pitt was encouraged by Kidson as Master in Charge of the Riding Team

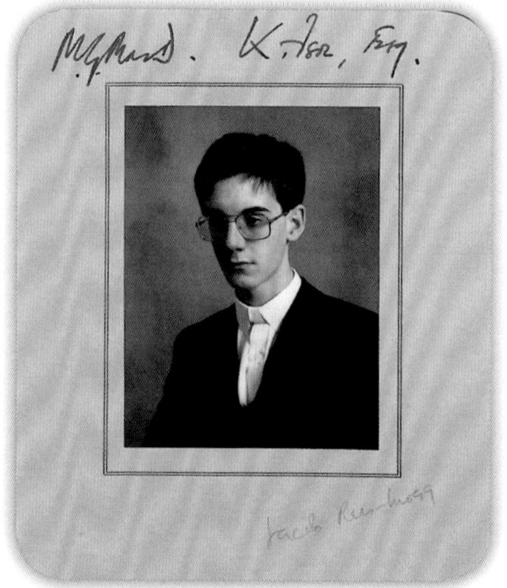

Jacob Rees-Mogg liked Kidson's anti-establishment attitude

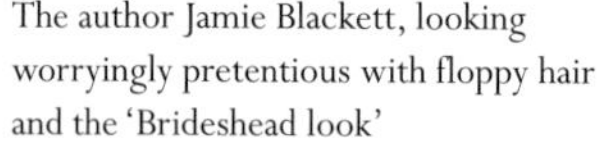

The author Jamie Blackett, looking worryingly pretentious with floppy hair and the 'Brideshead look'

Sir,

A million, million thanks for all you have done for me. There is certainly nobody else like you in this school, always so willing to

Mark Wiggin, whom Kidson helped out of a few scrapes

'A million, million thanks for all you have done for me. There is certainly nobody else like you in this school, always so willing to help, taking one to places, cooking supper and the countless other things you have done for me. I am extremely sorry about the trouble I caused over the Windsor Horse Show saga and will always be eternally grateful. Somehow I feel a lot of your pupils didn't appreciate you enough. Although tutorial essays may be a pain they are well worth it. Thank you for all you have done. Mark. S81.'

Cornelius Lysaght. Kidson's pupil and later, BBC racing correspondent

'Mr Kidson – Many thanks for the help and encouragement which you have given over the last two years, for which I will be ever grateful. Privates have been enormous fun whether we have been listening to music or playing some pronunciation game – If I learnt nothing else at Eton, I know there is no "t" in the pronounced "Hertfordshire" nor "often" – something which I am sure is vital for any person's future life! It will be difficult to set out in the "big, bright world", but I do feel that you will have been a great help, and a person to fall back to. I was told about two years ago that a beak was not to "break" the subject, but to "educate" – if so, you have "educated" with a great deal of care and vigour and I am sure it will still be obvious in a few years time. I do hope to keep in touch and see you before too long! Cornelius. S82.'

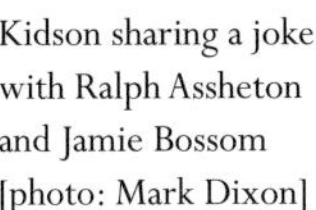

Kidson sharing a joke with Ralph Assheton and Jamie Bossom [photo: Mark Dixon]

Above: Kidson (centre) with pupils on an industry visit. Future racehorse trainer Nicky Henderson sits at his feet

Below: Kidson, in full flow, teaching history

Andrew Gailey
Now Vice-Provost of Eton

Jack Anderson
Lower Master

Jeremy Nichols
Later Headmaster of Stowe

James Cook
Later Vice-Provost of Eton

Michael Meredith

Michael McCrum
Head Master of Eton 1970-1980

Patrick Croker

Bill Winter

Sir Eric Anderson
Head Master of Eton 1980-1994

Beaks: Courtesy of Eton College Photographic Archive

Eton Beaks in the mid 1970s. Head Master Michael McCrum sits eighth from left

P.S. There is a very great deal of nonsense talked about the dangers of disease caused by dogs, whom we have lived happily with for 1000s of years. I am certainly not aware, in the Arboretum, that I spend very much of my time tripping on canine faeces.

Michael kept himself to himself in Gloucestershire, never really mixing with the county, although he followed the Hunt on foot at a distance.

Holidays were a chance to spend more time racing with ex pupils like Nicky Henderson, or in London browsing the salesrooms and bookshops of the West End. During the summer, he would drive to Worcester to watch the cricket. But best of all, they were a chance to continue his love affair with Scotland. His Northern tours were also a chance to keep old friendships in good repair.

Jane Torday: 'Michael spent many holidays in the North and Scotland. As I live in Northumberland, his progress would sometimes include us as a watering hole.[107] Unbelievably, he would still insist that I accompany him on late evening dog walks. You would think that once I was married with children and a home of my own, Michael's mockery would cease. It did not. At least I had the lead card – I knew where we were and he did not. It was on one of these occasions when he made some enquiries about the future education of my small sons.

'He listened as I put various options to him about independent schools which their father and I had considered. Then he swatted them all aside and suggested that if we were to spend all that money on education, it should be on the school which he considered to be the very best: Eton. Thanks to Michael Kidson's advice, an instruction nearly, that is the route we took – and a very rewarding one.'

Michael's next port of call was often with an ex-pupil, **Andrew Douglas-Home**, at the Lees, outside Coldstream in Berwickshire. Andrew remembers Michael turning up with a brace of unruly spaniels,

107 By this time, Jane was married to the writer Paul Torday (author of *Salmon Fishing in the Yemen*, and other works).

who would nearly always disgrace themselves inside the house. Michael would remain oblivious. They would spend a couple of days playing golf at the Hirsel, or latterly sometimes at the Roxburghe, spaniels charging up and down the fairways. Andrew once saw Michael rugby-tackling one of the dogs to bring it under control. Often, they would go down to the River Tweed for a couple of hours fishing, with Andrew rowing the boat and Michael doing his best to cast, while the two spaniels rolled around beneath their feet.

From Coldstream, he would head for Edinburgh, where he would stay at the New Club. There he would visit the galleries to see what was on offer: the Malcolm Innes Gallery and the Anthony Woodd Gallery run by Ant Woodd, an OE and brother of one of Michael's pupils, David. Ant recollects him coming in and the dogs peeing on the paintings piled up on the floor. Michael would sometimes buy a print and they would repair to the New Club for lunch together.

In Edinburgh, he would meet up with whichever one of his old pupils he had asked on a golf tour, perhaps David Pease, Peter Daresbury or Charlie Arkwright.

David Pease: 'It started when I was at Edinburgh University. Michael came up one half-term and took me off round Scotland, playing golf and "going antiquing" – searching for bargains in the antique shops and galleries he knew. We played all the major championship courses together over the years: St Andrews, Muirfield, Turnberry, Carnoustie, Gleneagles, North Berwick, Prestwick. They nearly all accepted dogs, which made Michael happy. We would usually stay in pubs. Michael found that much easier than staying in private houses, where he would have felt the pressure to perform.

'At Muirfield, we drove off on the first tee feeling that we were under the gaze of Captain Hanmer, the fearsome secretary of the Honorable Company of Edinburgh Golfers. We realised to our horror that we had driven towards the 18th green by mistake. Michael said, "Leave the balls and carry on walking," – the only time I ever saw him abashed!'

From the mainland, he would then go and lose himself on Mull.

Sometimes he was accompanied and **Peter Daresbury** calls to mind an idyllic week on the island with him, fishing and playing golf, but more often he had only his dogs for company. Mull appealed to his romantic nature and perhaps it was this, together with his rather cavalier view of the law, and sometimes a rather roundhead view of property, that led him into trouble on a 'John Macnab'[108] expedition.

Richard de Klee: 'He was apprehended wandering back to his car from our hill loch with a rod in hand! Ironically, if he had asked my grandmother, who was living there at the time (and whose brothers and father were all at our old school), she would have been delighted to have let him fish. I was up to him for at least one half for history (circa 1976) and a friend sitting next to me confronted him point-blank in the middle of a lesson (which greatly embarrassed me, of course) with the question as to whether he had poached on the de Klees' estate – which question he brushed aside almost as an irrelevance and did nothing to dent his flow! I noticed him in Tobermory with his spaniel a long time after I left Eton.'

Malcolm MacGregor remembers seeing a lone figure striding along the beach with two spaniels and was delighted to find it was his old tutor and that they were both staying at the Bellachroy hotel in Dervaig, where they enjoyed having dinner together. Malcolm was struck by how solitary Kidson had become.

Michael was never short of invitations to stay with boys' families and a lesser man might have taken advantage of the hospitality on offer. He did sometimes stay in some of the grandest houses in the country – at Floors Castle with the Duke of Roxburghe and at Raveningham Hall with the Bacon family. He was an acute observer of the aristocracy in the tradition of Evelyn Waugh, John Betjeman or, one of his heroes, James Lees-Milne, and these occasions provided wonderful opportunities for him to appreciate the minutiae of country house life, art collections and libraries, and Capability Brown landscapes. He relished these times,

108 I use the expression in the original poaching sense, I don't think he was attempting to bag three species.

although his natural shyness came to the fore and he sometimes found the pressure too much. Like Mrs Bennett, chatelaines often thought that it is a truth universally acknowledged that a bachelor Eton beak must be in want of being paired off with one of their single friends. He abhorred these attempts, and on one occasion fled before breakfast the next morning, leaving an apology for his hostess.

He was much in demand as a holiday tutor but rarely accepted. Although one holidays he tutored one of the Soames brothers in the British Embassy in Paris and helped Lady Soames with the proof reading of her book about her mother, Clementine Churchill. And another holidays, he tutored the Marquess of Salisbury's son **Michael Cecil**[109] at Hatfield House: 'I had been run over by a car and fractured my skull rushing back from playing the Field Game to get to my house before the hot water ran out, as it was prone to do. I then missed quite a bit of the O level syllabus. I was up to Kidson and I liked him enormously and through his excellent and idiosyncratic way of teaching, he was largely responsible for giving me my love of history. It was never dull and he managed us all fairly and with a sure hand.

'I asked him if he would come and tutor me in the holidays, so that I could catch up. He came with his quarrelsome dog Dougal, which caused waves with the other dogs and at least one fight! I came to know a quieter, more thoughtful side to him than I was used to from his div room performances. Kidson taught me thoroughly and then we would go for long walks with the dogs in the park and I enjoyed his company, but I missed the jokes and anecdotes that livened up the history divs. He needed a proper audience in order to perform. He obviously enjoyed being at Hatfield and took particular interest in the Muniments Room, where all the family papers are stored, including original copies of the Casket Letters, which incriminated Mary Queen of Scots. He got on well with my parents, but he was quite quiet and shy as a house guest.'

109 Kidson was punctilious in pronouncing his name correctly as 'Syssel'.

David Pease had a successful three-day eventing career and Michael went with the Pease family to watch him as he completed Badminton twice. But the only family with whom Michael really felt at ease was the Greenalls. Two of the Greenall brothers, Peter and Johnnie, became amateur champion jockeys and Michael often went with them to watch races:

Gilbert Greenall: I was never taught by Michael at Eton, but he had an extraordinary influence on my life, as our family house at Waltham in Leicestershire was on the route of his thrice-yearly 'pilgrimage' to Scotland. At the end of every half, Michael would make a slow journey to his club in Edinburgh and back, staying with the parents of his various pupils on the way. We always enjoyed his visits and so did our mother Migs, who spent many happy hours cheating while playing golf with him on the Melton Mowbray nine-hole course, and he found her eccentricity and the unusual life at Waltham a marvellous source of subsequent anecdote. It was a pattern that continued for more than twenty years.

What was special about Michael was his subversion and his mischievous sense of humour. All children knew instinctively that he was on their side. He was a magnificent story teller and the gift to me was the splendid vocabulary he used. Ludicrous, carbuncle, scrofulous, words at that stage in my life I had never heard – his stories were peppered with extravagant language that made the ordinary so much fun. My vocabulary must have improved as a result, for when I joined the army straight from school, my soldiers would say at the end of a briefing, 'Sorry, sir, we are not getting you,' or perhaps it was simply the general incomprehension of young officers' muddled orders.

There was another thing. For me, he introduced culture into our philistine home indirectly and there it found some traction. Suddenly, history was no more about dates that we had learnt dryly at school, but the things all around us, and the force that shaped everyday events. As we were ragging and jumping about on chairs, he would remark, 'Have a care, people have been sitting on those since the reign of George III.' History became alive and I realised what lovely things we had in our house.

Living with our mother in Leicestershire, the default conversation was exclusively hunting, racing and sex. Michael taught us that there might be other things to talk about, and even discussion might be an improvement on the 'shifting tangent argument' skilfully employed by our mother – arguments that always ended with us being shouted down as the most useless offspring any mother could have the misfortune to produce.

After over two decades, the friendship between my mother and Michael took a terrible blow. My mother, by then in her seventies, dropped in to see Michael at Eton when returning from a trip abroad. Always partial to a drink, she had a number of generous G&Ts. Clearly not in a state to drive, Michael tried in vain to get her to take a room in the hotel at the end of the High Street. She sailed off into the night and took the road back to Leicestershire. In the small hours, a policeman tapped on the window of her Ford Capri.

'What are you doing, madam?' said the policeman.

'About seventy miles per hour,' replied my mother.

'I think it would be better if you turned off the ignition and stepped outside.'

She had fallen asleep and run over so many cones at some roadworks that the back wheels were now in the air and she was oblivious to this new predicament. Needless to say, the bench were unimpressed, but sadly she chose to blame Michael for this unfortunate episode and their friendship never recovered.

It was a great sadness, he had been a wonderful companion, and although we had now grown up, we all still missed the visits.

CHAPTER FOURTEEN

Outside the Classroom

Kidson the cognoscente

We turn to Armies to preserve a nation, but we turn to teachers to preserve a civilisation.

Kemal Atatürk

One of Eton's great strengths is its extra-curricular activity. Societies abound and it is possible on almost any night of the week to go and listen to a cabinet minister, an actor or an artist sharing their thoughts, or to watch a play in the Farrer Theatre. Looking back, I have a pang of conscience that I did not take more advantage of the opportunities. Kidson's time at Eton also coincided with moves to modernise the curriculum and make boys look beyond the stereotypical careers in academia, or the armed forces. It speaks volumes for the narrow pool from which beaks at that time were drawn that Kidson, after his brief spell at Shell, was seized upon as someone who knew about industry, and he was tasked with setting up a business module with a programme of workplace visits. These are remembered with great enjoyment by his pupils.

Rupert Hancock: 'Business Studies, in that strange year after O levels and before the formal two-year A level course, was memorable, eye-opening and never less than entertaining. It may be common nowadays to make factory visits, but for us Kidson was the pioneer, and visits to Allied Biscuits, Mars, Hoare Govett and Horlicks, amongst others, opened all our eyes to a world which, until then, we knew nothing about.

'In his business class, the famous hurling of a wooden-backed board duster was unnecessary, as we were all immersed in the subject. Indeed, his dictum that "five per cent is the natural level for interest rates" is recalled by me to this day, every time I read of the Governor of Bank of England opining about the direction of monetary policy.'

Nicky Henderson has vivid memories of going on visits to the BBC and to industry with Kidson, and one in particular to Slough that went a bit wrong. Another member of that Business Studies group takes up the story:

Justin Cadbury: When I was about sixteen, I was amongst a group of young Etonians accompanied by Michael Kidson on a supposedly business education trip to the Mars factory in Slough, learning about the world of chocolate. Although I was interested in going, I had been round the much larger Cadbury Bournville factory many times with my grandfather, Sir Egbert Cadbury, since I was about six years old. Whilst we were walking around, wondering how we could pop a few bars of chocolate into our jackets, we noticed a few people running about the factory looking quite agitated. Suddenly, the security siren went off and a very loud voice boomed out across the Tannoy.

'Would the party of Etonians please stop immediately where they are and the [Mars] Team Leader make Security know of their exact location in the factory!'

We all thought that somebody must have pinched a bar of chocolate and we were all in deep trouble. Suddenly three very large people appeared, with one holding a clipboard. He addressed Kidson, who was looking deeply worried.

'Do you have a young Cadbury here in your group?' he barked.

My loyal friends unanimously turned and pointed at me, whereupon the biggest of the Mars team stepped forward, firmly placing my arm in a lock. He then marched me across the main factory floor, to the astonishment of the crowds of workers who were doing various jobs of making chocolate and wrapping it, and straight into a small room, where he asked me to sit down.

He said that I constituted 'a serious threat to the secrets and knowledge of making chocolate' and that I would have to spend the remainder of the time of the trip locked in this room, which ended up being about two hours.

When eventually the door was unlocked and the burly man from Mars explained he was taking me straight to the car park to meet up with my friends, who had replenished themselves with much chocolate, he did to his credit try to apologise and say that 'security was one of the highest principles and that he was only doing his job.'

I thought it would be helpful to put him at his ease – so I told him that I had spent several years going round our own chocolate factories and that he had nothing to worry about, because my grandfather had always told me that chocolate not made by Cadbury's had snippets of rat tails mixed in, so there would never be any chance that I would want to touch it!

A popular beak like Michael Kidson was often in demand to oversee societies.

Jacob Rees-Mogg: 'I set up the Stockton Society and Dr Gailey was the Master in Charge. He was then away on a sabbatical for almost a year and Michael Kidson took over. This was great fun, we had committee meetings and discussions about who to invite and attracted some fairly distinguished speakers – Lord Hailsham and Shirley Williams both came, among others. Kidson was a great enthusiast for what boys wanted to do, with a strong anti-establishment streak.'

Richard Cormack: 'When I was at Eton, I set up with two friends, Andrew Lillingston and Chris Denny, the Rous Society. The three of us were keen racegoers and felt that Eton lacked a society to feed this interest. The idea was to get trainers, jockeys and pundits to come and talk on a Wednesday evening – our first speaker was John McCririck, and other notable speakers while we were there included Henry Cecil, Charlie Brooks, Michael Stoute and Lord Oaksey. To set up a society at school, you needed a beak to sponsor you, so naturally we asked Michael if he would be prepared to do so and he said "yes", but under one condition: that it should be called the Rous Society, after Admiral Sir Henry Rous.[110]

'None of us had heard of Sir Henry – we were obviously "ignorant buffoons" – but in Michael's mind, he was one of the most important people in the history of racing, having designed the weight-for-age handicap system. Obviously, Michael took great pleasure in demonstrating his superior knowledge of the history of racing to many of our distinguished speakers, who would invariably ask the question, "Why are you called the Rous Society."'

The school also went out of its way to nurture journalistic talent. As well as the school newspaper, the *Eton Chronicle*, there were often 'ephemerals' – one-off magazines timed to come out on one of the School's two open days, the Fourth of June or St Andrew's Day. These had to have a beak as 'censor' – no doubt the school had learnt through experience!

Kidson censored one of these magazines, *White Horses*, in 1972. It became traditional on these occasions for the boy editors to burnish their editorial credentials by supplementing the articles and poems of budding writers in the school with pieces from famous people, so that the magazines often resembled *The Spectator* with a catholic cast of contributors.

On this occasion, the boys – **Andrew Bell**, assisted by **Anthony Webber** – hoped to assemble a stellar line-up of the great and good of the day: Sir Alec Douglas-Home, Lord Longford, the actor Robert Morley, cartoonist Kenneth Mahood, novelist Anthony Powell, Lord Egremont, Harold Acton and racing journalist Roger Mortimer. Kidson wrote to them backing up the boys' requests. Most accepted, although Douglas-Home, charmingly and Powell, less so, turned down the request. Longford agonised over it, then also turned it down. It was a chance for Kidson to renew his friendship with Roger Mortimer. Mortimer replied:

110 The Rous Society is one of the few Eton societies not named after an Etonian; the Admiral was at Westminster.

Budds Farm,

13 August *Burghclere*

Dear Michael,

I enclose a contribution. If it is no good, buzz it back or tear it up. Please, if you use it, correct errors of grammar and spelling. I cannot think of a suitable title. 'Stray Bats from an old Belfry'?

Jane seems very happy living in the outer suburbs. Charles, as far as I know, is eking out a living as a second-hand car spiv in Devonshire. I am departing shortly to take the waters at Baden Baden.

Yours ever,

Roger

A copy of *White Horses* survives in the archives and Michael Meredith, now retired from teaching and installed as the Librarian in College Library, kindly finds it for me. It is a good read and Meredith confirms that it is one of the better ephemerals to have been produced over the years. The editorial team is listed inside the front cover and it included the future historian **Noel Malcolm**. At the bottom, in capital letters so as to stand out, perhaps as a subtle way of highlighting his contribution, is – Censor: MICHAEL KIDSON Esq.

The editorial preface ventures, rather heavily, three functions for the magazine: entertainment, exhibition and edification, and it seems to succeed on all three fronts. It contains a number of very good poems and short stories by boys and I am amused to see that one of the stories is by **Charlie Seymour**, now my insurance broker. There are photographs by a budding photographer, **Richard Ehrman**, later to be a journalist. The outside contributors did not disappoint either, Acton on philistinism, Mortimer on memories of schooldays illustrated by Mahood's cartoons, Egremont on fortune. Morley has written a short story about a cannibalistic beak eating small boys.

The magazine stands the test of time and I enjoy my half hour reading it, while Lupton's great bell chimes away beside me. Then I look up the review of *White Horses* in the *Chronicle*. Calamity! It is a reminder of the testosterone-fuelled aggressiveness with which tall poppies are cut down at Eton:

> Would, your correspondent wonders, *White Elephant* have been more appropriate? ... Only Mahood fails to disappoint ... Acton's tone belies all the qualities for which one might have admired him ... insensitive and tediously reactionary in its attitude to the modern art of the Stedelijk Museum ... Morley is an accomplished actor, but his humour is decidedly second-hand ... a wearisome couple of pages ... Lord Egremont writes at least with brevity, if not originality. His remarks on Fortune are platitudinous and his emphasis on his heritage distasteful ... But perhaps we should be thankful for small mercies. Andrew Bell provides future editors with a horrifying example of how not to begin an ephemeral. Never have I seen an editorial which uses such long words, yet contrives to mean so little, or be so sententious ... Had I not promised to write about it, I for one would not have read it all.

Wow! I now understand why so many Etonians reach the top of the journalistic tree. It is the real school of hard knocks.

Afterwards Roger Mortimer wrote:

> *Dear Michael,*
>
> *Thank you so much for 'White Horses', which I shall read with interest. I remember Harold Acton*[111] *at my preparatory school; in certain aspects of life, he was six years older than most of us. I seem to remember a little trouble at Eton over an unflattering picture of his dame in an Eton magazine; the caption underneath was:*

111 Sir Harold Acton was a writer and aesthete. He was one of the inspirations for the character of Anthony Blanche in *Brideshead Revisited*.

'At the head of the table looking fresh
Sat a charming mound of human flesh.'

Jane seems happy in Highgate, not a part of London that I yet know well. Charles is at least beginning to realise what an ass he has been and that his chance of obtaining profitable employment is remote in the extreme.

Yours sincerely,
Roger Mortimer

Sometimes we would arrive for Private Business at Kidson's flat in the High Street to find him on the telephone. He would wave us to help ourselves to a drink and sit while he conversed, partly it seemed for our benefit, with some cognoscente of the London fine art world, probably a former pupil of his,[112] about a lot in a forthcoming auction. Or at other times, he would be eager to share with us details of his latest trip to London – 'I stayed at the Rag,[113] of course' – and invite us to have a look at his latest purchase, a limited-edition print bought at Christie's for a song. Or he would show us his things; Edward Harley remembers Michael once getting his shotgun out to show them, a Purdey, of which he was very proud. He made us look at art and appreciate it. He convinced us that we could not be true men of the world without appreciating it and probably without spending part of our waking hours acquiring an impressive collection into the bargain.

Kidson was an avid collector. He had a very good eye and was generous with his time in helping to pass it on. His own collection, constrained as it was by a schoolmaster's salary and the confines of a small flat in Eton and a cottage in Gloucestershire, was nevertheless full of treasures. His walls were covered in sporting art. He had a keen eye for a bargain and would go to great lengths to get what he wanted. His most prized possession was a Thomas Bretland oil painting of a grey hunter. He had taken French leave

112 Almost certainly Dave Ker or Guy Morrison.

113 The Army and Navy Club – his London club and bolthole.

from Eton one half and driven all the way to Norfolk for a country house sale, when Lord Suffield sold off the contents of Gunton Park. Often, he would be given things by boys and their parents. He also collected good Georgian furniture and clocks, and his bookshelves were crammed with first editions – normally books about art, sport or history.

For a time, his hobby proved to be a very shrewd investment as prices soared. His collection was valued at its height at £280,000, but alas, by the end of his life, the fickle cycle of fashion had made 'brown furniture' and sporting art much less valuable. At one time Kidson set himself up in partnership with an art dealer in Hartley Witney as a sideline from teaching, his only commercial foray. They once took a large punt together on a Jan Brueghel the Elder painting at Christie's.

Clues about Kidson's life are provided by his pocket diaries, usually Smythson's finest. They show how every year he went through the galleries' and auctioneers' calendars and eagerly scribbled in details of forthcoming exhibitions and sales that interested him. If they fell during the half, he would usually try and take boys with him. It was an important part of his mission to civilise us.

Often there would be no warning, as **Mark Wiggin** relates: 'I was walking along the pavement on my way to lunch one day, minding my own business, when Kidson's car screeched to a halt beside me – "Wiggin, get in!"

'Forty minutes later we were in the West End of London. I had been kidnapped, still wearing my school uniform, and I recall feeling rather self-conscious, dressed like a penguin, as he took me into Fortnum and Mason for something to eat. We then went to a Christie's sale and wandered around a few art galleries before returning to school. It helped me to pass my History of Art A level, which I certainly would not have done without his help.'

Tom Birch-Reynardson: 'He loved sporting art, and he was wonderful at encouraging us to look at paintings in the numerous catalogues that were sent to him by London dealers. He was particularly fond of Herring (he had one – or at least, he claimed it was!) and the Fernleys, possibly also Sartorius, and of course, Stubbs. His favourite dealer was Richard Green, and I remember wandering down Bond Street one day in the Christmas holidays and finding Dougal sitting on the pavement outside the gallery. Eventually Michael came out – "What the hell are you doing loitering, talking to Dougal – do something useful for a change and have a look at that picture!"'

A number of Kidson's pupils have subsequently made a living out of selling art, antiques and books.

Adrian Gibbs: One of the reasons that Michael quickly became such an important person in my life is that, although he clearly attracted the cool, confident boys to be their tutor, he was equally welcoming to the radar-ducking, un-starry boys, like me.

I remember being surprised that, when the offer was first made to join Michael on a half-day trip to London, only a couple of others in our group came. But while I was enthralled, I am pretty sure that no other boy ever joined us on the many other trips to town for the next two years.

You always had to rendezvous with Michael on the dot of when he said, otherwise all you saw was the rear of the white XR3i disappearing up the Slough Road. We would drive up and park in the underground car park at the Army and Navy Club, where the faithful Joseph Yeboah would keep an eye on the dogs if they had to stay, but normally they would come with us.

Others, I am sure, will have recalled fond memories of Dougal and Boodie bombing along the pavements of St James's, unleashed. I know Michael enjoyed the squeamish reaction from me every time one of the dogs would squat and shit outside some grand establishment. I loved being in his slipstream when we swept into Christie's, the dogs rushing up the main staircase, with harassed staff not knowing how to react. The studied disapproval giving way to, 'Oh, hello, sir,' as a young man would recognise Michael and the unique dispensation that he and his dogs had earned – partly by shaping the career choices of that same young man and half a dozen of his colleagues in the building!

We would wander round St James's in what felt like a parade of his old pupils. It always amused me how he would treat them with aloof indifference, and these titans of the art world would stop being aloof and indifferent themselves in their galleries and start behaving towards him like fourteen-year-olds! Then we would go back to the Rag for tea, before driving back to school.

I had such a great time on those trips with Michael (perhaps twice a month) that I came to an agreement with my housemaster, David Guilford [DJSG], who allowed me to travel to London on my own at least once a week, to pursue those interests in museums and galleries that Michael had first awakened. It helped DJSG in making that allowance that, a) I offered him nothing in the way of sporting contributions to the house, and b) I was obviously square and unlikely to embarrass him with drinking or smoking, let alone drugs!

When I left school, Michael arranged for me to get my first job working for Christopher Elwes at Christie's in South Kensington, where I was a porter.

Ian Marr: Despite all the amusement and diversions of Private Business, he obviously noticed me looking at his packed arrays of antiques, pictures, books, and so on. On the occasions when we had to do essays for him (such as 'Are the majority always right?'), he would get us round one-to-one to go over them. The usual thing when I turned up was, first, not to let Dougal out if he was in, or not to let him in if he was out. Then, as often as not, Kidson was involved with something else (preparing a monastic or Spartan meal of poached egg on toast, or a long phone call; sometimes he was not even there), and again, he probably noticed me taking in the adornments. This eventually resulted in his asking me to go on one of his high-speed trips to Hartley Witney, the village in Hampshire that had a number of antiques emporia.

One evening, I was summoned to the study of my housemaster, Charles Impey. A summons like this was usually bad news. Impey was a strict disciplinarian, and occasionally quite frightening. Anyway, I turned up at the appointed time, and Impey said, 'Michael Kidson says that you're an antiques expert,' (this was news to me), 'so, I have devised a test for you.' At this, he triumphantly produced a silver tankard. 'What age do you think it is?'

I really had not the faintest idea, but ventured a guess.

'Eighteenth century?' I quailed.

'Well,' he said, 'that's not much good; can't you be a bit more specific?'

I was completely horrified and rooted to the spot, and to this day I do not know how I arrived at an answer: '1728,' I said.

Silence, then, '1728?' spluttered Impey. 'How did you know? That's the exact date!'

Naturally, I did not tell him it was a fluke. The point is that a grilling like that, thanks to Kidson dropping me in it, becomes a defining moment that you do not forget, and I did subsequently discover that I had a gift for assessing historical objects.[114]

Later on, I concentrated on books. Kidson encouraged this, and once took me to meet his bookbinder, Mr Day, in Old Windsor. Day was a second- or third-generation bookbinder to the royal library at Windsor Castle. It was a meeting I well remember, because Day only had one thumb, and from what he showed me of the bookbinding process, this must have made life very difficult.

After leaving Eton, I did keep in touch with Kidson by phone and through visits, and there was always talk of his latest or planned acquisitions. When I worked as a Director for Marlborough Rare Books in the 1990s and early Noughties, he (and the dogs) occasionally visited. I sent him catalogues, and he would sometimes ring up to see if we had the decimal point in the correct place on the price of a book he wanted.

In sitting down to write this, I have had to think hard about his influence on me, and see that it is actually more subtle, deeper, and greater than I had supposed. I loved history anyway, he could see that. But he

114 Impey was, in fact, an acknowledged expert on silver and sometimes acted as a consultant to auction houses.

somehow imbued in me the idea that history is alive and around us all the time; and that a proper and full appreciation of it is both rewarding and life-enhancing, to the point of being almost essential.

I cannot say that he specifically steered me in the direction of antiquarian bookselling, but neither can I say that he did not. He knew me better as a young man than I did myself, and he knew exactly how to employ subtle encouragement without me even realising it. It is fairly typical of the enigma that was Michael Kidson that, in short, here I am, aged fifty-six, knowing that I owe him a great deal, but without exactly being able to explain it!

Dave Ker, now doyen of the London fine art world, was another who had his interest awakened by Kidson on trips to London to see the *France in the Eighteenth Century* exhibition at the Royal Academy and visit Christie's and Sotheby's: 'I had not originally intended to go into the Fine Art world, but when the opportunity arose to work for an antique dealer, the brief apprenticeship I had had as one of Michael's pupils stood me in good stead and I never looked back. Michael had a good eye. He had one Herring, and several that purported to be, but he tended to concentrate on finding good value among the lesser-known artists, such as Crawhall, Webb, Bretland and Fothergill.'

This education in art and antiques was not preserved exclusively for his pupils. Peter Daresbury, then **Peter Greenall**, had a different Modern Tutor, but used to go round to Kidson's flat for drinks with friends who were pupils, and soon became a lifelong friend:

'I was very interested in sporting art, as my grandfather had amassed quite a collection. Kidson immediately spotted this interest and nurtured it. Not long afterwards, he asked me to go to London with him to see Ackerman's Sporting Art Exhibition. Later, Michael came out to Limerick with me to stay with my grandfather.

'But it was clocks that became my real interest and that is entirely due to Kidson. He always had good clocks and was very knowledgeable about them, more so about the furniture of them than the internal workings. He really knew his stuff and he taught me about Thomas Tompion and other English clockmakers. He took me to Hartley Witney, where I bought my first clock, a bracket clock that still keeps wonderful time, and over the years I went on a number of buying expeditions with him. My clocks have given me enormous pleasure and I always think of Michael when I look at them.'

As time went by, more and more old boys started working in the salerooms and galleries of the West End, and he was able to combine hunting for a bargain with bumping into old boys like Humphrey Butler, Charles Cator, Dave Dallas and Johnny van Haeften, now at the top of their fields in jewellery, furniture, landscape and Dutch old master paintings respectively. They would cap him in the street and stop and have a chat.

Guy Morrison worked at Spinks in the picture department after leaving Eton: 'I saw a huge amount of Michael, as whenever he came up to London, it was always to visit galleries and sale rooms. Invariably he would bring pupils in to see exhibitions, and then take them (and me) to his club, the Rag in St James's Square, for lunch. He would leave Dougal at the front desk at Christie's and view the sales, with all his former pupils then working there appearing out of the woodwork to see him. He would express amazement at the "absurd" prices which various works of art were fetching, and loved to appear to be confused by a price of £2,000 for £20.'

Dougal was generally left at Christie's, rather than its rival auctioneers Sotheby's. **Henry Wyndham**, former Chairman of Sotheby's, explains: 'I was taught History by Michael and we became friends at school, mainly because I was a cricketer and we had great arguments about the respective merits of my hero Colin Cowdrey and his, Tom Graveney. I remember being impressed by this man of the world, who clearly appreciated the good things in life.

'When I later went to work in the auction houses, I liked seeing him on his trips to London and our friendship continued. Eventually, I became Chairman of Sotheby's and was put in a difficult position. His dogs roamed around the building off the lead and I received representations from different departments asking me to take action, no doubt prompted by health and safety, or concern for the priceless items on show. I felt I had to support the party line and, as I later came to regret, I wrote asking him to tether them somewhere out of harm's way. I received a rather extravagant letter in response and, very sadly, our relationship was never quite the same again thereafter.'

Philip Harley was one of Kidson's pupils – 'I remember being bewitched by his flat in 134 High Street and he detected a glimmer of interest in art history in this listless adolescent' – and recollects what it was like to be an ex-pupil in the art world:

'Jill at the front desk of Christie's still recalls how those dogs would sit still for an hour or more in the hall, while Michael went round the sale. Then they would start to wag their tails excitedly as he came down the stairs, but not move until he gave the word of command. I would know he was coming, because I would get back to my desk a few days before and one of the girls in the office would come looking completely ashen, and say, "I think you had better ring a Mr Kidson straight away, he is very cross with you and was very rude on the telephone ..."

'When he arrived, I would always forget that he had once told me you should never ask someone how they are. The reply was always "very moderate". We might then go and look at some pictures together, "far too expensive for an old hack like me". It was always embarrassing if there were any large women in view, as he was apt to say rather too loudly, "Look at that. They've completely let themselves go." He absolutely detested modern art and it was always a good wind-up to send him a press release for a Cy Twombly coming up for auction. He often took me to the Rag for lunch and on rare occasions I managed to persuade him to join me over the road at Brooks's.'

Kidson's generosity was what everyone remembers most. He felt much more comfortable giving, rather than receiving, and being on his own turf. **James Faber**, now an art dealer, says that Kidson invariably refused to be taken out himself, although he could sometimes be persuaded to accept lunch at Wiltons, which he liked.

The last memory that most of us have of Michael is of the cultured boulevardier striding through clubland, pinstriped and spanieled, *en route* from the Rag to a gallery.

Postscript

While writing this book, I heard that henceforth it will not be possible to study History of Art for A Level; the exam boards will no longer be setting papers. Instead of letting young people find subjects that interest them and using that interest to develop powers of critical appreciation and expression, the civil servants have usurped powers to restrict the curriculum to subjects they condone. Perhaps they think the subject too 'elitist', and no doubt there will not be a requirement for artists or architects in their vision of the new world order.

The irony is that it *will* now be elitist, as some private schools will still offer it and those in the state sector will be denied the opportunity. It is too early to say whether this move will enrich the cultural life of the nation or help to maintain London as an important trading centre in the global art market, but it looks doubtful. It makes the role of someone like Kidson, in nurturing an aesthetic awareness outside the curriculum, even more important.

CHAPTER FIFTEEN

The End Game

His was the function of a catalyst to liberate in others their latent capacities for fusion.

Anon, from Kidson's commonplace book

The largest files in Kidson's desk by a long chalk contained the reference letters he wrote for boys trying to get into university or the Army, or even, years later, when they changed jobs. Sometimes they were for boys who had not even been at Eton: younger brothers of his pupils who had been elsewhere and whom he had befriended in the holidays. He was driven by a desire to 'hitch his pupil's wagons to the stars' and went to enormous lengths in the days when letters had to be handwritten, or bashed out on an old typewriter. Each letter has a tick or a cross scrawled across it, to indicate whether it was successful or not – most have ticks.

The vast majority were to Oxford or Cambridge colleges. In those days, boys stayed on at Eton for an Oxbridge half after A levels and left at Christmas. It was a huge disincentive to apply for Oxbridge for boys who were rapidly outgrowing school, and the rest of us left in the summer, many of us reasoning, in our arrogant Etonian way, that we were already well-enough educated and if we were not going to Oxford or Cambridge, there was no point in going to university at all.

Kidson, who would have cut heaps of mustard as a headhunter in another life, made it his business to know his way around the Byzantine world of college admissions. He networked shamelessly. He knew what individual colleges were looking for and which buttons to press. In the unlikely event that this book is reviewed by the *Guardian*, no doubt it will say, 'Aha – this is what we have long suspected, proof of an establishment conspiracy and of the need for regulation.' But talking to Admissions Tutors, I am interested to hear that, even in these days, they like to receive such letters as they help them to differentiate between applicants, and I suspect they are more than capable of judging well-taught Etonians against bright pupils from the state sector, who have not had the same opportunities.

He was also shrewd in advising boys on their choice of course. Several of his pupils have become successful lawyers and are very grateful to him for preventing them being put off law by studying it at university.

During his time at Eton, the competition for Oxbridge places became very much fiercer. The hereditary principle withered during the 1960s, after the Wilson Government brought in means-tested grants to widen access. Then in the 1970s, all-male colleges started to admit women, so that boys were competing with their earlier-maturing and harder-working sisters. The advocacy of someone like Kidson became increasingly critical.

Eton has responded to the competition by gradually raising the bar at common entrance, so that their raw material mostly has Oxbridge potential, and by increasing the intellectual rigour of the education. The knock-on effect has been that fewer sons of Etonian fathers have gone there. When I visited the Alma Mater the other day, I was impressed to find that between 70 and 100 boys out of a year-group of 250 still go on to Oxford or Cambridge each year.

Although he always did his best to get his pupils in, he was a shrewd judge of whether they were likely to succeed or not. He wrote to one boy's housemaster saying, 'I don't feel that he is an entirely serious or confident candidate today. It will need some gentle and amiable dons if he is to survive unscathed next week's inquisitions. I hope my pessimism is confounded, but it seems to me that he is not quite ready.' Sure enough, the candidate relates twenty-five years later, 'Sadly, no such gentle and amiable dons were present when needed!'

References were always written by housemasters and so Kidson had to write as an additional referee, sometimes without the housemaster's knowledge or approval. I had cause to be grateful myself for the balance that Kidson sometimes added to the mix.[115] I attended the Regular Commissions Board at Westbury and after three days of writing essays, solving problems, giving lecturettes and levering barrels over pretend gorges, the moment came for the interview with the Brigadier. I marched in front of him and stood to attention. The great man looked up from the papers on his desk.

'Well, your housemaster didn't seem to think much of you.'

Damn, I had not expected this.

'The feeling was mutual, Sir.'

I passed and went to Sandhurst a couple of months later.

Martin Humphreys: 'I was not an academic. Nor was he, perhaps this is what made him a great teacher. When I finally plucked up the courage to seek his advice on universities, the conversation went like this:

'"Sir … I was thinking of applying to Cambridge."

VERY LONG SILENCE

'"Good God, Humphreys, Dougal has more chance of getting into Cambridge." … LONG PAUSE … "If you must, for God's sake apply to an all-male college. No point in competing with women. Somewhere deeply unfashionable … I suggest Downing. And forget History, apply for some absurd course … I suggest Archaeology and Anthropology. Do you know how to spell that? Do some reading and come to my flat at six tomorrow."

'Excellent advice, as it turned out.'

Andrew Dalrymple points out that Kidson was a very serious history tutor: 'The only time when I did not much enjoy my visits to his flat was in my Oxbridge term. I was a marginal candidate, especially in his view. "Dalrymple, you're much too stupid for this. Trinity is totally out of the question. The best that we can possibly expect is to squeeze you into some third-rate establishment like Downing!"

115 Thirty-three years later I discovered that, typically, Kidson had rung up one of his former pupils in my regiment. Hugh Boscawen remembers the conversation: 'I've got a boy here. He wants to join the Army, in fact the Coldstream Guards. What do you suggest? His name's Blackett – d'you know him?'

'So began a half of nerve-wracking history essay submissions, which were invariably, and probably correctly, described as "useless and hopeless" at best. I will never forget sitting unhappily in the chair beside his desk, listening to the many clocks ticking, as he reviewed my disappointing offerings, followed by a long monologue on their deficiencies, which inevitably left me much demoralised.

'Nevertheless, as was always the case with Michael, he really pushed for me, and as he had correctly predicted, Trinity did turn me down, and I scraped into Downing College (in fact, not at all a third-rate place), the day before admissions closed.'

This success was in fact the culmination of a carefully planned campaign that had started seven months earlier in May, when Kidson had written to the Admissions Tutor at Downing:

Dear Horton,

I'm sorry to be formal, but I don't know your Christian name. Nor do you know me, but you might conceivably have heard of me.

I have a pupil, Andrew Dalrymple, who is thinking of trying for Downing next Michaelmas. We are anxious to try to place him carefully: he has no obvious Cambridge connexions, he is a good beta candidate, and a very promising oar (rowing bow in the current eight). He and I could think of no better idea – since I too know little of Downing – than to write to you and ask whether you thought they might be marginally more sympathetic to an oar than some colleges. The Cambridge alternative might be St John's, but Eton somehow has never struck up a very harmonious relationship with them.

I'm not suggesting that you personally can help! However, – clutching at straws – we thought that your success might make Downing look twice at an oar.[116] *Andrew thinks of Pt I Arch & Anth and then something else. He ought to get two or three B's: he is a dour Border Scot,*

116 This was prescient. Andrew Dalrymple won two Cambridge rowing blues and helped Downing to reach Head of the River the year after he graduated.

very nice, a man I've a high regard for in every way.

Would it be a bore to scrawl me a line if you can think of any encouraging advice?

Yours sincerely,

Michael Kidson

Tom Birch Reynardson recalls: 'Kidson was incredibly helpful to me in my efforts to get into Oxford, although I think he would have preferred me to go to Cambridge, where he had very good connections with dons at Magdalene. I will never forget the appalling dressing-down I got from him, having submitted the first draft of my personal statement to him for approval – "This is quite simply ghastly and must be consigned to Pseud's Corner [of *Private Eye* fame]." It was indeed awful, and thank goodness no one other than MGMK got to read it.'

Tom was a little discomposed and then delighted to find that his letter has survived:

E.H. Burn, Esq.
Tutor for Admissions,
Christ Church,
Oxford *17th November 1974*

Dear Burn,

Would you allow me as the boy's tutor to add a word or two to my colleague Callender's recommendation for Thomas Birch Reynardson, who is shortly trying for Christ Church, and as a candidate for the Timmis Exhibition?

It may well be that David Callender has not quite done him justice. In the last two years, he has worked extremely hard and made large progress (as A,B,C at A level indicated), and, at his best, is a very competent historian. I have no doubt at all that he is well capable of a respectable class in History.

Nor, I hope, will you be put off by his associations with the Beagles here (and, I dare say, at Ch. Ch.!) He is not the kind of idle Etonian that we have, alas, sometimes sent on to you. He is level-headed, sensible, and honest. In all ways, I should like to recommend him.

Yours sincerely,
Michael Kidson
(M.G.MacD. Kidson.)

Tom Birch Reynardson continues: 'His kind letter to Christ Church, in contrast to the less complimentary, but perhaps more accurate appraisal from Callender, certainly would not have done the trick had the first draft of the personal statement not been torn up and substantially revised with all the "psychobabble" (as Kidson described it) removed!

'As a postscript to Michael's supportive letter to Holman Fenwick, my first employers, I recall that Charles Stewart, the renowned history don at Christ Church, wrote that "he appears to prefer beagling to the Bodleian". Again, I suspect Kidson's helpful letter saved the day!'

Gerald Wellesley was the beneficiary of another helpful letter: 'I have fond memories of Michael demonstrating the human qualities and empathy that have been spoken about in recent months. We all enjoyed his pomposity, because we knew it was not real. I was by no means a star student, but he became a mentor in a way that my housemaster never could. Thus, after leaving, when applying to Williams College, a leading US Liberal Arts College, I asked him to provide me with a reference. He did so and wrote a letter to me afterwards in his typical style containing a phrase that has stayed with me all my life – he wrote that he had "perjured himself generously" on my behalf. Generous, indeed, since I gained entry to Williams, notwithstanding very average A level grades.'

CHAPTER SIXTEEN

After Eton

Others will fill our places,
Dressed in the old light blue;
We'll recollect our races,
We'll to the flag be true,
And youth will be still in our faces
When we cheer for an Eton crew.

William Johnston Cory, ***The Eton Boating Song***

There is an Eton tradition that when you leave you give your friends, including the beaks you feel have helped you, a photograph of yourself with a message. Kidson kept boxes of leaving photographs or 'leavers'; it is testament to the affection in which he was held that he accrued an awful lot of them in thirty years. Going through the boxes with Dave Ker was a hilarious experience. Dave looks like Billy Bunter in his and in mine I look horribly pretentious in a cricket sweater with floppy hair, no doubt trying to look like Jeremy Irons on the cover of *Brideshead Revisited* (it had just been on the television).

Justin Welby looks a bit serious in school uniform and I am pleased to see that he did not get his stick-ups either.

David Cameron has written: 'I know you think that I know less History than your dog, but all the same I greatly enjoyed being taught by you for the two years of specialisation. As you once said, I fear the Oxbridge dons may well be more perceptive than the A level markers, but the strangest things can always happen. Thank you once again for everything. Love David.'

Whilst **William Fox-Pitt** writes: 'Sir – just a note to say goodbye and many thanks and sorry for letting you down at Hickstead last year. I won't this year I hope. See you at Hickstead – William.'

Joel Cadbury has perceptively captured Kidson's likeness in a poem:

An Enigma
Weird but wonderful,
Strange but sartorial,
Unreasonable yet refined,
Tiresome yet kind,
Lonely but lovable,
A friend when in trouble,
A man beyond rhyme,
Eternally lost in a world without time,
Arrogant, eminent, confused but intelligent,
Golfing, shocking & invariably mocking,
The end draws near and I'm running out of time,
So please forgive this humble rhyme …

Tutors had to write leaving reports to the Head Master about all of us prior to our last (and, for some law-abiding boys, first) meeting with him. The actor **Dominic West**, in a loud Pop waistcoat, has written: 'Sir – I steamed open your letter about me, to the Head Master, & have duly made several alterations.'

There are themes to most of them along the lines of: 'I can't thank you enough for what you have done for me and I hope that one day I shall be able to repay your kindness.'

Or: 'Despite the way you have treated me, I remain very fond of you; quite an achievement on your part.'

Or: 'Believe it or not, I really have become genuinely interested in 19th Century Britain.'

Quite a few competed to see how many split infinitives they could jam in to the space provided. Nearly all of them include an address and express the hope that Kidson will 'come and stay if ever in ——shire'.

I saw him a few times after I left, either at Eton or in London. I was reminded of the line from the 'Eton Boating Song': 'Others will fill our places.' It was difficult catching him, because for the next twelve years he was still teaching, so either busy keeping his current crop of pupils on the straight and narrow, or off travelling in the holidays.

Once I bumped into him with my mother-in-law. I introduced them to each other and he fixed her with one of his thespian poses, 'Well, I had better tell you he's the *idlest* boy I ever taught, I can't *begin* to tell you how idle.' It seemed to confirm Aura's worst suspicions of this callow youth who was intent on marrying her daughter.

After I got married, we moved off around the globe and disappeared into a vortex of children, housebuilding and careers and, I think like many of his pupils, alas, I was bad at keeping up with him. Although every now and then we would all catch a glimpse of Michael in the letters page of the newspapers:

Letter to the Times, 16 Jan 2001

From Michael Kidson

Sir, It is hard to agree with the suggestions (letters, January 8, 10 and 12) – and your leading article (January 9) – that it would be a good idea for the recipients of civil (and presumably also military) honours to advertise them in public. The British are not generally keen to flaunt their achievements or their good fortune: and there is no pressing need to add this parenthetic dimension to the Government's European ambitions.

Although in Bonaparte's words, 'it is with baubles that mankind is governed', our

whole honours system excites widespread
amusement rather than admiration, so
multifarious and confusing are the inequities.
They should not be compounded by the
frivolous temptations of personal vanity.
Yours faithfully,
MICHAEL KIDSON
Ivy Cottage, Westonbirt,
Gloucestershire GL8 8QT

Once a mentor always a mentor, he continued to help his boys whenever they needed it. **Mark Wiggin** had a job in the bookshop Truslove and Hanson in Sloane Street, while he was waiting to start at Cirencester:

'On my first day, they gave me the job of writing a review of some fearfully complicated history book for their promotional material. Of course, I did not have a clue, so I hit on the idea of calling in on Michael at Eton on my way back to Hampshire for the weekend. Naturally Michael wrote the most brilliant review, ready for me to hand in on Monday morning. The only fly in the ointment was that they thought I was an absolute genius, so Michael ended up being my ghost writer for the rest of the summer!'

Pupils would always try and seek him out if they were visiting Eton, and for the American **Harley Walsh** it was a memorable occasion:

'I ended up proposing to my wife at Eton (on the steps to the Head Master's garden), and went by Michael's apartment afterwards to introduce her – so he was the first one to know officially of our engagement. I loved my year at Eton, and Michael played a central role in making it memorable.'

Michael was especially keen to help those who had left Eton under a cloud. **Charlie Mortimer** continued to keep in touch as he lurched through various crises in his life, including drug addiction. His morale was bolstered when Kidson went to visit him in hospital after he suffered severe liver failure:

'I saw a lot of him after I left. I took a car home and resprayed it for him. One of my friends had a terrible drink-and-drugs problem, and Kidson was always very good with him. He would say, "So under which hedgerow are we sleeping tonight?" Another of our group was Charlie Shearer, the only man to be sent straight from Eton to Borstal. He later became Chief of Police in the Dominican Republic and was killed in a helicopter crash. Kidson never gave up on anyone.'

And he would always be there at times of trouble, as **Luke Douglas-Home** reveals:

'Ten years ago, in hospital and coming out of a long coma in London, I wrote a letter of thanks to him, having been out of touch since 1989, when I had left Eton. My short-term memory was non-existent then. The next day, I was woken out of my bed by a ward nurse, who took me to the phone. "A call for you – and this number is not for public use," she said testily, while handing me the receiver.

'"Hello?" I said. "Who is it?"

'"Who do you think it is?" the voice said, and then he could not play any longer. "Why are you there? What have you done to yourself?"

'And our friendship resumed, until he died.'

While Michael remained an emotional prop for many, so did he continue to rely on the friendship of his pupils long after they had left.

Lachlan Campbell recalls: 'At some stage in my appallingly moderate military career, or shortly afterwards, Michael rang me up out of the blue weeping unashamedly over the telephone. I was shocked and could not work out what he was saying. Gradually I "twigged" that he was telling me that Dougal had just died.

'I was deeply moved, not least because someone whom I cared for was so upset, and my paltry efforts to cheer him up seemed totally inadequate. It was the first time that I had been in that position and it left an indelible impression on me.'

Others have treasured memories of encounters with him:

John Everett: I came to Eton via the Fleming Scholarship scheme, which was then being organised by Hertfordshire County Council – I had previously attended Hitchin Boys Grammar School. I came straight into E and struggled to make ground on the academic front, but eventually managed to make considerable headwind and started getting decent-to-good Trials results.

My time at Eton was a difficult, but essentially happy one for the first two years in E and D. In C, I really came into my own and began to enjoy Eton life immensely. But sometime towards the end of the academic year, and on into B, I felt increasingly alienated from the general culture of Etonianism, preferring the company during vacations of those whom I considered to be from my own background.

In retrospect, I blame mostly myself for my final troubled year at school and it is hard to decide whether or not the angst I felt had any genuine justification or not. I ended up experimenting with LSD, which had disastrous results and left me in a state of breakdown and depression. I left school a couple of months before my A levels, on account of my mental condition.

I kept in quite regular contact, however, with several beaks from school, not least because I had a girlfriend in Slough whom I had met during social services at a youth club, and I needed somewhere to stay when I used to travel across on my little motor scooter to visit her. Bob Baird and Roger Royle often accommodated me, and I regularly had tea with Michael as well, traditional English tea on a Sunday afternoon; occasions when, for the gastronomic pleasure of his guests, he would produce freshly ordered, sumptuous cream-cakes, still in the boxes in which they had been delivered from Fortnum and Mason. To have been invited back to his lodgings for Sunday afternoon tea was an honour indeed.

I took my A levels the following year at Stevenage College and got semi-decent results (at least, as it was back then: three Cs). Michael had been an enormous encouragement and kept faith in me. Of particular long-term importance was the quite remarkable reference from him in the application I made for university entrance.

The reference he gave me spoke glowingly of how I had managed, against considerable odds, to pick myself up and get fairly decent A level results. He recommended that the top-flight universities should give serious consideration to my application. Thanks to this, I was invited to an interview at Exeter – which had been my first choice on the UCCA form. Before the interview, however, I was offered an unconditional place by the University of Kent and was so thrilled that I accepted it immediately, still thinking the academic rigours of a place like Exeter might well be beyond what I could cope with.

When, on a passing visit, I told Michael that I had accepted a place at Kent, he entertained me with a supreme performance of theatrical indignation, rather like an angered peacock displaying the full glory of its brilliant plumage in a statement of mastery. He drew out from his filing cabinet the reference he had written and thrust it in front of me, insisting that he would never have been so effusive in his praise had he thought for one moment that I would accept a place 'at a … at a … at a second-rate university, god-dammit!'

I have no way of knowing how genuine this display of pique was, but it was by no means out of character, and revealed much of what he stood for and believed in. I managed to persuade myself that beneath this 'front' he was actually very pleased for me. Had I really thought my choice of university was totally without his blessing, it would have been a sad day for me indeed.

Charlie Spencer:[117] My last meeting with Michael Kidson was in the late summer of 2004. I was walking along King Street, in St James's, London, when I saw a sight I had not witnessed for over two decades: the ever-dapper MGMK in a dark suit, white shirt, striding in his inimitable, slightly lopsided gait – as if walking into the teeth of a gale – with a duo of spaniels at heel. (Dougal was long gone, of course.)

117 This is our old friend Alltrup from Chapter Two.

Kidson entered Christie's, and I followed. He was already comfortably seated in a chair he clearly knew well, his dogs flopped at his feet, obedient, loving and loved.

Me: 'Hello, sir – how are you?'

MGMK: 'Good, Charlie, thank you – and you?'

A feeling of sudden and uncontrollable pride ballooned inside my chest. I burst out with: 'Well, you won't believe it, but I've written a History book, and it's currently a *Sunday Times* bestseller!'

I awaited the inevitable praise – the delight of a master on learning that a pupil from long ago had prospered in HIS subject, making those years of teaching thousands of disinterested Etonians really mean something.

Kidson's eyebrow arched in surprise, as memories evidently returned of my not having been a particularly stellar boy historian. 'Really? What period?'

'The battle of Blenheim.'

High amusement danced across his eyes, before his swift rejoinder: 'Bloody boring period, Blenheim.'

It was pure, delicious, Kidson.

Charlie Metcalfe: In 1988, about seven years after leaving Eton and having read history at Yale (much to Kidson's surprise, although he had helped me get an A grade in A level), I met him in NYC where I was working.

To be precise, I took him to lunch – along with Mark Dixon – to the Brook Club, just off Park Avenue.

It was a very humid summer's day and MGMK arrived in a particularly rumpled, but otherwise elegant cream linen suit.

The Brook in NY is a bastion of East Coast snobbery. It is much smaller and more exclusive than the Knickerbocker or Metropolitan clubs and it makes White's look democratic!

One sits at a long dining table, laden with one of America's finest silver collections, taking the next empty place along.

We had a jolly lunch, although Michael was berated throughout by some liquored-up member who gave him a hard time about his suit and droned on about his wartime experiences in England.

After, as we three stood on the sidewalk and said our farewells, Kidson turned to me and said, 'Well, Metcalfe, it's not often one travels over three thousand miles to get away from tiresome fellows with small minds, but you managed to find America's world champion club-bore and sit me next to the blighter. I hope you never do that to me again. Farewell.'

With that, he took off down Park Avenue with that distinctive slope-shouldered walk. I never saw him again.

Matthew Gordon Clark saw Kidson only once after he left: 'I was late for a dinner at the Cavalry and Guards Club and I was dressed up in my grandfather's dinner jacket. I loved it – it had been made for him in 1929 but he had been five inches taller than me and had been a great deal thinner than me, so I certainly did not look as dapper as I liked to think I did. As I was walking along Piccadilly, he was walking in the opposite direction, his dog and that strange gait of his making him unmissable. It was a very short exchange.

'"Hello, sir."

'"Hello, how are you?"

'"Late as usual."

'"Well, you'd better get on with it then. By the way, why on earth are you so FAT? You should take more exercise, you know. I hear that rowing is TERRIBLY good exercise ..."

'By this stage, he was twenty yards beyond me and disappeared into the throng, arm waving a cheerful goodbye. I had been wondering if he had remembered who I was, but clearly he had. And he hadn't called me Gordon-Lennox, either!'

David Shepherd-Cross last saw Michael at New Road, Worcester: 'I spotted his dogs before I saw him. We watched the cricket for a while and discussed a recent obituary, of whom I cannot recall. I commented that I liked the *Telegraph* obituaries, to which he replied, "I cannot abide having to wade through those pages of middle-class names."'

It occurred to me that we had all been indelibly marked by Kidson in some way, so I started casting about for people who would explain it.

Charlie Arkwright: 'Although I did not remotely recognise it at the time, he became a quasi-father figure to me (my very own Darth Vader!). Perversely, a good deal of what he was and how he behaved was anathema to me (my brother could never understand what he saw as my misguided loyalty towards him), but I believe you had to know him, REALLY know him, manage the intimidation, and experience his own, very singular form of kindness, to get him. My own father was severely invalided when I was twelve and thereafter, through no fault of his own, he was a patient rather than the patriarchal figure that he had been up until then. With hindsight, that may have left me susceptible; I have never thought of it this way before, but I think Michael, wholly unwittingly to both of us, partially replaced him for me. Not exactly pithy or profound, I am afraid, but the best that I can come up with.'

Richard Forwood: 'Just a small memory from someone Kidson constantly despaired of as "totally spineless" ... so not polite! But instead of causing me to despair, it gave me the impetus not to be – it is a regret I did not keep in touch and let him know that after the usual bouncing around I set up business in Vietnam as one of the first foreigners allowed in, twenty-five years ago, and now have a wonderful furniture factory of over a thousand workers. It was Michael and his completely disparaging description, which I always saw as being a challenge from a good and much respected friend, who was so often behind me, driving me to make the whole enterprise work. He still does!'

Next I contacted Boden Towers, to see whether **Johnnie Boden** had learnt anything from Kidson. He writes: 'At one stage, I did rather fancy his dress sense: the rather bold tweeds, etc. Indeed, Abdul Faridany, my house captain and dapper Iranian (or Persian, as he liked to be known) copied Kidson and, unlike me, could afford to. I was made Male Fashion Editor of the *Harpers and Queen* teenage edition in August 1977 and based my article on Abdul's splendidly British, Bertie Woosteresque dress sense. With hindsight, every piece came from Kidson's wardrobe.

'I am occasionally asked to speak to schools about business. Many sixth-form children are intelligent and ask good questions, but what defines Etonians is their wit. At a recent talk at Eton, I was teased mercilessly about some absurd things I had said. Westminster boys want to get to the truth, but Etonians want to entertain, too. "Banter, banter," as my children would say. Knowing how to use humour and levity whilst retaining seriousness of purpose is a vital management skill. At the risk of sounding off, I do think this gives Etonians an edge. No one wants to work for a bore. And Michael Kidson was the maestro. We respected and enjoyed his approach in helping us to understand the subject but, subliminally or otherwise, it also infected our own manner.'

Then I looked in the House of Commons. **David Tredinnick** MP is one of Kidson's ex-pupils in Parliament:

'His oratorical style in the classroom is what I remember most. It has definitely been a useful influence on those of us who have gone into politics and I find myself sometimes using his style – the unusual pauses, grimaces, shaking of the head, and dramatic changes of tone and direction. He was a very effective communicator and brilliant at drawing attention to himself. Something he had in common with Donald Trump! That and his legendary put-downs: "rebarbative boy" and "pusillanimous creature"!'

Then **William Sitwell**, food critic and star of the television series *MasterChef*, gets in touch:

'I so remember being in his school room ... that grand way of talking about history, full of drama and attitude and opinion, although I was so rapt by the way he spoke that nothing ever seemed to sink in. It was teaching from another era, no visual aids, just the power of words and imagery. The fact that thirty years later I can still hear him describing the smell of the morning dew before some great battle says it all.

'He did give me a little private tuition when I was struggling in history and I recollect how lovely his rooms were – like the sort of study you might expect at some grand country house with its paintings and furniture ... and his dog, which he addressed not as a dog but as a sort of ancient and disobedient retainer. His bookshelves were lined with books I never knew existed by my relations and you can imagine how rude he was about that.[118]

'He was very kind to me and talked about my great aunt Edith and had that aristocratic and quite idiosyncratically rude way of addressing one – telling me quite how useless I was and how hopeless and ignorant … in a way that I was sure I detected a smile and which just made me laugh.

'I think Kidson embodied the spirit of independence that is said to typify Etonians (and which can so easily spill over into arrogance). He bristled with energy and bombast. As a writer and journalist and television presenter, I often have to talk with confidence and colour and hold an audience. I have never had a lesson in public speaking, but you could say that knowing Kidson was that lesson.'

If you want to know the truth about somebody, ask a priest. So, one dark December afternoon, I went to see Father **Alexander Sherbrooke**. I had noticed on the 'race card' for Michael's memorial service that Fr Alex had said the prayers at the service and, knowing that Michael had been an Anglican, I had been intrigued. I was worried that it might be shut up, but St Patrick's Church in Soho had a trickle of eclectic-looking parishioners saying their prayers and lighting candles. (Why is it that C of E churches, by contrast, are always empty between services?) Feeling like a character in a Graham Greene novel, I rang the bell to what I assumed must be his office to one side of the porch.

Alex had been one of Michael's pupils. While he finished issuing instructions to his secretary, I noticed a spaniel curled up on a dog-bed in the corner, the mark of a true Kidsonian. The only concession in the room to a life before ordination was a picture of a house that I recognised, Traquair[119] in Peebleshire, which turned out be his maternal family home.

118 This refers to the literary siblings, Osbert, Edith and Sacheverell Sitwell. Kidson's commonplace books are full of Osbert Sitwell's descriptive prose and he had a full set of bound first editions.

119 Scotland's oldest inhabited house and perhaps its most romantic. It has been a staunchly Catholic house throughout its history and is riddled with priest holes. The famous Bear Gates have been closed since 1745, never to be opened until a Stuart Monarch sits on the throne again.

Fr Alex has a natural air of authority and it comes as no surprise to learn that he was at Sandhurst, bound for the Royal Hussars, when he heard the call. I can imagine him gently but firmly telling his parishioners to pull themselves together, much as Kidson might do.

Kidson had helped him to go to Edinburgh University to read History before the Army. When Alex had dropped out of Sandhurst to start preparing for the priesthood, Michael had tried hard to dissuade him.

'He wrote to me and he said, "You're mad, you need to stop and think about this." But when he realised that this was what I was going to do, he supported me to the hilt and came to see me being ordained. I suppose he felt he had a sort of parental duty to test my vocation, but ultimately he wanted everyone to do what they were meant to do.'

I ask him if he feels that Kidson has been an influence on him in his pastoral work and he agrees.

'Oh, without a shadow of doubt he has been. He helped me not to take life too seriously; when you see a lot of human suffering, that is useful. He also taught me a lesson in human respect: that if someone is prepared to make an effort with you, then you are duty bound to make an effort with them, and if they come to you for help, you must leave no stone unturned to help them.

'I was also influenced by his complete probity. His moral compass was absolutely straight. I think his sense of humour has helped me as well, and his ability to prick pomposity. He was able to stare down a grand person and make them feel that they were not as grand as they thought they were. There is still a lot of Barchester Towers in the modern church and Michael could laugh at that, so that you avoided being on a pedestal. When he took me for lunch at the Rag, he pretended he did not know where Soho was. We live in a rule-obsessed world, and Michael would have said that too many rules stop people being the people they are meant to be.

'My first job after being ordained was in a sixth-form college in Ladbroke Grove. Michael would never have thought that he would have influenced a Catholic priest working with inner-city kids, but he did. He had an uncanny knowledge of child psychology.'

We talked about Michael's faith and Alex confirms that Michael was not a strong believer.

'He used to say, "I believe in the mystery of life," which I think is a bit of a cop out. But he was a very righteous person and he had an extraordinary kindness. He would take enormous trouble over things that one finds onerous – writing references for people, cooking meals for them. I think his love of nature and of dogs was also very Godly. He had a naturalness and a purity and simplicity about him. On the other hand, you cannot really avoid the conclusion that he was a snob – but he did it well!

'Of course, we would not have shared some religious language at all. Michael was steeped in Anglicanism and so thought that Catholics were dodgy!'

I wonder whether Michael, who must have had terrible personal anxieties of his own, had ever unburdened himself to Alex.

'No, several times he asked me to help others, pupils of his who were in some kind of trouble, but never himself. I am not sure that I could have been any help to him.'

The awful thought occurs to us both that Michael, who was the father confessor to so many, may never have had anyone to turn to himself.

The Baron and Bailiff of the Manor of Northstead is someone else who felt Kidson's influence. **David Cameron** – for it is he – meets me for lunch in the wake of his resignation from the House of Commons.[120] Cameron Minor had been two years below me in my house at school and, although I had barely seen him since, I was relieved to find that Dave was still Dave, the irrepressible boy I remember. Dave seems to enjoy laughing about old times after the turmoil of the Brexit Referendum and later he writes to thank and say how good it is that everything changes, but everything stays the same.[121]

120 As Kidson once explained to me, MPs cannot resign from the House of Commons directly. They are either appointed, in rotation, to the stewardship of the Chiltern Hundreds or the Manor of Northstead and they keep that appointment until the next but one resignation.

121 It occurs to me that this was quite a scoop as I believe it may have been the first and only interview DC gave after his resignation. I'm claiming it as a worldwide exclusive anyway.

He has just started on his memoirs and we are comparing our experiences of writing, when a woman comes up to our table and says shyly, 'I'm sorry to butt in – I hope you don't mind – I just wanted to say, on behalf of all my family, well … thank you … for everything you have done for this country, we really appreciate it … and good luck with everything in the future.'

As she returns to her table, I say, 'That was nice,' and he grins, 'Yes, I pay someone to come and say that every hour to keep my morale up.'

We start by chatting about Eton and talk, as parents always end up doing, about our respective children and their schooling:

David Cameron: In some ways, it was a handicap, I started my political life as 'the Old Etonian David Cameron' and it was only when I became Prime Minister that they started to see me for who I am. But it was definitely worth the handicap. We were very lucky to go somewhere that gave us a fantastic education, yes, but also all that independence and responsibility. I have noticed that Etonians have a great sense of social responsibility; we were not taught it, it was just imbued in us. I was determined to try and bring some of the values and practices of the independent sector into the state sector, and if you were to visit Toby Young's Free School down the road, you would recognise lots of the things that are good about Eton, a structure of houses and tutors, and so on. I really hope that is going to continue, for all children, not just the ones going to grammar schools.

I think Eton's still a great school. I worry that it has become too academically selective, I think one of its great strengths was that it had some very bright people, and also some who were really quite thick, but often they were the real characters. I hope there is still room for eccentrics and it has not become too conformist. I have noticed how some of my friends, even some who absolutely hated Eton and were very unhappy there, have nearly killed themselves to afford to send their sons there. We haven't decided yet, I would be very happy to send him there, but there are lots of factors to take into consideration and we will have to see what is right for him when the time comes.

Kidson was a very big influence on me. All that stuff I said about him bringing the characters to life, he really did. His passion for the subject definitely inspired us. It is absolutely true that when he read to us about Gladstone's death from Magnus, he had tears streaming down his cheeks. And, of course, the humour never leaves you – Rommel and Hofmeister – and I was in the div when Kidson gave Ben Weatherall that ticket: the noxious fumes! You never forget stuff like that.

I was bang in the middle of the div academically and so perhaps he took less interest in me than in the very bright boys writing brilliant essays, or the ones struggling at the bottom. I played golf with him once – that extraordinary swing of his – and went round to his flat for drinks a few times. I remember his post-modernist approach to criminal justice and the rehabilitation of offenders when dealing with some of my friends! He was an intriguing character, outwardly he seemed like a swivel-eyed, reactionary Tory, but he was really very progressive, a small 'l' liberal, one-nation sort of Conservative.

You know he left me his Gladstoniana in his will? I have them in my study: his bust and biographies by Magnus and Morley, with lots of annotations by Kidson in the margins, wonderful things to have.

I wonder where he stands on the Great Man Theory. Europe has just done for him as it did for Thatcher and Major, was it one of those irresistible forces that might be said to disprove the theory – like Tariff Reform or Irish Home Rule, which destroyed some of the statesmen Kidson taught about? But he is dismissive. 'No, you cannot think like that. Sure, there are social trends and forces, but ultimately history is made by humans making decisions.'

We talk about the way History was taught then and now, and I voice my concerns. He is quick to pick up the point:

David Cameron: I was very aware in government of the long march of the Left through the curriculum and the attempts to replace the History syllabus with a Marxist programme. We did try and rectify it and I think if you saw the stuff that my daughter is learning in a London comprehensive school now, you would see that narrative History is making a comeback. But it will remain a concern.

Kidson gave me that broad sweep of History, which was a great foundation for everything I learnt later doing PPE at Oxford. The other beak was Andrew Gailey, who was my Modern Tutor, he helped me to connect things in my mind through to the present day. When I was Prime Minister, Andrew would send me brilliant insights comparing the problems I faced with ones from the past. I owe them both a great deal. It is so important, as a politician, to be able to stand back from problems and see them in a historical context. And all that stuff that Kidson taught us about Home Rule helped me to understand Ireland much better. Also, it helps you to understand the Tory party if you know about the splits between Peel and Disraeli, and then the events of 1922 and later appeasement, and he taught me all that.

I took a little bit from all the 'Great Men' Kidson taught me about. I liked Disraeli's flair (but I think the modern equivalent is probably someone more like Boris Johnson); Gladstone, although he was a bit pious for me; Peel, Baldwin and so on.

I guess you could say that a lot of what I have achieved in life was down to Kidson, as he really got me working, all those jibes about Dougal writing better essays than me, and I really wanted to get that A Grade in History for him, because I genuinely liked him, and that set me up in Oxbridge and so on. He was one of those extraordinary characters you meet in life who leave a very big stamp on you.

I tried to get him to come and stay at Chequers, but I left it too late, he had got too old, and that is a big regret.

CHAPTER SEVENTEEN

Retirement

I used to think (being deceived like most people, by the poet) that old age came gradually and gently upon a man, like mist over the California mountains; instead of which it attacks one by jumps like a diseased and malignant monkey, snapping and biting and wounding with its yellow teeth.

Hilaire Belloc, from Kidson's commonplace book

From: The Head Master
To: M.G.M.K. *16 January 1992*

Dear Michael,

I would be devastated if you dreamt of retiring one day before you have to. That is the quick answer, but by all means come and talk.

Yours sincerely,

Eric

Despite the Head Master's hopes that he might carry on longer, Kidson retired from Eton at the end of the summer half in 1994. We read about it in the *OEA Review*. The Vice Provost, Tim Card, wrote in his 'Vale' that Michael 'had a reputation for tutoring Eton's most difficult boys', no doubt eliciting wry smiles over breakfast tables up and down the land. He packed up his flat in the High Street and moved to Ivy Cottage permanently, taking as a memento the Rackets Courts sign from Eton, which he hung on the door of the garden shed. He also had the bathroom in Ivy Cottage retiled to include a bas-relief tile of Gladstone. He told people that he shaved in front of Gladstone every morning.

Before he left Eton, the then Provost and his wife, Sir Anthony and Lady Acland, paid him the rare compliment of throwing a dinner party for him in Provost's Lodge, to which he could ask twenty guests. He asked one beak, Michael Meredith, and all the rest were ex-pupils. The Aclands remember being very impressed when every single one made the effort to come, some coming from halfway round the world to be there.

Released from the confines of his flat, Michael took the opportunity to have two spaniels in retirement – Bertie and Charlie succeeded Boodie – and his world revolved around them, tramping the lanes around Westonbirt, or striding down the pavements of St James's with dogs at heel.

Michael's routines remained: Scotland every summer, frequent trips to the salerooms, and Worcester Cricket Club, and he also found more time for racing, and reading his extensive library of history books. Gardening became a passion, he was a good and knowledgeable plantsman, and just as the jumble of books and pictures inside Ivy Cottage reflected his collector's passion, so the garden became crammed full of rare plants. It also gave him an opportunity to correct people on the pronunciation of his clematis and camellia.

June and Geoffrey Goatley saw more of him and would look after his dogs on the rare occasions when he was unable to take them with him, such as when he had his hip replaced. When Geoffrey died, June remembers Michael's great kindness to her in bereavement and saw, as so many had seen before, the huge sympathy that lay behind the rudeness. He would take her off to see gardens and architecture and help her to see things anew.

June was very good to Michael in turn. She recalls the ritual of the preparation for his trip to Mull each summer. 'He would invite me round to "advise him on his packing". Then we would go up to his dressing room and he would show me a pile of un-ironed shirts and he would say, "These are the shirts I would really like to take." And then he would show me "his favourite sweater" with a hole in it. And he would persuade me with one of his legendary gin and tonics to iron his shirts and darn his sweater!'

Another of the most important women in his life was his housekeeper, **Julie Wodecki**. Julie, pretty and cheerful with a natural warmth, is a nurse at Tetbury Hospital and for seventeen years helped him with his cleaning and ironing, navigating the minefield of antiques and *objets d'art* and Michael's idiosyncrasies with charm and humour. She became a rock and a confidante ... except for a couple of occasions.

'Mr Kidson was sometimes very rude to me and I was not prepared to take it, so twice I walked out on him. A couple of weeks later, he turned up on my doorstep with strawberries and cream and gave me a big kiss, and said, "I can't cope without you and I'm really sorry for my behaviour," – so I went back.

'I thought he was arrogant and a male chauvinist to begin with, but as I got to understand him, I became fond of him. He needed mothering really. When my sons were younger and having problems, he would always ask after whichever one was in trouble and show a genuine interest.'

Ben Sheppard captures the atmosphere of a visit to see Michael in retirement:

> A dog walk, often through some secluded valley, with lots of stopping to admire the view, or to be lectured on history or grammar, or on one's stupidity and ignorance.
>
> Then a quiet, empty church to drop into, with the dogs careering up and down the aisle.
>
> Lunch always in the Cat and Custard Pot pub.
>
> Always ham, egg and chips.
>
> Back to his cottage for loose-leaf tea and cake, surrounded by piles of books and the sound of ticking carriage clocks.
>
> Later, a farewell in the lane outside, and a friendly parting word: 'Nice to see you. Do TRY to pull your socks up.'
>
> 'Yes, sir, I will.'

The master/pupil relationship did not seem to miss a beat and 'boys' were frequently put to work on arrival, as once happened to **Hugh Boscawen:** 'On a visit to Ivy Cottage, I remember being asked to help put up a picture given to him (generously) by a "pupil of mine who is now in New York". Putting this one picture up necessitated moving about a dozen others.'

On rare occasions, ex-pupils stayed with him. **Adrian Gibbs** visited several times: 'I stayed in his tiny spare room, which had a chest of drawers in it. I opened it up to find dozens of wedding invitations from ex-pupils, none of which he had accepted. He always had an interesting programme planned for the weekend, I remember going to Dyrham and various old churches. The day would always end with his ritual of leaving two eggs on the garden wall for the fox. I think he had that English thing of loving animals more than people.'

Any danger of falling into a life of rural obscurity was prevented by Nat Rothschild. Nat repaid Michael's many kindnesses with great generosity. John and Marion James remember the arrival of the annual Rothschild hamper from Fortnum and Mason and Michael sometimes sharing the contents over the garden fence. The baskets became gifts for people and Julie has one in her cottage big enough for a welterweight hot-air balloonist. Nat spirited Michael abroad on a visit to New York, and they toured India together in Nat's private jet with another Kidson pupil, Hugo Guinness. The Rothschilds gave Michael a share in a racehorse they named Modern Tutor in his honour and it gave Michael immense pleasure to go with Nat and watch him run.

His love life remained as enigmatic in retirement as it had been at Eton. Julie Wodecki remembers being intrigued, as his pupils had once been, by occasional visits from lady friends, one of whom brought him a soft toy. But as you now know, he never married. It was increasingly a source of regret to him that none of his relationships had ended in marriage. Shortly before he left Eton, I got married and we invited him to the wedding. He bought us a very handsome Portmeirion teapot from our wedding list, that we still use, but sadly he could not come. He replied formally to my mother-in-law and wrote to me to say:

My Dear Jamie,

I'm late replying to your kind invitation because I'd hoped very much to be able to get leave off to come. Alas, no: it is on the 1st Saturday of the half, & there are too many boring tasks and people to see etc., so, sadly, I can't get away.

I hope that you are happy & well & enjoying life – & that it's all brilliantly compounded[122] *after 25 April. Being a bachelor is a very unsatisfactory* *<u>modus operandi</u>.*

All good wishes.

Yours,

Michael

The consequence of his celibacy was that he faced the challenges of retirement and old age alone. Others in similar circumstances often have nieces and nephews to look out for them. Michael had no family, but the boys he had taught over the years did their best to fill the gap, and many of them became almost like surrogate sons. There was David Pease, scion of a Quaker banking family, there is a Quakerish kindness and gentleness in David. Then there was Dave Ker, art dealer, bon viveur and savant, always the life and soul of any party; Nat Rothschild, mercurial, glamorous and eternally grateful to his old saviour; and Charlie Arkwright, loyal and decent and always happy to drop everything to drive Michael somewhere.

He also gathered a very loyal band of local people, attracted by the magnetism of his eccentric character, just as so many boys had been in his history lessons over the years – neighbour June, gardener Rick, Ken at the pub, the two Julies, Jeremy the carer – they saw through the cantankerous outer shell and appreciated the innate goodness within. Good Samaritans all, theirs is a remarkable story of devotion to an old man who was often extremely difficult, but never dull.

---

122 I had never heard the verb compound used in the context of marriage before. Fowler gives 'mix, combine, make up into a composite whole'. Michael had hit the nail on the head as usual.

I motored down to Gloucestershire to find out about his twilight years and, adopting my best Detective Inspector Barnaby manner, went around to Michael's local pub to make some enquiries.

The Cat and Custard Pot in Shipton Moyne is one of those pubs that, along with the Church and the Beaufort Hunt,[123] forms the three legs of the stool on which that part of the Cotswolds rests. I go in and order a pint of Elmers and as Julie behind the bar pours it, I ask her if, by any chance, she knew Michael Kidson. She gives me a sharp look of appraisal, decides I am not from some agency of the Government, and nods.

'Oh, I knew Michael Kidson. He was a lovely man … well, he was a lovely man and he was a terrible man, if you know what I mean. He didn't like us ladies much, did he? I mean he was very rude, he was always correcting the way I spoke.'

I nod sympathetically, 'He used to do that with me, too.'

I tell her about the book and as we chat, it becomes clear that Michael has worked his magic on her as well. **Julie Spruels** and her brother, Ken Grey, the landlord of the pub until his retirement, had been part of the faithful band of disciples who helped Michael through his dotage, and she had clearly been very fond of him.

'He used to get me to run errands for him. I remember once he rang up and said, "Julie, I need to watch the racing on the television and the remote's not working. Leave that other girl[124] to run the bar and come and fix it, will you." So, I went down to his cottage and had a look at his remote for him and there was nothing wrong with it – he had that many books piled up in front of the telly that the signal couldn't get through!'

We giggle like old friends at the memory of this irascible old man and his telly, and soon a gaggle of regulars gathers round to join in.

'Oh, I remember Michael. He used to bring his spaniels in here, didn't

123 In fact, the name of the Cat and Custard Pot comes from a famous meet in Surtees's novel *Handley Cross*.

124 In fact, Michael knew the 'other girl' Aly Walker's name perfectly well. She was another of his local friends.

he? They used to lift their legs everywhere and he was always shouting, "Come here, you bloody dog!"'

'Yeah, and you always knew to pull over onto the verge if you saw his BMW coming. Lethal he was.'

Then Julie remembers, 'One time he came into the bar and he said, "Have you got a shovel, Julie?" and I said, "Why?" And he said, "You see, one of my dogs has just done the most enormous shit on your lawn!"'

She shows me the pub's address book and in the back, there is still a list of Michael's pupils who were to be rung if anything happened to him: Nat, David and Dave's numbers are there and I feel a pang of guilt and admiration for their devotion to their old tutor.

We chat for a while and I tell them a little of the legendary schoolmaster whom they had known in his declining years. As I make to leave, Julie pulls down a photograph of Michael from behind the bar. He is standing side-on in the doorway of the pub, bent with age, but it is unmistakably him in a pair of baggy corduroys and an old jersey. Around him there is a sea of hounds – the Hunt had been meeting there that day – and it reminds me of a picture from my childhood of St Francis with his animals, serenely at one with them. And then I walk out into the night and go in search of Ken.

Ken Grey remembers Michael coming into 'The Cat' because it was dog friendly. They soon became firm friends through their mutual love of racing. Ken had horses in training with John Tuck at Didmarton and he would take Michael to watch them on the gallops and racing.

'He would come in regularly and order a pot of tea with three bags, or sometimes a bottle of beer, crisp bacon, egg and chips, no tomatoes. Sometimes he would have former pupils with him. I remember once going over and asking him if everything was OK. "No, it clearly isn't."

'And he pointed at two fifty-something year-olds opposite him. "Look at these two boys' table manners!"'

A blow to Michael's morale came when his brother Ian died in 2005. He wrote to the manager of Ian's home:

Dear Mr Foster,

Thank you for the letter telling me of Ian's death.

It is impossible to try to express sentiments that perforce one cannot really feel. I did not know of his existence until I was fifteen years old, when our grandfather tried to tell me, and he was never mentioned again. Grandfather was essentially Victorian (when he came down from Oxford in 1878, Gladstone, perhaps the archetypal Victorian, still had twenty years to live). Ian was hopelessly lost to the agenda of my painfully fractured family (which heaven knows affected me, too). It was a blessing, at least, that he was so well looked after at Normansfield.

After getting comprehensively lost in a part of London I had never ever been near, I got to the crematorium in good time. The actual venue, and the service itself, were better than its awful environs. It was then very clear that Ian had some kind supporters and friends. From what was said about him, it sounded as though he was a happier man than many of us whose faculties are relatively intact. If Heaven exists, he will have an easy passage.

Yours sincerely,
Michael Kidson

As the years went by, the garden at Ivy Cottage became more of a strain for Michael – and for his neighbours. June Goatley remembers wielding the pruning shears under Michael's instruction:

'Left a bit, now up, that's it, that one … no not that, now look what you have done. You have ruined my tree!'

Not long after that, in a stroke of genius, in 2007 June recruited **Rick Hewitt** as Michael's gardener. Rick is a talented musician and not long before had given up his job as a director of a marine diesel company to develop a new life teaching music and tending people's gardens. He is also a keen historian with a love of antiques. They hit it off straight away, although naturally the relationship was often a stormy one.

'My first impressions were of a very prickly man. I was working in the garden on the first day when a lady walked past with her dog. Michael leaned over the fence and said, "Can I just ask you what on earth possessed you to buy such a bloody ugly dog?"

'I soon realised, though, that you had to give it straight back to him and we enjoyed a bit of banter together. I did resign several times when he was being unreasonable, but always went back.'

Michael enjoyed Rick's company, referring to him as 'My Man', or sometimes, when there had been some disagreement over the herbaceous border, 'That Bloody Man', and to Rick's wife Sue as 'Mrs Rick', and they went off to antique sales together and argued about history.

As time went by Michael also came to rely on Ken Grey.

'He would ring up and say, "Ken, I'm in the shit. The car's tax has run out." And I would find his MOT and insurance and do it online for him. Then a few days later, he would ring and say, "Ken, a bloody miracle has happened. They've just sent me a tax disc through the post. There's no need for you to do anything."'

Michael's driving had always been a source of alarm, but it became more serious as his eyesight deteriorated. **Gilbert Greenall** recalls a visit late in Michael's life: 'He was still at the cottage and was about to move to the new house. He wanted to show it to me and led in his car, which did not look as though it had moved for some while. He set off at such speed that I, in an Audi Quattro, had trouble keeping up. At least twice in the mile-and-a-half journey, he cut up other drivers so badly that they were visibly pushed off the highway.'

There was the time he was found reversing up the hard shoulder of the motorway by the police on his way back from a lunch party at the Rothschilds. Then the occasion he drove into a parked car in Tetbury.

It was after a trip to the vets in Wootton that Rick came upon the scene of one of Michael's accidents.

'I somehow knew straight away that it was Michael. I stopped and went over and a man told me that the driver had been very posh, and had been making a fuss about his dogs when they were trying to put him in the ambulance. With my heart in my mouth, I rushed to the hospital, where I found complete pandemonium. A nurse came out and said, "Are you his son? Will you please take him away, he is causing problems on the ward!" Apparently, he had accused one of the nurses of stealing his walking stick and been very rude! Michael was very tickled about them thinking I was his son. It is such a shame he never had a real son.'

Rick hid his car keys after that and the two Davids backed up this decision. David Pease organised for the car to be repaired, and continued to insure it so that others could drive Michael around.

The Wootton accident could have been much worse, but Michael's driving licence was a casualty, much to his distress, as it spelt the end of his independence, and so were his front teeth. For the rest of his life, Michael had dentures fitted and Rick remembers the problems they caused, as he frequently put them in the wrong way up.

Ken Grey was telephoned one evening. 'Ken, it's Michael here. Can you come round here and put my teeth in? I can't get them in.'

'No, Michael, I am not going to put your teeth in for you, but I will take you to the dentist.'

Ken made an appointment and took him to the dentist, then sat in the car and read the paper while he was in there. A few minutes later, an agitated dental nurse came running out, 'Are you Ken? I think you had better come.'

Worried by what might have happened, Ken hurried in to the treatment room, where Michael was in the chair, with the dentist waiting to fit his denture back in.

'Ah, there you are, Ken. Now I want you to watch carefully to see how he does this, so that you can do it in future …'

When Michael could no longer drive, his reliance on others became even greater. He used to ring up Ken late at night. 'Ken, what are you doing?'

'Well, I have just had my dinner and I'm going to bed.'

'Lucky you. I have no provisions at all.'

'OK, well, shall I take you to Tesco's tomorrow then?'

'No gentleman has ever shopped in Tesco's.'

And off they would go.

Taking Michael to the supermarket was an experience that none of his friends ever forgot. Latterly his carer, **Jeremy Sinker**, whom Michael knew as 'the boy', was one of them:

'He would "eye up" the strawberries and freshly baked cakes but, try as I might to persuade him to buy any, he would always say he did not know who had touched them. He would ask the price of other items and then say, "Far too expensive, I should be in the workhouse if I bought them." If any of the other shoppers were on the large side, much to my embarrassment he would say very loudly, so that they could hear, "I can't understand how anyone could be that fat!"'

Rick Hewitt says that the staff at the supermarket came to know Michael pretty well, because of the chaos he caused. Especially the young lad who retrieved Michael's wallet from the recycling bin where he had posted it.

The vets were another local business to view his custom with mixed feelings. The Malmesbury practice banned him after he was rude to one of the female vets – hence why he took the dogs to be seen at Wootton under Edge.

One day, Ken took Michael to the opticians. All went well until he was asked to pay, and the startled receptionist was told, 'I can't possibly pay that. An old pupil of mine is now running the country, send the bill to the Prime Minister. He will pay it.'

Michael was intensely proud of having taught David Cameron and took great pleasure from his achievements. Neighbours remember seeing a book about Cameron on his table and Kidson saying, 'I'm in that book, you know.' Of course, there was no question of old age softening his stance on giving praise to his pupils and he was never going to blow Cameron's trumpet for him. Sir Anthony Acland once called in to see him.

'I said, "I hear you taught David Cameron, what was he like?"

'Kidson curled his lip in that way beaks sometimes have when talking about boys. "A totally unremarkable boy," was his reply.'[125]

---

125 I told Cameron this story and he threw his head back and roared with laughter and insisted that it should go in the book.

Others remember that when asked about Cameron, Kidson would take delight in growling that the Prime Minister's A Grade in History A level (this was before the days of A*s) was 'among the most inexplicable events in modern history'.

In September 2009, Dave Ker organised an eightieth birthday party for Kidson at White's.

Nicky Dunne: 'There we were at White's gathered for what for many of us turned out to be a final performance. We were greeted by MGMK with familiar gruff disdain. We all grinned as he winced. It took one straight back to his divisions. The years of increasing solitude had not been wholly kind to Michael. He looked older than his age, his appearance not helped by the blue frilly dress shirt and oversized black tie. But there was still a sparkle, an edge to his sidelong glance.

'After dinner Dave Ker rose and toasted Michael fondly and amusingly, and concluded by reading the letter of tribute that David Cameron, then Leader of the Opposition, had found the time to write. At the end we clapped and cheered, perhaps sixty of us around one table in the main dining-room of the old club, which had been commandeered for the purpose.

'Michael rose to respond. He began to speak, but his voice quickly faltered and fell away. Overcome by the emotion of the occasion he quickly sat back down, his cheeks, for the first time I had ever witnessed, wet with tears. His adoring pupils similarly affected rose as one, banging the table and roaring our appreciation for long minutes. It was the last time I saw him.'

On another occasion, he was picked up and taken to a party. The politician Lord Mandelson, then at the height of his fame, was introduced to him and Michael stared at him as if trying to place him.

'Were you at Eton?'

Mandelson was rather discomposed by this and, fearing an Ancient Mariner situation with this strange old man, suddenly caught the eye of someone he urgently needed to talk to on the other side of the room and made off. As he retreated, Michael was heard to say in one of his deafening stage whispers, 'He's a very unsatisfactory man, you know.'

His iconoclastic tactics were still intact.

Always devoted to his dogs, as old age crept up on him, they became even more central to his life. The neighbours in Westonbirt remember them going missing once, not long after a spate of dog thefts in the area, and were haunted by the vision of a distraught Michael combing the parish for them, before they returned unscathed from a hunting expedition.

Another time they saw him walking back to his cottage soaked to the skin. The dogs had gone into the River Avon at Easton Grey and Michael had gone in after them.

The year 2008 was an *annus horribilis* for Michael, when Charlie and Bertie both died in quick succession. His diary entry for the day of Bertie's death in Scotland reads: *Bertie died today in Perth; a desperate day.* Michael buried him in the garden of a pub where he liked staying and drove south alone. Ken Grey remembers Michael being very upset and saying to him, 'I don't think I will live without them. I might shoot myself.'

It seemed to Michael's friends that he was in terminal decline, especially as his health was not good at that time, but the arrival of two more spaniel puppies, Jed and Faddy, gave him a new lease of life.

It became a worry for June when he took to walking the dogs at night and sometimes fell, and had to wait for someone to pick him up. One night the Headmistress of Westonbirt and her husband drove home after dinner and found him lying in the street with a gash on his head. There was a scene when he refused to go to hospital without the dogs.

A red-letter day was his appearance, as guest of honour, at a dinner held by the Old Etonian Association at Blenheim Palace for OEs in the south of England. But he rarely went back to Eton. Andrew Gailey, by then a housemaster,[126] organised a dinner party for all the retired members of the history department. He did not think Michael would come and was flattered when he accepted.

126 Boys in his house included TRH Princes William and Harry.

'We had a jolly evening, which was enlivened by Paddy Croker going down on one knee before Robert Franklin, saying, "I bow to your academic genius." Michael seemed to enjoy himself and wrote a thank-you letter, saying, "I had such a good time that I missed my turn-off from the M4 on the way home and ended up in Wales."'

He still kept up with a few beaks, although he turned down several invitations from Eric Anderson, because he did not want to see his old colleagues *en masse*. A Christmas card from Michael Meredith in 2013 reads:

> **Overheard in College Library on St Andrew's Day two weeks ago:**
> **'Is Michael Meredith dead?'**
> **I was standing two yards away, unrecognised.**
> **Hope time is being kinder to you.**

Kidson wrote one to Nigel Jaques that read:

> *Nigel,*
>
> *Welcome if and when you like. I'm in London from time to time & could bring you one way at least. I've not been on a train (in England) for over 40 years, & they tell me the cost of fares is prohibitive. However, from Paddington to Kemble is 1½ hours & relatively efficient, I'm assured.*
>
> *I hope all goes well. I'm hanging on by a tenuous thread, tho' finding daily some horrendous Blairite inspiration that nearly causes ultimate choler. God, how I hate this government.*
>
> *This is a poor Christmas message, I'm afraid.*
>
> *Best wishes,*
>
> *Michael*

As Michael aged, it became clear to Dave Ker that the time was approaching when he could no longer look after his own affairs.

'Bills were not being paid – "it's a preposterous amount, I threw it in the bin" – with the result that his utilities were being cut off. It was not for lack of money, as his pension was piling up at the bank. I discovered that there was over £80,000 in his account. When I said, "Michael, you really mustn't leave that sort of money sitting in a current account," he replied, "I like to have some ready money." As if he was hoping for a Herring to pop up at Sotheby's. But in reality, he was not spending money on anything apart from the dogs, who were starting to grow fat, and often there was no food in the fridge. And the house was cold.'

It is a conversation that children often, reluctantly and with embarrassment and trepidation, broach with elderly parents, but it is perhaps unique for pupils to come together as surrogate siblings to look after one of their old tutors. Dave Ker and David Pease sat Michael down and talked things through. It was arranged that they and Michael's solicitor should have power of attorney over his affairs and from then on Michael, who had been a guardian angel to so many boys, was himself the recipient of great kindness behind the scenes. The two Davids kept in constant contact with Rick, Julie and June, and as life became more difficult for Michael, arranged his care. Nat Rothschild was also a great support, making his private office available for the routing of correspondence and the payment of bills.

His visits to London became harder to arrange and Joseph at the Rag remembers Michael saying sadly, 'I haven't got any family on this earth, the only friends I have are those who look after me. My only real friends are these two dogs.'

Pupils continued to drop in from time to time to see him.

Charlie Mortimer: 'I last saw him a couple of years ago, just before he lost his driving licence. He kindly drove me to a pub for lunch, and "hair raising" does not begin to cover it.

'I also gave him a copy of a book I had recently published called *Dear Lupin*. Like a fool, I asked him if he would like me to inscribe it. "Why on earth would I want you to desecrate a perfectly decent book?" came the instantaneous response.'

Jamie Norman also visited occasionally: 'I saw him perhaps only six times. The last visit about four years ago was to Ivy Cottage and perhaps the one I will treasure the most. He commented on my rather battered and scratched people carrier. I explained we had privately educated four children purely out of earned income and it had been quite tough.

'He replied, "Well, I'm very sorry, but what it tells me is that you clearly haven't been very successful."

'The frisson of pleasure at being mildly insulted remained undiminished after forty years.'

Benjy Mancroft bumped into Michael in Sherston and introduced him to his son Arthur, who was about to start at Eton. He was struck by the way that Michael immediately established a rapport with him, asking the boy questions and showing a genuine interest. The gift that Michael had for communicating with the young had clearly never left him.

The last time that Benjy saw him was out hunting. Hounds had checked near Westonbirt Arboretum. Benjy saw a stooped figure walking up one of the rides with unmistakeable sloped shoulders and spaniels at heel. He rode up to him and started chatting, Michael behaving as if they had only met the day before, in his matter-of-fact way, even though it had been a while. Then they heard hounds begin to speak again and Michael said, 'Don't stand here talking to an old man, you get on, Ben, don't dawdle.'

They never saw each other again.

Andrew Dalrymple returned to Eton to see Michael several times after leaving, when he was still living in London:

Andrew Dalrymple: It was always fun and I remember rather nervously introducing my fiancée to him, thinking he might be rather fierce. I need not have worried. There was then a very long gap in our relationship, as I lived in Asia and then Scotland.

But about two years ago, hearing that he was deteriorating somewhat, and with a nagging conscience, I wrote to him to say that I would like to come and see him in his house at Westonbirt, since I was going to be in the area. He actually rang to say how nice that would be, and I remember being shocked at how frail he sounded. Upon arrival at the appointed hour, he was nowhere to be seen, but the house was not heavily secured, so we thought he must be nearby. Sure enough, about ten minutes later, he appeared round the corner, accompanied by his two spaniels, walking rather slowly, in that familiar way, with one shoulder down.

In all honesty, I cannot be sure that he necessarily recognised me, but he was pleased to have some visitors, and we settled in to a cup of tea. I had brought some grouse, and a saddle of roe deer, despite advice that he rarely cooked, or indeed ate much, but he seemed pleased to have them. Quite understandably, he was extremely preoccupied, and entirely traumatised, by the impending removal of his driving licence, on account of a recent accident in Tetbury. I asked him about it, to be told that he had collided with a number of cars, perhaps as many as five, in the High Street. "But I can't see what on earth all the fuss is about, they were most inconsequential little vehicles!"

He showed us round his house, and it was good to see so many of the familiar pictures again, amidst the usual sea of books, so strongly reminding me of his flat in Eton.

As we parted, he rather sweetly asked my wife, a little unsure of her greeting status, if he might have a kiss. And that, sadly, on a dark November evening, standing at his door, was the last time I saw Michael, an unforgettable tutor and friend.

CHAPTER EIGHTEEN

I Can't Stand the Preliminaries

I don't mind death, but I hate the preliminaries.

One of the last entries in Michael Kidson's commonplace book

Not long after Andrew's visit, it gradually became clear to Michael's friends that Ivy Cottage, with its steep stairs, was becoming too much for him. June started to realise, when she popped in with some food, that he had slept in an armchair rather than going up to bed. An upstairs bathroom made life difficult. Nat contacted Dave and with characteristic generosity told him that he would pay for a bungalow for Michael and they could repay him from the proceeds of Ivy Cottage when it was sold.

No doubt Michael, with his sense of history, was tickled at the thought of the Rothschilds, who had financed the Napoleonic Wars, now bridging him; although he continued to be as rude as ever to Nat, calling him an 'unreliable boy'. He became very excited at the thought of moving and ordered the particulars of remote cottages in the middle of Exmoor, so Dave had to remind him gently that the object of the exercise was to find somewhere easy to manage, and where he could be supported by his friends.

Eventually a bungalow came up for sale nearby in Willesley, a semi-detached part of a barn conversion, and the team of pupils and helpers assembled to move him. It was close enough for Rick and Julie to carry on going in – she would take Michael a roast every Sunday – and for June to pop round to keep an eye on him. For a couple of years, the new arrangements worked well, although it was a constant worry for them all that Michael might burn the house down. He was not good at remembering to feed himself, but he would cook up meat for the dogs in his old saucepan, with its accumulated layers of fat, and this would sometimes fill the house with smoke and set off the fire alarm. Twice the Fire Brigade had to attend.

David Pease organised a roster of carers to look after Michael that included Julie Wodecki. It proved hard to find people who Michael got on with, and vice versa. They would make him tea in mugs, rather than in bone-china cups, and find it hard to rekindle the relationship after such a deplorable error! Fortunately, Dave Ker heard about a local man while shooting at Badminton and Jeremy Sinker arrived to take charge as Michael's main carer. A countryman, well-read with a highly developed sense of humour, he proved to have exactly the right down-to-earth approach and Michael took to him straight away, christening him 'The Boy'.

Michael's mind started dying before the rest of him, a cruelty for someone who derived so much pleasure from using it. Julie lost him in Cirencester one day. She had driven him in to buy some Christmas cards and hovered on a yellow line while he went around the corner to the shop. To her mounting horror, he reappeared one and a half hours later from a different direction. June also noticed that something was wrong. She took a cake round to Willesley for tea and could not find him. She came upon him sitting quietly on a stile with the dogs at his feet and, when she went over, she got the idea that he did not know her. Both of them were terrified that he would wander out into the busy Bath road, which runs fifty yards from the door of the cottage.

The last time Michael visited the Rag, he was without the dogs, the only time Joseph had ever seen him dogless. 'Someone brought him in. He told me, "I can't look after the dogs anymore. I haven't got long for this earth." It was a very sad day.'

It had reached the point when it was no longer possible for the arrangements at Willesley to continue and full-time care was needed. With characteristic thoughtfulness, the two Davids arranged for Michael's ex-pupils to be kept informed via the OEA Office:

From: Jackie Tarrant-Barton *Mon 13/04/2015 12:20*
To: MGMK Pupil List
Subject: New address for Michael Kidson

David Ker (AJM, RDM 69) has contacted me to say that Michael has left his house at Willesley in Gloucestershire and is now living at: Hunters Care Home, Cherry Tree Lane, Cirencester GL7 5DT.

According to David, 'Michael is extremely frail. However, I think he really benefits from visits, even if it is for a very short time. I find what he likes is if one chats away, but one should not expect a great deal of interaction. Some days are obviously better than others. David Pease and I who look after him are keen for people to visit as we think it keeps the care home on their toes when people turn up unexpectedly. Hunters is easy to find and there is plenty of parking. It is very accessible from both the M5 and the M4.'

Kind regards,
Jackie.
Clerk to the Old Etonian Association

The dogs, Jed and Faddy, were given to Rick's sister-in-law to look after. Initially, Jeremy took them into Hunters so that Michael could see them, but stopped when it appeared to upset him and they caused havoc by chasing a rabbit around the garden.

Dave Ker remembers Michael's mordant wit on the occasions he went to see him.

'He would point to the other old people and say, "Of course, they won't be here next time you come."'

As he faded, a number of his old friends made the trip to Cirencester to say goodbye. June was the last of his friends to see him alive. She held his hands on the last night and she remembers him squeezing them tight as she left for the last time.

The following day, Michael died peacefully in his sleep.

CHAPTER NINETEEN

Vale

In sadness then remember him, but mark this epitaph,
His gift was not to make men grieve,
It was to make them laugh.

Michael died on 20 June 2015. In this part of the book I have tried to distil the many conversations and email exchanges with Michael's pupils and friends into a chapter on what he meant to all of us.

I have included below just some of the things that people said about him:

He is the reason that I have a copy of Blake's *Disraeli* on my shelves, that I know how to pronounce 'orang-utan', that I can't think of Palmerston without Michael's final quip entering my head ('a tawdry end to a magnificent career'), and, probably, that I ended up teaching History myself.
Martin Humphreys

We loved him but, of course, we were of a generation that could not say that. I hope he knew how much he was loved. He really was one in a million.
Father Alex Sherbrooke

He was one of those extraordinary characters you meet in life who leaves a very big stamp on you.
David Cameron

Behind that acerbic wit, there was the kindest man in the world. I hope he is in some celestial library in front of a nice warm fire reading a favourite piece of Victorian history with all his spaniels at his feet.
Jamie Norman

He was the king of enigma.
Charlie Arkwright

At a school where the teaching of life was as significant as the teaching of subjects, it is not surprising that Kidson's boys appreciated and remembered him in the way they did. We and they were lucky to have crossed his path.
Jeremy Greenstock

In thirty years of running the pub I met some remarkable characters, but Michael was different to all of them. He was a great man.
Ken Grey, retired landlord, The Cat & Custard Pot

He was a remarkable man – quite unperturbed by the opinion of others and so obviously determined to live his life according to his rules. In a place like Eton, that is an achievement all in itself.
Matt Pinsent

If you had to go to a department store to buy the ideal schoolmaster, Michael would be the one you would choose – but it would have to be Harrods.
Andrew Bell

What a dude he was.
Alex Bonsor

He was a very kind gentleman. He was like a grandfather to me.
Joseph Yeboah, formerly car park attendant, now hall porter, at the Army & Navy Club

Christmases will never be the same now that I do not get a Christmas card coming on the back of mine with the traditional message, 'I see your handwriting is as bad as ever.'

Richard Cormack

Bless him, he might have been subliminally responsible that I can laugh at most things, even if too often it is only at myself. He was delightfully serious about not being too serious. A valuable training in having a sense of proportion, perhaps?

John Watson

One of life's great characters, with impeccable judgment and foresight.

Eliot Woolf

He was a great teacher, and a great Eton beak. Michael Kidson was one of those rare men to whom the cliché, 'They don't make 'em like that anymore', could truly apply.

Tom Parker Bowles

Michael was indubitably one of the handful of beaks to leave a lasting impression on me. Besides an infectious enthusiasm for History, in which he schooled me to an A at A level, he taught me punctuation and pronunciation ('westcut, boy, not waistcoat'). Above all, I remember the humour.

Charlie Egerton-Warburton

For me, his abilities to enthuse and to amuse meant that I could see the importance of things that I would otherwise have ignored. It was always a pleasure to 'sit at his feet'.

Mungo Mansfield

His was an extraordinary influence. If I look back, I think it is almost entirely due to him that I studied History, did Politics as a degree, and

then did a short stint in the Army. I was under no great illusions that I was ever going to become one of his 'great men', but he made the prospect of being among them so exciting.
Matthew Gordon Clark

To this day however, always has a comma.
Napier Marten

Nobody, but nobody, I knew ever had a bad word to say about Michael Kidson; he was the embodiment of kindness and fairness, commanding unparalleled respect from one and all. I can only ever think about him with great fondness and affection.
John Everett

Michael Kidson: A gentleman, an inspiration, I think we were all incredibly lucky to have met him and to have known him, so many fond memories.
Tom Goff

Michael was the first adult to give me an inkling that it is OK to be an individual. Until I had him as my tutor, my childhood had been very much one of towing the line, and doing what one was told through blind subordination to hereditary prejudice. Everyone deserves an iconoclast like Michael in their lives.
Anthony Slessor

My memory is very strong that Mr Kidson taught me a very important rule in life unrelated to history, which I still follow today. The rule is that if you have to write a difficult or important letter or email (e.g. accepting or resigning from a job) always sleep a night on the letter/email. Never write such a letter or email and immediately send it off: you may regret it later. Whenever I write such a letter/email, I think of Mr Kidson looking at me and consider the matter carefully.
Andrew Parker-Jervis

I will always remember a letter which I received shortly after graduating from Oxford in History. I had done well in my Finals and the letter of congratulations he sent me was one of the most genuinely affectionate I have ever received. There was no egoism in it all, no sense that one of HIS history pupils had cast honour on him, as it were. Just an utterly authentic happiness and warmth at my success.
Darius Guppy

Legend.
Harry Nuttall

Once I remember him sensing that I was rather down, and it was at that moment that I first appreciated his perception, support and good advice. I am sure that many, perhaps even most of Michael's pupils, would have numbered him as one of the very first people they would have turned to for help and wise counsel in adversity. Indeed, as testament to that, I recall him once telling me, very sadly, about how he had spent an entire night talking to one of his former pupils, but that this had still not been enough to prevent him from jumping over Beachy Head soon afterwards. He had an ability to listen sympathetically, and well, and it was a most endearing quality. One of his favourite sayings, and one which I now use with my children, was 'consider one year hence, what a small moment this will seem'. Good advice, and a good maxim.
Andrew Dalrymple

There were numerous anecdotes about his ability to make Eton a more amusing place. One old boy remembers seeing a note on the Lost & Found Board in Cannon Yard, which said simply: 'One watch of humble aspect, found on Agar's Plough. Please contact MGMK.'

Rupert Hancock put his thoughts into a letter to Michael, written after his death for this book:

Dear Michael,

You would be intrigued to see your OBIT in the OEA Review, along with Paddy Croker and Richard 'Ollie' Bull.

But for me, your passing is a profound closure, as single-handedly you were the most significant influence in my life.

Uniquely, I had the benefit of your guidance both at Eton and at Papplewick.

At Papplewick, your advice that Common Entrance 'is probably the most important exam that you will ever take' rings true to this day. We both know that without your skills and care, I would not have had a chance of passing Eton entrance, and for me the double benefit was the best education in the land, and your continuing tuition through the A level years as my Modern Tutor.

At Eton, I was fortunate to join your group for Private Business: as is recorded elsewhere, you were always oversubscribed as a Modern Tutor, in my case, almost certainly your willingness to take on lost causes made all the difference. And it did. I recall you asking if the last, and typed, essay that I wrote before A level had been written by me, as apparently it was on the right track.

Your attempts to civilise us were perhaps only partly successful, but galleries and 'The Winter's Tale' remain vivid memories and undoubtedly influenced my own behaviour as a parent.

Success in life is hard to define, but a measure has to be the positive impact that you have on others.

Yours is immeasurable and enduring as this book will attest.

Thank you, once again, for everything,

Rupert

I am still beating myself up about missing his service of thanksgiving at St Mary's Church, Lasborough on 3 July 2015. The church was packed and Mark Wiggin told me that he had never seen such a rogues' gallery of Eton characters from three decades.

I went to Lasborough the following spring. The rooks were wheeling noisily around their building site in some beech trees and blackthorn blossom in the hedgerows spoke of new life beginning. The church sits by an ancient cedar tree in an enchanted valley, at one with the landscape, like the sheep safely grazing the old turf of the surrounding parkland. It was chosen, not because Michael was a regular worshipper there, but because he walked his spaniels in the valley, and I could understand him feeling closer to his Maker there than anywhere else. The church is described by Pevsner as Victorian and so it was fitting that he should pass back through the Victorian Anglicanism that had formed part of his early life.

Rick the gardener, faithful to the last, played the organ to a packed church. For those, like me, who missed it, I have included the two eulogies. One from Nat Rothschild on behalf of his boys and one from Sir Eric Anderson, Head Master and later Provost of Eton. Had I been there, I would have found it hard to hold back the tears.

Nat Rothschild spoke first:

> I arrived at Eton alone – for the first year I did no sports, because 'I slipped through the net.' When others were playing football or rowing, I sat in my room. I had no idea I was supposed to be on a pitch or in a boat.
>
> By my second year, I had been bullied, beaten three times and rusticated. My best result in my first two years of exams was last place pass.
>
> Then I met a man called Michael Kidson, who inspired me. I looked forward to his lessons, his humour, his rages. The way he taught us lightened up my day.
>
> I catastrophised about him not wanting to be my modern tutor. Why would he possibly want to choose me? But he did.
>
> I was on the road to recovery.
>
> Once Michael was my modern tutor, my life definitely got better. My grades improved. I was happier. I enjoyed something. I made new friends. And most importantly, I was granted twenty-

four-hour access to his flat. The key was located above the door. And I knew when Michael was teaching, because he left his schedule on his desk. I would go in most mornings to make myself a cooked breakfast, using a saucepan that was never washed and full of decades of old grease. I always marvelled that Michael lived to eighty-five, given that saucepan and its contents.

In my last term, I was 'asked to leave'. My recollection is that I moved in a split second from JJB to the spare room in Michael's flat, and a camp bed. It was from there that I took my A levels. I lived with Michael and just loved it. Why? Because he treated me as an equal. He did not order me around, or tell me what to do. He mocked me sometimes. He was, in essence, an early cognitive behaviouralist, self-taught. This was a very remarkable feature.

I would never have gone to university, or even finished my A levels without him.

After I left and he retired, we kept in close contact. Why? Because he was great company. I was unbelievably proud when he came to visit me in New York once. I enjoyed so much seeing him in Gloucestershire and I admired the beautiful house he made for himself in his retirement in Westonbirt. He was incredibly funny, and he knew it.

Only in the last couple of years, when he drove his high-powered BMW like a battering ram down Westonbirt High Street, did Dave, David and I know that his days were numbered. But even last month, when we watched the Derby and the Oaks together, you could see the old Michael – the passion, the will, the excitement in his eyes were still there. As I left, I hugged him and said goodbye.

He was the most inspirational person to me, and he totally changed my life.

And then **Eric Anderson** spoke:

Michael Kidson, MGMK, whose passing we mourn and whose life we celebrate at this Service was a remarkable, but complicated man. Just how remarkable and complicated I did not fully appreciate until this last ten days, when a great number of you – and several more who could not be here this afternoon at such short notice – kindly sent me memories, stories and reminiscences. I cannot repeat them all in a short address, but no doubt they will be told and retold in the Cat and Custard Pot afterwards.

He was, according to those who have been in touch, inspirational, unconventional, indiscreet, dismissive, confrontational, outrageously opinionated, sarcastic, rude, politically incorrect, contrary, sartorially correct, charming, kind, generous, shy and deeply private.

He was private, even mysterious, about his early life, which he did not talk about. We know he was born in 1929, lost both his parents very early, did National Service, read History at Cambridge (and, we presume, played Rackets there), worked for Shell for a few unhappy years, and had a brief, successful spell at Papplewick, before coming to Eton at the age of thirty-six.

The next twenty-nine years were what mattered most to him and mattered to many of you. He taught history brilliantly, as an exciting story of Great Events, of dramatic moments and movements, and of Great Men (I think there were not many Great Women in his version of the past). How wonderful to be in a gathering as large as this, where everyone knows all about Gladstone.

To be up to MGMK for History next div was something to look forward to for even the most reluctant scholar. He was a showman. The performance would be unpredictable, but might include tantrums of temper, the muddling of boys' names, a board-rubber or that block of wood from his desk flying through the air; and – with luck – one of those well-heralded explosive sneezes. It would not be a dull forty minutes.

It was an extraordinary History Department, a mixture of mavericks, scholars and teachers of genius, most of the masters qualifying for at least two of those titles: among them Giles St Aubyn, Tim Connor, David Evans, Robert Franklin, Bill Winter, Andrew Gailey, Tim Wilson-Smith, Ray Parry, Patrick Croker and Michael. They were by no stretch of the imagination a united team. They were individuals, and that was their strength; each went his own way – and that exactly suited MGMK. It has to be confessed that he did not enormously like them and made some show of not even knowing their names.

(If those of you here who cared for him so devotedly in his last years and months, carers, neighbours and visitors, found that he did not always use your correct names, please do not take it to heart: he told many of those who visited him how excellently you looked after him. We are all grateful to you for that, and so was he.)

He particularly enjoyed, I suspect, his relationship with Patrick Croker.[127] This is not the occasion on which to rehearse the Great Staircase Scandal – whose dog was to blame? – but here is a story I can tell. MGMK angrily upbraided one boy and told him that he could put up with him no longer. He must go next door and tell Mr Croker that he was now joining his division instead. The boy returned to say that Mr Croker would not accept any of Mr Kidson's rejects, and pleaded for reinstatement. MGMK, as he usually – I think always – did, relented, but on condition that the offender would never again, ever, do what he had done in the feeble and hopeless essay which had caused the row: split an infinitive.

What would he have said last week to the OEA office which, in sending out notices of today's Service, as you will all have noticed,

127 Poor Paddy died a few months later. I am pleased that they will be reunited with their beloved dogs and able to continue sparring as they walk them on the Elysian Fields together.

somehow managed to include an infinitive and to split it?

However little he liked his colleagues, he did like the boys he taught. He may have been appointed as a teacher of History, but actually he was a teacher of boys. And that is much more important. Private Business with Michael Kidson, one of his pupils told me, 'encapsulates everything that was wonderful about Eton'; several others asserted that he was 'the biggest single influence' on their Eton careers.

For me, as Head Master, he was very, very important. All schools have some boys who need an awful lot of attention – because they are idle, or disaffected, or bored and unmotivated, or a disciplinary nightmare. Most beaks do not really enjoy teaching them and many housemasters – in my experience around the ninth week of each Half – think their lives would be pleasanter if those boys were to … leave.

The Head Master (who admittedly sees less of them: just a few minutes in his Schoolroom before lunch most days) knows that they include some of the most interesting boys in the school, lively and good fun and full of unused talent, potentially among the most worthwhile, therefore, if the school can put up with them long enough to straighten out some of their problems.

To have Michael Kidson on hand was a gift from the gods. He seemed positively to want as pupils boys whose work was 'feeble' or 'hopeless' and whose already lengthy Bill record was 'deplorable'. Of course, he was also a popular choice among the decent, responsible, well-rounded characters, well represented in this church, who go on to become the backbone of their businesses and their local communities, and who might occasionally include in their number the sort of boy who becomes a successful entrepreneur or famous actor, or prime minister or racehorse-trainer. But he never turned away the others. He threw out a lifeline to the strugglers.

In his words, he tried to 'civilise' them, by cramming them

into his car for a sudden visit (in school dress) to Waddesdon or Claydon, or a trip to London, by assuming that opera and English furniture, or clocks and books, would fascinate them as they did him, and by cooking them breakfast on a Sunday served off fine china under the array of sporting prints acquired at Sotheby's or Christie's and – although I can't approve of this headmagisterially – by sometimes pouring them generous measures of ... other beverages.

He civilised all, and he saved some. A boy in trouble had an advocate in Michael, who would stand by him. Come what come may, he was on his side, even if he continued to be horribly rude about his work, gave vent to spectacular tantrums of wrath, brushed aside the gratitude of those he had helped, and would profess astonishment at their success:

'Dear Mr and Mrs X, A major miracle has taken place. Your son has passed his A levels. An extraordinary achievement for a great thick-head.'

They all knew he cared about them, whether or not they realised that the outrageous bluster, and the insults that so amused us all, were a means of concealing how deeply he cared about them. His comments about other masters and his willingness to ignore the usual rules were a kind of guarantee that he was not on authority's side, but the boys' side.

What he did, for instance, one St Andrew's Day typifies the sort of tutor he was. Two of his boys pointed out that Arkle was running in the Hennessy Gold Cup at Newbury on St Andrew's Day when, of course, there was no leave out for beaks or boys. Michael agreed, however, that Arkle would probably be more entertaining to watch than the Wall Game. They piled into his little car – I think it was a Morris Minor at the time – and took up their station by the last fence, where they saw Stalbridge Colonist and Arkle (who was giving thirty-two pounds) jump it neck and neck. Stalbridge Colonist actually won, but they had seen the great Arkle, got back with time to spare before Absence, and they had got away with it … Until, that is, the *Sunday Times* came out the next morning with a large photograph of Arkle taking the last fence and three very recognisable faces in the front of the crowd.

It would not be appropriate to conclude this memorial address without saying that Michael Kidson loved his boys, but also his dogs. He was pretty good at training them, too. I once met him, walking down Bond Street with two springer spaniels at his heels, not on leads. I can believe the story that at Christie's he left the two of them sitting at the top of the stairs while he went off round an exhibition of sporting prints, and returned to find them being stroked by the Queen Mother.

The usual advice for speakers on an occasion like this is: *de mortuis nil nisi bonum*. If any of you have difficulty in translating that, MGMK would, I am sure, be outraged and insist that he could go into Tetbury, pull the first old lady he met off her bicycle and she, of course, would immediately know a simple thing like that: 'Speak no ill of the dead.'

But in the interests of a little shade in the corner of the portrait, I feel constrained to tell you that those who played golf with him – I'm sorry, those who played 'goff' with him – report strange experiences when they were close to beating him. He might unfortunately be overtaken by one of those thunderous sneezes just as they were at the top of their backswing, and Dougal (normally best-behaved of springer spaniels) might uncharacteristically run across their line as they were putting for the hole.

How do you measure a good life? I don't know – but I know this was a good life, well lived by a good man who did good things. Few have influenced more people for good than Michael Kidson and he did it at the most formative moment in their lives.

He did not go back often to Eton. That was because for him Eton was not a place, not buildings and rackets courts and fields and colleagues and community. Eton was you: 'his' boys. His relationships with you were what Eton meant to him. Your loyalty and continuing friendship was his reward, and he died – I am certain – happy in the knowledge that he had mattered and had made a difference to so many of you.

Jamie Blackett: I will go last, as that is the narrator's perk. It has made me smile, as I have burnt the midnight oil writing his biography, to think that in death Michael has got me to work much harder than he ever managed in life.

His last act of generosity to any of his pupils has been, whether he knows it or not, to me. He encouraged me to write and fostered a love of words and wordsmithing, but I would not now be a published author if he had not bestowed on me a book that has largely written itself. Few writers have ever been handed on a plate such a compelling and quirky character, or such an incredible plot. Pulling it together has sometimes caused me to double up in laughter, and at others has brought a lump to my throat. But I would not have got off my arse and written it if he had not meant a great deal to me. It has been the greatest privilege to be the one of his pupils to tell his story.

He got under all our skins. Many of us admitted, to our eternal shame, that we had not seen him for years, yet confessed to thinking about him nearly every day. It is almost impossible to fix a comma into a sentence, or frame an insult, or pronounce a word without him hovering at the back of our minds; pernickety little things that mask the bigger truth that he has been a rock to all of us. Struggling to write the stickier parts of the book, I have found myself wishing that I could take it round to his flat at the top of 134–135 Eton High Street, let him pour me a stiff drink, and talk it through with him. He was always there for us and we all knew, if we went to see him, that we would pick up again as if we had seen each other yesterday, and that he would walk through a blizzard to help us if we needed it.

We all need mentors in our lives and for many of us that was Michael. He deserves his bit of fame, much as he might be horrified by it. Maybe in future, instead of saying 'a Mr Chips', who was a fictional character, as shorthand for an inspirational schoolmaster, people will say a Mr Kidson instead.

I hope so.

Epilogue

Michael Kidson's legacy: The boys he tutored and taught

Michael is dead, but his influence lives on. The Kidson diaspora is spread across the world. At the time of writing in 2016, most of us are now in our forties, fifties and sixties. I reckon there is another forty years to go before the Etonians he helped to unleash on an unsuspecting world have finished making their mark, and memories of our old mentor start to fade.

He is remembered frequently in conversations in the clubs around St James's Street. If you walked into the Stewards' Room on most racecourses and asked if anyone knew him, you would probably get a response. (Probably also if you were to pop into the Priory, or go to an Alcoholics Anonymous meeting in one of the more fashionable shires, you might also meet some of his pupils – but we will not go there).

There is no typical Kidsonian, although they generally have an ability to laugh at the world and at themselves. When they meet, even if they are twenty years apart, they tend to find that they share the same values and sense of humour. There should be a tie really, something suitably unorthodox, like an OE tie with spaniels cavorting between the stripes.[128] In the following list, I have restricted the names to those whose leavers were found in his papers. I have attached an asterisk to those who had the perspicacity to choose Kidson as their Modern Tutor.

128 Thanks to the good offices of Johnnie Boden, there now is one: it depicts Kidson and Dougal on an Eton blue background.

They include itinerant dukes, denizens of all parts of the racing industry and the fine art world, farmers, builders, actors, writers, MPs, and the Convenor of the Standing Council of Scottish Clan Chiefs, *Sir Malcolm McGregor of McGregor. They are scattered through county Lieutenancies and the High Sherriffdom: in 2015, Oxfordshire felt Kidson's influence through the Lord Lieutenant, Tim Stevenson (taught by Michael at Papplewick before going to Canford), as well as the High Sherriff, *Tom Birch-Reynardson, and one of the sitting MPs. Four of his pupils have been ordained. Some have been detained, at Her Majesty's pleasure. Quite a few have been successful entrepreneurs. There is a marked shortage of accountants and a striking number of wine merchants.

Often, they have done well in life. When I interviewed Kidson's colleagues, many of them said, 'Of course, Michael never taught the top divisions with the brightest boys.' But it is apparent that Eton actually put some of the ablest boys into the lower divisions, quite cunning. The grungey and gauche teenagers of yesteryear have morphed into some of the great and the good, as Kidson always knew they would, sometimes the only one, it seemed, who did.

The countryside and parts of the equestrian world have been administered by his protégés. In recent years, the Country Landowners' Association (*George Hervey-Bathurst and Harry Cotterell), the Countryside Alliance (Barney White-Spunner and *Benjy Mancroft), the Masters of Foxhounds Association (*Mancroft again), Vote OK (*George Bowyer), the Grand National (Peter Greenall now 4th Lord Daresbury), the Hurlingham Polo Association (*David Woodd), the Historic Houses Association (*Edward Harley), the Royal Horticultural Society (Sir Nicholas Bacon), and the National Beef Association (*Duff Burrell) have all been led by boys he once taught.

The interest in racing that Kidson nurtured during schooldays has borne fruit. *Nicky Henderson has fully justified Kidson's decision to take him to watch Arkle on St Andrew's Day. He has been champion trainer three times. The late *Alex Scott was another of Kidson's pupils to whom he was very close. He had established himself as one of the leading trainers on the flat before he was murdered at the age of thirty-four. Trainers *Jonathan Pease and *Ed Dunlop were also Kidson pupils; there was the famous occasion of the 2004 Arc when Pease won it with Bago and Dunlop came third with Ouija Board. Former trainer and champion amateur jockey Tim Thomson-Jones and trainer George Baker were also taught by him. *Cornelius Lysaght is a racing journalist and BBC racing correspondent. Charlie Brooks has made his mark on the racing world as a jockey, trainer and journalist.

Sir Matthew Pinsent is one of our greatest Olympians. He repaid Kidson's flexibility by winning four consecutive Olympic gold medals. *Hugh Matheson also rowed for Great Britain, winning a silver medal in the Montreal Olympics..

William Fox-Pitt is another famous Olympian whose encouragement by Kidson has paid off. He has so far collected two silvers and a bronze medal for three-day eventing and in 2014 he was ranked first in the world.

Johnny Barclay, once a golfing opponent of Kidson's, captained Sussex CCC, whilst Matt Fleming was captain of Kent, played for England in eleven One-Day Internationals and is now President of the MCC.

*Benjy Mancroft (now 3rd Lord Mancroft) has been tried by his peers, not as might once have been predicted, for committing a capital offence, but to determine his suitability to sit in the reformed House of Lords. His name was read out fifth in the ballot of hereditary peers and he is a respected working peer, particularly on issues affecting the countryside.

*The Rt Hon Sir Hugo Swire was Minister of State for the Foreign and Commonwealth Office and The Rt Hon Sir Oliver Letwin was Chancellor of the Duchy of Lancaster along with other MPs in the House of Commons who were influenced by Kidson who are Sir Henry Bellingham, formerly Parliamentary Under Secretary of State at the Foreign Office, rackets player Richard Graham, *David Tredinnick, Philip Dunne and Jacob Rees-Mogg. Another of his rackets players, David Faber, was also an MP, but is now Headmaster of Summerfields.

HH Sheikh Mohammed al-Moubarak al-Sabah is Minister of Cabinet Affairs in the Government of Kuwait.

Andrew Gilmour is Assistant Secretary General for Human Rights at the United Nations.

Dr The Hon Gilbert Greenall CBE MD has had a successful career in humanitarian aid with Oxfam, DfID and the United Nations.

Few have taken up Schoolmastering. *Martin Humphreys was a housemaster at Shrewsbury and the Headmaster of King William's College, on the Isle of Man.

Magoo Giles is Principal of Knightsbridge School.

*Henry Hood (now 8th Viscount Hood) is a solicitor and a Lord-in-Waiting to the Queen, in which role he is often deputed to look after visiting Heads of State.

*Dominic West is an accomplished actor, star of *The Wire* and *The Affair* and numerous films.

Justin Welby has learned to spell and is now the Archbishop of Canterbury.

*Father Alexander Sherbrooke runs a Roman Catholic Mission in Soho, London.

*Nat Rothschild is an international financier.

Johnnie Boden has done quite well in the rag trade. His eponymous brand is the preferred choice of 'Boden Mums' everywhere.

Timothy Melgund (7th Earl of Minto) is CEO of the retailer Paperchase.

Rupert Soames has been CEO of Aggreko and is now CEO of Serco.

*Henry Pitman founded Tribal Group plc and co-founded African Century, an investment company based in East Africa.

*Joel Cadbury is founder and CEO of the restaurant group Longshot and formerly owned the Groucho Club. He is also CEO of KidZania.

*Andrew Bell is CEO of international oil-exploration-and-mining company Red Rock Resources.

*Andrew Dalrymple, Bertie Gore-Browne, Richard Cormack, *Hylton Murray-Philipson, *Julian Colville and *Jeremy Harbord are among many Kidsonians at the top of the banking and the financial services industry.

Kidsonians at the Bar are represented by *Alex Hutton QC

and *Eliot Woolf.

*Hugo Guinness is an artist and writer living in New York. His screenplay for the comedy film *The Grand Budapest Hotel* was nominated for an Oscar. *Sir Lachlan Campbell Bt is also an artist and illustrator and author of the definitive history of the Field Game. Oliver Preston is an acclaimed cartoonist with a Kidsonian sense of humour.

*Geoffrey Carew runs a building company in the West Country.

*Mark Wiggin is a partner of Strutt and Parker.

Lieutenant General Sir Barney White-Spunner retired as Commander of the Field Army.

*Major General Sir Edward Smyth-Osbourne is a former SAS officer, who commanded the Household Cavalry Regiment in Afghanistan and was the Major General commanding the Household Division.

*Major General Robert Talbot-Rice commanded the Welsh Guards and is Director Land Equipment in the Ministry of Defence.

Kidson's uncompromising insistence on literary style and grammar has helped a number of writers and journalists: Hugo Dixon on the *Financial Times* Lex column and then online media company Reuters Breakingviews; Rupert Uloth, Deputy Editor of *Country Life*; food writers Tom Parker Bowles and *Masterchef* star William Sitwell, writer and photographer Mark Dixon, and writers *Christopher de Bellaigue and Edmund Marlowe. Minter Dial is a professional speaker, author and film-maker.

*Charlie 'Lupin' Mortimer is also now a successful author in his own right and co-founded The Thimblestitch and Bramble Art Foundation.

Charlie Spencer (9th Earl Spencer) is a best-selling historian and runs a literary festival at Althorp in Northamptonshire.

Henry Wyndham was Chairman of Sotheby's, *Dave Ker is a director at Dickinson. *Adrian Gibbs is Deputy CEO of the Bridgeman Art Library (Bridgeman Images), and *Philip Harley is Director of the Modern British Paintings Department at Christie's. *Edward Gibbs is a director of Sotheby's.

He passed his love of books onto *Ian Marr, who is a leading antiquarian bookseller, and *Nicky Dunne, who runs the Heywood Hill

Bookshop in London.

Simon Mann got into a number of scrapes at Eton with Kidson which helped to prepare him for life as a mercenary and jailbird. His failed coup in Equatorial Guinea was no doubt partly inspired by Kidson's tales of Palmerstonian gunboat diplomacy.

David Cameron overcame the stigma of being an Old Etonian to lead the Conservative Party and was one of the very few Prime Ministers to win a second term with an increased majority. He rescued his party and the British economy and vanquished the other two English parties, before resigning after failing to win a mandate for his solution to the problem of Britain's relations with Europe. His small 'l' liberal, one-nation Tory values seemed remarkably similar to Kidson's own. The education reforms pursued by his government have been so successful that they may yet be the biggest threat to Eton since Edward IV.

The Royal School Wolverhampton has just become a Free School.

In his memory, the British Sporting Art Trust has renamed its annual essay, 'The Michael Kidson Sporting Art Essay.'

Portraits of Michael Kidson now hang at Eton and in the Cat and Custard Pot, Shipton Moyne.

Michael's ashes are scattered on Mull, on the hills where he walked his spaniels.

A Bursary Fund in Kidson's name has been established at Eton to help with fees. Priority will be given to boys whose lives have been disrupted by divorce, or the death of a parent. Part of the proceeds of this book are helping to endow the fund. Donations can be sent to the Michael Kidson Memorial Bursary c/o The Development Office, St Christopher's House, Eton College, Windsor, Berkshire, SL4 6DW.

Appendix

History Matters

History is the essence of innumerable biographies.

Thomas Carlyle

After Kidson died, Dave Ker delivered Michael's collection of 'Gladstoniana' to David Cameron. As he describes, it was one of his more memorable tasks as an executor.

Dave Ker: 'The Prime Minister invited me to Chequers and I took my grandchildren along. David Cameron was very appreciative and made a great effort with the children. He produced one of the treasures of Chequers for the children to see – Oliver Cromwell's life mask. The children were fascinated by the ghoulish mask, but it fell a bit flat for me as, to my horror, it rapidly became apparent that my grandchildren had not an earthly clue who Cromwell was. I was shocked to the core.'

As Kidson would have said, it is 'deplorable' that the History syllabus today is 'a constant disappointment'.

Kidson thought that history really mattered and, of course, it does. It is very hard to decide which way to go if you have not the foggiest notion of where you have been. That is not an original thought, far from it, but it is a timely one. We seem to have hit the age of referenda in this country: Scottish independence, Brexit, and other important issues, such as whether to change the voting system, are now put to the people in plebiscites with increasing regularity. Yet increasingly, one wonders whether the population still has the historical toolkit to make an informed choice.

If you wonder why this matters, consider Kidson's beloved Scotland. Scottish schoolchildren – and especially Scottish students – come away with the Mel Gibson[129] version of Scotland's place in the Union. There is a selective approach to history. The anniversary of the Battle of Bannockburn was given huge prominence by Alex Salmond before the referendum, despite being, as George Galloway pithily reminded us,[130] 'a battle between two Frenchmen, with Scots fighting on both sides' – Kidson would have enjoyed that and written the quote into his commonplace book.

The Highland Clearances are evoked regularly in discussion of public policy, most notably the Land Reform Act.[131] The decline of the mining and manufacturing industries is laid at Mrs Thatcher's door, simply because it happened on her watch, without any regard for the malign influence of nationalisation or the abuse of trade union power beforehand. Scotland is not so much a prisoner of history as kept captive by a partial, and often flawed, version of history.

The nationalist establishment likes to keep it that way. They do not want people to be enlightened about the Enlightenment – a senior civil servant in Edinburgh recently told a friend of mine that the Enlightenment was a Unionist fallacy. It would come as a surprise to the majority of Scottish schoolchildren to be told that the Union came about because a Scottish king inherited the English crown. Or that the Act of Union was at the behest of a Stuart queen. It is convenient to forget that Galloway and Shetland and Orkney have only been part of Scotland since the Middle Ages, and might secede themselves, rather than be ruled by the diktat of the central belt. Any mention of the Darien Scheme would be unhelpful for their prospects and is banned accordingly. It is politically correct to ignore the extraordinary contribution of Scots to the building of the Empire and the astonishing wealth accrued by Scotland in the process.

When the Union seemed lost at one stage in the referendum campaign,

---

129 Gibson starred as William Wallace in the film *Braveheart*.

130 The *Spectator* Debate in Edinburgh.

131 And nationalist historians are busy promoting the notion of Lowland Clearances as well.

David Cameron came out fighting. It is instructive that he instinctively turned to his knowledge of History when he made this speech:

> It would be the end of a country that launched the Enlightenment, that abolished slavery, that drove the industrial revolution, that defeated fascism, the end of a country that people around the world respect and admire, the end of a country that all of us call home.
>
> And we built this home together. It has only become Great Britain because of the greatness of Scotland. Because of the thinkers, writers, artists, leaders, soldiers, inventors who have made this country what it is. It is Alexander Fleming and David Hume; J.K. Rowling and Andy Murray and all the millions of people who have played their part in this extraordinary success story – the Scots who led the charge on pensions and the NHS and on social justice.
>
> We did all this together. For the people of Scotland to walk away now would be like painstakingly building a home – and then walking out the door and throwing away the keys. So I would say to everyone voting on Thursday, please remember. This is not just any old country. This is the United Kingdom. This is our country.

It was a fine speech, at least I thought so, anyway; Kidson might have grudgingly given it a C+, but a C+ with a twinkle in his eye. What was significant was how little traction it had with the voters he needed to sway: people who either did not know what he was talking about, or were determined to cling to their own version of history.

Perhaps this ignorance of history has also started to undermine our sense of Britishness. We bemoan the failure of immigrants to assimilate into our society, but maybe they have failed to buy into the British identity, partly because we have been having an identity crisis ourselves. Many of them have come to Britain as a consequence of our own colonisation of their countries. The British Empire, with all its splendid achievements and grotesque crimes, is what we have in common.

It also explains much of what goes on in the world around us. Why the tele-sales operative rings from Mumbai in English, just as we are sitting down to lunch. Why democracy and the rule of law flourish across large parts of the globe, but also why countries like Iraq are a mess of warring tribes surrounded by arbitrary borders. Why the Archbishop of Canterbury seems to spend much of his time trying to find compromises with African bishops. Our imperial history hovers above the pitch at rugby and cricket internationals. Yet the average schoolchild is probably unaware there ever was a British Empire, let alone that its extent was so enormous that the sun never set on it. It is a guilty secret, never to be mentioned in a classroom, and thus large chunks of our history have simply been deleted. If it is mentioned at all, it is in selective case studies on the Amritsar massacre, or the slave trade, designed to inculcate guilt and self-hatred.

History also gives us a sense of perspective. We are better able to recognise the sinister ambitions of the authoritarian or the mountebank. When we read of some politician's sex scandal, we think of Palmerston on his billiard table and realise that we have seen it all before.

Kidson described himself as a 'Great Man Historian', as many of them were in those days, but even then, they were swimming against the tide. Social history was all the rage.

Darius Guppy encapsulates the two arguments: 'I had always loved history as a boy, but there is no question that Michael made it by far and away my favourite subject. In particular, I think it was his focus on individual heroism and adventurous acts that made his classes so exciting.

'Nowadays, human agency is frowned upon as a defining force in history. It is all about social movements, developments in technology, economic factors and so on, which are seen as the real determinants. Individual actors such as Wellington, or Elizabeth I, or Cromwell, are merely people in the right place at the right time. If they had not been there, someone else would have been, and history would have moved in the same direction. In short, determinism, as opposed to human agency, is now the vogue.

'In this respect, Michael's world view accorded with the Classicism that suffused the Eton I knew as a young boy. It dovetailed perfectly with the view of the ancients – the Greeks, Persians and Romans. There was, therefore, something heroic in the way Michael taught history and his well-known refrain 'They were giants in those days!' accords with this view.'

Kidson realised that young people need heroes. Perhaps he had been helped through his own childhood by the inspiration of people who succeeded against all the odds. He also had a small 'l' liberal and a big 'C' Conservative distrust of the Big State and a clear belief that individuals should have the opportunity to shape their own destinies.

I fear that heroes have been proscribed. The focus now is on how ordinary people lived in past centuries. A fuzzy awareness of the domestic arrangements of Victorian slum-dwellers has replaced the sharp detail of Nelson dying on the orlop deck, or the Charge of the Light Brigade. Ignorance about historical figures is matched by a keen interest in 'celebrities'. Society is less interested in what 'great men' thought and said in the past, than by the ephemeral tweets of today's actresses and pop stars.

Instead of tracing the twists and turns of our island story, children are now served up bite-sized chunks of text, normally about some worthy subject like the Poor Laws, and asked to analyse them. It is hardly the stuff to inspire young people to take an interest in history. Though they were well-taught, neither of my children wanted to read it at university, and who could blame them? Revisiting History as a parent in the noughties and early teens, I was depressed by the modern syllabus, and throughout the whole dismal experience I thought I could hear the sound of my old history beaks banging on their coffin lids.

It is very perplexing, as History is supposed to be one of the Humanities. Studying it is meant to help us to understand the human condition. Kidson helped his pupils to learn what makes people tick. He invited us to consider the strengths and weaknesses of the principal actors in the great dramas of the past. Gladstone, Palmerston and Peel were presented as great statesmen, Disraeli as a mountebank. A boy who discussed Disraeli's principles in an essay prompted Kidson to write in the margin: 'Had he any "principles", I wonder?'

Tom Goff recalls: 'David Cameron has spoken about MGMK and Gladstone. But I think Sir Robert Peel was another great man who inspired Michael. Peel obviously became a bit of a martyr figure after the repeal of the Corn Laws and the split of Conservative Party. This definitely appealed to Michael's romantic side.

'So when he read us "The Death of Sir Robert Peel", Michael wept as he recounted the ten thousand people waiting agog outside Peel's house for any news, after Peel had fallen from his horse in Hyde Park and had suffered awful injuries. Michael could not conceal his emotion, as he pulled his spectacles from his face and told us that the great man had, in fact, died. What mattered to Michael was that Peel was a man of principle, not motivated by high office or money. Doing the right thing was what mattered to Peel and to Kidson.'

Kidson once set an essay entitled 'How Greasy was Disraeli's Pole'. One wonders what the Ofsted inspectors would make of that now. The *double entendre* was no doubt intended, but woe betide anyone who produced a flippant answer, or who failed to produce a reasoned and rigorous analysis of Disraeli's character and his rise to power.

The change in the way history is taught now is all very frustrating, and if you will not believe the incontinent scribblings of a Galloway farmer, then quite a few others are starting to say the same thing. The last Head Master of Eton, Tony Little, recently bemoaned the fact that school children nowadays no longer have knowledge of the 'great sweep' of British history. He said his daughter knew about the Mexican revolution, but not about the Tudors.

Great sweep? Seeing my children go through school,[132] I wondered whether there had been a deliberate conspiracy to ensure that they knew nothing at all of our history. Centralised control of the curriculum has given the politicians and the Guardianistas in the Department for Education and the exam boards the opportunity to squeeze history quietly

132 It may be that things have improved since then, in England anyway, as a result of the Cameron government's reforms, but the ideological struggle will go on.

out of the way. It has always been on the Left's agenda to wipe clean our folk memory, so that they can re-programme us. Tony Blair displayed all the ruthlessness of William the Conqueror, or Henry VII, in ensuring that everything that went before 1997 was viewed as the dark ages and the educational establishment rowed in behind him with glee.

Artfully and disingenuously, they have successfully argued that what is important is not in knowing any history *per se*, it is in developing the skills of a historian. There is a subtle deceit in the emphasis on process. It is easy to argue that learning narrative history for its own sake is less important than developing the skills of textual analysis.

There is less emphasis now on learning facts, dates and quotes, along with fewer exams and more coursework, which strikes me as an open invitation to unscrupulous parents to do the work for their children. It may explain why day schools in more ambitious parts of the country do so much better in league tables. When I went to see Andrew Gailey, who taught me A level History, he ruefully accepted much of my analysis. There is evidently a move towards computerised marking, which needs a templated approach. Apparently a very bright boy, who deserves an A*, can end up with a D because his highly original answer does not fit the template. Eton's response has been to seek out exam boards carefully, so that they can still teach some History, and to move more towards doing pre-U courses rather than A levels.

Most insidiously, social history provides an excuse to insert 'social-ist' history. Undue emphasis on various 'movements' – Labour, trades unions, suffragettes, civil rights and so on – important though these are, creates the impression that the whole exercise could be retitled: 'How we arrived at the smug *Guardian*/BBC consensus that underpins the doctrine that all right-thinking people subscribe to now.'

Kidson's great hero Gladstone believed in leaving money to 'fructify in the pockets of the people,'[133] and he actually tried to abolish income tax. In

133 Though the phrase, often attributed to him, is not actually his.

an era when there is a consensus between all the political parties that fifty per cent of all income above a certain level should be expropriated by the state, in defiance of Adam Smith's unseen hand and Arthur Laffer's curve, it would appear that the apparatchiks of the educational establishment think that the less known about him, the better.

Hitler is studied assiduously, because he was a right-wing monster – those other, and more prolific, mass murderers of the twentieth century, Stalin and Mao Tse Tung, are allowed to hide in the shadows. One could argue that the biggest lesson from the last century is that socialism, whether of Hitler's variety or of Harold Wilson's, harms the very people it is supposed to help, and the more extreme the socialism, the more brutal the suffering. You might disagree – it is still a free country – but is any schoolchild or student ever given the opportunity to examine this hypothesis? It is said that the millennials are more likely to be seduced by the false hopes offered by socialism than baby boomers or generation X. It is not hard to see why.

Today, I am told, teachers are encouraged to be 'facilitators rather than pedagogues' and they are supposed to have a reflective style, whatever that means. Kidson was firmly in the pedagogue camp and would sometimes deliver lectures more in the style of a university course than boys of sixteen were accustomed to hear. The notes for the two lectures below were found in his effects and they would have been delivered to boys in the bottom division at the start of their history module on the Victorian Age, among them a young David Cameron. Whilst he brings the 'Great Men' to life, he is careful to explain the social history at the same time, and beneath the bluster there is balance.

By now you know him well enough to imagine the well-rehearsed, but seemingly spontaneous stagecraft. You can see him in your mind's eye, as he occasionally plays with his spectacles, or stares out of the window for theatrical effect, while he recalls some important point. You know that if you allow your eyelids to droop, there will be a half-croquet ball winging its way towards you. You will be alert to the seismic indications of an impending sneeze. You know that he is the most liberal of men beneath the conservative façade and so you do not take seriously his political incorrectness.

So, I will not attempt to dramatise these two lectures and I will leave it for you to read them. They have been edited for this book, for they were much longer, but hopefully you will come away knowing a bit more about the Monarchy and the Victorians:

> The Crown today remains, of course, a vital part of the constitution. I say vital, because there is life and meaning still in the Queen's example and leadership. But the Monarchy is most relevant in terms of precept and example, and not constitutional activity. We respect it for its history and tradition, its happy family example, and that feeling of stability and continuity. That is probably a simplistic explanation of the Crown today – but it is broadly near the mark.
>
> Let us turn back the clock to the nineteenth century. George III's long twilight period started from about 1804, during his third illness, and about the time that Pitt returned to office. His eyesight began to fail, though until his final illness in 1811 his brain remained clear. He was probably never mad in any real sense – that is, not mentally ill – and medical option today hazards the view that his illness was a classic case of porphyria, a disease unknown until the twentieth century. Talk of madness was understandable, when we consider the brutal medical treatment he was subjected to.
>
> On 25th October 1810, he had ruled for fifty years, and his popularity reached a zenith with the celebrations for the event. But his last illness was upon him and he sunk slowly into oblivion. On 5th February 1811, the Prince of Wales (with irksome limitations to his power for a period of one year) was proclaimed Regent, and so the last decade of the reign is his story. The old king passed out of history, and spent the last years of his life here at Windsor; he was still able to find some solace in music, especially in Handel,

and he chose for the anthems in his chapel all the passages from that composer connected with blindness and madness. He died in January 1820.

George III was the only one of the first four Georges to achieve more than transient popularity. At least he was a God-fearing, humble, decent, honest man, who like most of us, led a dull domestic life. His profound sense of duty kept him hard at work. He married Charlotte of Mecklenburg-Strelitz, a formidably dim and ugly creature. Plain and undesirable as she was, the King doggedly and pertinaciously fulfilled his marital duties and remained loyal to her: his brood of fifteen legitimate children was a record for an English king.

His influence and importance in the twenty years after his accession – punctuated by the loss of the American colonies – are obviously nothing to do with us today. I would only say that posterity owes quite a lot to George III: he founded the Royal Academy (it is true that not all artists today are grateful); his splendid library is now the King's Library in the British Museum; and in the realms of science, his patronage of William Herschel enabled the great astronomer to build his telescopes and produce his important observations of the universe.

His successor on the throne, George Augustus Frederick was, at fifty-seven, the oldest monarch until that time to have ascended the throne. He and his brothers were a pretty grim lot, and probably few monarchies have struggled under the weight of such vulgarity and indulgence.

There was the Duke of York, with his mistress Mary Clarke, who dealt in commissions like a broker, and was publicly exposed so that his military career was ruined. He spent the rest of his life pursuing the elderly Duchess of Rutland, building palaces he couldn't afford and never lived in. The Duke of Clarence was simply absurd, with no sense of propriety or position. Having retired from the Navy, he lived at Bushey Park with his actress,

Mrs Jordan, who produced ten Fitzclarences to swell her family of illegitimate children. Like all the princes, Clarence was utterly broke and hopelessly in debt.

The Duke of Kent was a frightful martinet, who caused a mutiny in Gibraltar through the severity of his discipline – he simply loved savage punishments. His sexual life was insatiably licentious: after spending twenty-seven years in the arms of a French–Canadian mistress, he married a Princess of Leiningen and sired Princess Victoria. The Dukes of Cambridge and Sussex were innocuous: Sussex went in for daft marriages, Cambridge lived mostly in Hanover and was eccentric and not very nice. He was actually the only prince who lived within his means – but that was only because he *was* mean.

The Duke of Cumberland was the most unsavoury member of the family, and even his brothers spoke of him with horror. Indeed, there are only several of us here today old enough to comprehend his wickedness – and it's certainly not my business today to run the risk of denting your virgin innocence – but among his less heinous activities was the reputation of a child begotten by his sister and the bloody murder of his own valet.

A right crew. It would, I think, be true to say that the Royal Family was held in almost universal contempt from 1812 to 1837.

George IV resembled his father in his prejudices and obstinacy. His hatred of Canning in the early years of the reign stemmed from his natural loathing of Canning's liberal principles, as well as for his support of Queen Caroline. George had been persuaded to marry Caroline, Princess of Brunswick, in 1795, mainly to get his debts paid off and to increase his income, as well as to produce a legitimate heir.

The mistake was in the choice, for Caroline was simply awful – coarse, flamboyant, dirty and highly sexed. To climb into bed with Caroline was almost worse than going to the gallows. Caroline hardly ever washed or changed her linen, and smelt powerfully.

Naturally the Prince was appalled: he who was supposed to be the conscious advocate of good taste and refinement. He was overcome on meeting her, turning to Malmesbury, saying, 'I am not well, get me a glass of brandy.'

On 8 April 1795, he went through the marriage ceremony, drugged with drink and looking like a corpse. He probably slept with her just that one night, a dreadful penance – it was perhaps the one really brave thing he ever did – and after a few weeks of mutual recrimination they parted forever, the Prince to fresh sexual adventures, mostly with ageing women, the Princess also to other Ugandan activity. In 1814 she drifted abroad, much to the Regent's relief. She lived among the Gondolieri in Venice in doltish and vulgar ostentation.

Then, quite suddenly, George III died; the Princess was now technically Queen, and, supported by various troublemakers in England, led by Brougham, she returned to claim her heritage. No one had been more rapturously received since Charles II landed at Dover in 1660. She entered London in riotous triumph. Each day she drove in state to the House of Lords cheered to the echo. The new King, hiding at Windsor, was prostrated.

Anyway, I must pass over this sad and sordid affair: very soon the fickle public deserted Caroline: by the summer of 1821, George IV judged that excitement had died down sufficiently for him to stage his Coronation, which was a very grand affair. The half-crazed Queen Caroline died in the summer of 1821, shortly after Napoleon on Saint Helena. On his death on 21st May, the Lord Chamberlain rushed into the Palace and cried dramatically, 'Sire, your greatest enemy is dead!'

'Is she, by God!' said the King.

George IV was, of course, intransigently opposed to the parliamentary reform which now approached. He was lucky in that a large and influential section of his subjects agreed with him about all questions of reform – still, the example of his father should have taught him that monarchs must not support a dying cause. The fact remains that after the death of George IV, steadily but inexorably, the powers of the monarchy declined.

And a final word on George IV, as Prince of Wales his debts were monumental: all his life he was profligate and extravagant – English kings in the eighteenth century, compared to their continental brothers, lived in modest, old-fashioned buildings, poorly furnished and containing few good pictures. To a man like George IV with such a taste for splendour, this was awful, and he decided to compensate for his ancestors' meanness and philistinism. The result was Carlton House, the Pavilion at Brighton, the Royal Lodge here at Windsor, the virtual rebuilding of Buckingham Palace, and finally the restoration of Windsor Castle on the grandest scale. To these monuments, you can add some beautiful additions to London: Regent's Park, the Nash Terraces, the now-despoiled Regent Street, Carlton House Terrace.

And building wasn't all: he was an excellent judge of art, making a superb collection of seventeen-century Dutch paintings, and he was mainly instrumental in the Government purchasing for three hundred thousand pounds the 'Angerstein Collection', which became the nucleus of the National Gallery. It needn't worry us today that his motives were principally ostentatious vanity and self-esteem.

George IV was succeeded by Prince William Henry, the third son of George III and formally Duke of Clarence. Sometimes known as 'The Sailor King', he had actually been present at the Battle of Cape St Vincent: probably he was a competent officer up to the rank of Captain – though a very stern, if not brutal, disciplinarian – but the Admiralty felt that was about his naval ceiling. Thereafter, he and his mistress, Mrs Jordan, lived in happy domesticity at Roehampton and Bushey, breeding like rabbits, producing five boys and five girls.

Eventually he jettisoned her, and, after many humiliating

rebuffs, married Princess Adelaide of Saxe-Meiningen in 1818. She was a typical, buxom German female, without a sense of humour, but virtuous and sensible – and she guided William into more sensible courses than he had managed so far.

George III's second son, York, had died in 1827, and William was in his sixty-fifth year when he became King in June 1830. He was very different from his predecessor: he hated extravagance and flamboyance. He even didn't want a Coronation, but was overruled; but it cost a mere £30,000, against the £200,000 of George IV's.

Although by instinct a strong Conservative, William was prepared to make an attempt to adapt. He was certainly not a clever man, but he had lots of dry common sense. In the end, he realised that no government could withstand for long the emotive urge for reform; above all, he was in nearly everything prepared to allow his ministers to make the ultimate decisions. He accepted Lord Grey with a good deal of apprehension in 1830; he wasn't anxious to have the constitution meddled with in any major way.

When Melbourne succeeded Grey as PM in the summer of 1834, there were difficulties with the King, who was no longer very happy with the Whigs – if he ever had been. The Government lasted just four months before the King dismissed them – of great interest, for it was the very last time a British monarch exercised this prerogative.

So much for William IV. He died in June 1837 – he was certainly not a good King, nor a very bad one. He had succeeded to a distinctly wobbly throne; he had steadied it a little, and left his successor with a chance of success. But still, when Princess Victoria came to the throne – she was just twenty-one – the throne was an object now largely devoid of romance and dignity. And when she handed it on in the next century, more than sixty years later, it was an extraordinarily valuable commodity.

From 1837 to 1841, the new Queen was largely under Lord

Melbourne's influence, then for the next twenty years under the Prince Consort's – her husband Prince Albert of Saxe-Coburg-Gotha, whom she married early in 1840. He was in many ways an impressive man, though a German: Disraeli, particularly, thought very highly of him. After his death, she acted as a constitutional monarch off her own bat, becoming steadily more matriarchal and independent.

What sort of woman was Queen Victoria? I should think that, like our own Queen today, she was full of ordinary common sense and intelligence, without in any way being remotely highbrow or intellectual. She was no Queen Elizabeth I, who could speak six languages fluently. Her favourite author was Scott, not much read these days, and she enjoyed Jane Austen, which is a feather in her cap. She didn't care for poetry, even the straightforward heroic stuff of Tennyson, and she never read modern authors. She liked Mendelssohn among composers – hardly of the first rank – the theatre had to be pretty straight theatre, and she had little appreciation of art. A woman of great honesty, as she saw things, perhaps not always far removed from a pretty steady prejudice.

The Queen's relationship with her ministers was a very real one. After initial distrust, she came to have great affection for Disraeli, for instance, who laid oriental flattery on with a trowel, which the Queen loved.

Conversely, the relationship between her and Gladstone was very sad. She didn't like his pacifism or his high Anglicanism. And the Queen only saw politics in one dimension: she was too isolated to be anywhere near the hurly-burly and infighting of the political scene – as Gladstone said, 'Lofty isolation kept her apart from the all essential dynamism of politics.'

In general policy, Queen Victoria was always ready to take sides and to offer her advice, but her direct influence was nugatory. In foreign affairs, she had, of course, a very wide dynastic interest. The German Emperor Wilhelm II was the Queen's grandson;

the Tsar, Nicholas II had married her granddaughter, a princess of Hesse; four of her other grandchildren became Queens – of Greece, Romania, Norway and Spain. And so, inevitably, European affairs were truly the Queen's affairs – here again, she was always ready with warnings and advice.

And so, whatever her shortcomings, her influence, her prejudice: she presided over this country and its great Empire through more than sixty of the greatest years in its history. Monarchs, of course, are always more than life-size, however ordinary as people. Queen Victoria was an ordinary enough woman; but I think she was a great Queen, wonderfully at home with her people in the Victorian age.

And now for the Victorians …

A year or two ago (and actually I did it again the other day), driving back from Scotland, I decided to visit a property in Northumberland, then fairly recently bequeathed to the National Trust, called Cragside, an extraordinary Victorian house hewn literally out of rock and cliff by the first Lord Armstrong, begun in the 1860s.

Lord Armstrong was of that present-day beleaguered and endangered species, marked out for early extinction by our more radical socialists in this age – a man of vision, industry, initiative, genius, a man determined to make enormous money, to build a successful industrial empire – in fine, to use his talents to get on in life – for whatever the Victorian age was, it was not a world of disincentive. If you were brave enough, ruthless enough, bold enough, determined enough, greedy enough, willing enough to work your pants off – then there was no ceiling to your endeavours.

Armstrong was at once tycoon, philanthropist, gunmaker, versatile inventor. He became the British equivalent of Krupp, producing and manufacturing arms for sale to anyone in the world who would buy them. And Cragside, begun as a comparatively small house in the 1860s, is the Victorian monument to his extraordinary success.

It was the first house in the world to be lit by electricity derived from water power. Other examples of his ingenuity in the fields of hydraulics and engineering are scattered about the house and grounds, which are particularly beautiful: he made thirty-one miles of carriage drive and planted seven million – yes, seven million – trees. *That* was the sort of thing you could do if you were successful in the Victorian age.

As we walked round, I heard a buxom Northumbrian biddy say to her estimable and bucolic consort: 'I wish I'd lived in them days.' Presumably she envisaged herself as part of Lord Armstrong's personal entourage – or, at worst, a happy member of his Cragside ménage – in which case, yes, she probably would have been a reasonably happy creature – for happiness in the Victorian age was certainly not confined to those who lived above stairs. And at *that* level, too, the historian G.M. Young also was in no doubt that around 1850 was the time when *he* would have wished to come into the world.

Today, in various ways, we are industriously reassessing the Victorian age – but we shall never manage to get it very accurately, in spite of endless eloquent archives and evidence of one sort or another. Its very span and variety defy the kind of absurd generalisations that we so often hear. To some extent, I've always felt at one with the ancient, short-sighted Lord Portarlington, who once said to an astonished Queen Victoria, 'I know your face quite well, but dammit, I can't put a name to it.'

The Industrial Revolution meant far more to England than the mere creation of new industries, new wealth, new towns, new mines and the expansion of London and other cities into the surrounding country. Together with its ancillary developments – canals, roads, railways – it profoundly affected the economic and social life of the countryside, and, indeed, the country generally. And in doing so, it divided England into two strongly contrasted social systems – the one aristocratic and rural, the other democratic and urban. The breach it created between town and country has never really been closed and I think has bedevilled domestic politics ever since.

That's another story – I'm not a political creature – but what a world of difference there still is between the independent, rough-hewn country yokel – and there's nothing snobbish about that: it means any of us who are endemically countrymen, whether lairds or gamekeepers – and his urban counterpart, living perforce compartmentalised cheek by jowl and forced to abdicate his individuality, so far as he's got it, to trade unions and other cartels, and to ambitious and ruthless local politicians.

The Industrial Revolution had given men a new conception of power, but had shown what can happen when power gets into the wrong hands. The world was alarmed: the labour troubles of our own day are to some extent the price we've had to pay for failure then to consider adequately the just claims of working people – or at any rate, to advance those aims quickly enough or effectively enough. But, again, to emphasise the contradictions in the Victorian age, don't interpret the fate of the working man only in terms of what someone like Cobbett had to say, or Dickens, among novelists.

One of the great strengths of this country – at least until this century – and still essentially perhaps, I'm not sure – has been the extraordinary flexibility of much of our social system. The rich and the poor lived very differently, but they were never as far apart as, for instance, in France. The upper classes in our country in the nineteenth century were sensible enough to notice some of the signs and the dangers – or some of them were – to adapt, to accept trespass in their territory, and, as the century went on, to be prepared to shed some power, an evolution made tolerable by their immense prestige and wealth.

When Taine, the distinguished French historian and philosopher, visited England in the 1860s, he was greatly impressed by the way the upper classes had changed: 'They realised that they must set their house in order.' He found no hostility between the upper and middle classes. Robert Owen, that pioneer among industrialists, had told Taine that it is 'not our aim to overthrow the aristocracy: we are ready to leave the government and high offices in their hands. An aristocracy was trained to rule and lead – they had a quality of dash and style. But we do absolutely insist,' he said, 'that all positions of power be filled by able men. No mediocrities and no nepotism. Let them govern, but let them be fit to govern.'

That was the view expressed by a rich and successful industrialist, who had a real care for, and interest in, his own workforce – in fact, far ahead of his time. And so we need not be surprised that the Whig cabinet of thirteen that presided over the 1832 Reform Bill contained eleven peers – or that as late as Lord Salisbury's second cabinet of 1886, eleven of fourteen were titled.

Equally we mustn't think it very odd that parliament contained no working men until very late in the century; or, for instance, that Jews were not admitted until 1858. After all, when we moralise about the shortcomings of the nineteenth century, there are anomalies in our own time that need rectifying - for example, that in spite of our large ethnic minorities, there are as yet no coloured MPs. And that seems to me just as odd.

So far you may think that I am rather gilding the lily. What, in fact, I am intent on doing is encouraging you to look at the age as dispassionately and objectively as possible: of course, there was often very rough justice, cruelty, inhumanity, tremendous inequality – there still is. Every century is one of contradictions; the nineteenth, I believe, more than any.

Among industrialists, your Owens and Armstrongs were the exceptions, not the rule. Here, in contrast, is Lord Radnor epitomising his ruthless ideology in a statement to his labourers, in which he explained why he would not increase their pay. He said: 'If you cannot live upon the wages I and my tenants give you, it is sign that you are not wanted here. Go to Lancashire, where wages are higher, and where, consequently, it appears you are wanted.'

This is the obverse side of the industrial coin, and such brutal attitudes only occasionally survived the legislation and humanity of later Victorian England. As time went on, and though social privilege diminished only slowly, more enlightened society recognised in Robert Hawker's lines:

Our poor have hands, feet and eyes,
Flesh and a feeling mind;
They breathe the breath of mortal sighs,
They are of human kind.
They weep such tears as others shed,
And now and then they smile.

Broadly speaking, then, the government of the country throughout the first half of the nineteenth century remained essentially in the hands of the aristocracy and the landed gentry, though middle-class and monied men like Peel and Gladstone were a novel development. As a class, they remained pretty firmly entrenched behind historic and ancient privilege: this is NOT something that came to an end after the 1832 Reform Bill.

But in this country, perhaps, more than in most countries, every class seeks unremittingly to gain acceptance into the one above: and the new rich of Queen Victoria's reign bought land, got themselves into parliament, sent their sons to public schools and the older universities, bought themselves commissions in the better regiments. And so, in these years, the base of class was enormously broadened.

It follows that changes in education were a central feature of this century. New schools, better teachers, more careful control were as vital as new railways, or new machine tools. But here again, progress was very slow: not until 1856 was a department of education set up, a new office created under the crown – effectively a minister of education, though not actually in name. By 1860, the Newcastle Commission had established that, among the poor, only about one in twenty received any sort of education after the age of thirteen. The Reform Bill of 1867 underlined the importance of better education for the masses. The result was Forster's celebrated act of 1870 – a great, though modest milestone, as it was limited to children under thirteen. Secondary education was still limited to the middle and upper classes.

However, slow as progress had been since the first modest parliamentary grant soon after the Reform Act – by the end of the century, the country was in sight of universal education. And so, wherever you look, English society in the Victorian Age was far from static, as, broadly speaking, it had remained in the previous century.

You wouldn't believe it from listening to trite generalisations still ubiquitous – but the arts signally flourished throughout the Victorian Age: Dickens, Thackeray, Tennyson, the Brontes and many more were producing timeless literature. Painters like Constable, Turner and Cox[134] – to say nothing of later developments – were enriching British art. Most of the credit for the patronage which made this rich output possible belongs to the upper classes again, but so does the blame for much of the architectural vandalism of the time.

The pulling down of countless country houses – for reasons very different from the similar, sad vandalism of our own day – and their replacement with more pretentious houses, to which the

134 David Cox, a leading member of the Birmingham School of landscape artists (1783–1859).

Gothic revival gave so much encouragement, was as chargeable against the county landowners as against the vulgar plutocrats who had invaded their preserves. The elegance of the Regency was soon lost to the English countryside.

However, I have always believed that the word Victorian has unfairly assumed a pejorative sense in so many ways, and especially in the visual arts. In general, each age dislikes and derides the art of its predecessors up to about a century preceding. In contemplating the Victorian Age, we shall never do justice to its enormous invention and variety. If we assume the premise, presented as an axiom, that its art was *bad*, you might just as well claim that all art of the Italian Renaissance was *good*.

And now a word or two about the place of *women* in the Victorian world. It is a truism as well as a truth that Victorian women were expected, on the whole, to do as they were told. In that sense, I suppose I'm a Victorian ... because I certainly expect women to do as they are told ... and they usually do.

But whenever I talk about this period, it strikes me as extraordinary that we hardly ever talk about women – unless we are speaking of someone – for different reasons – above life-size, like Queen Victoria, or Elizabeth Fry, or Florence Nightingale, or Harriet Martineau. It amuses me that four of the principals in our period – Palmerston, Peel, Disraeli, Gladstone – all made extraordinarily happy marriages, without which they could certainly never have been the same political creatures or personalities – but their wives are lost in the limbo.

Disraeli, predictably, made the most incongruous marriage to the widow of a dim, back-bench Tory MP, Mary-Anne Wyndham-Lewis, eleven years older than he was. Her social gaffes were famous and ignored with iron resolution by her husband. But as she lay dying, she said, 'I knew, Dizzy, that you married me for money' – as he assuredly did – 'but, if you had to marry me again, it would be for love.' And that was true. And Gladstone, the only one to enjoy a golden wedding anniversary (fifty years), like Pam was hugely oversexed and could never have survived as he did without the solid comfort and support of a virtuous woman. And so, Victorian women should not be allowed to go totally unsung.

If I've a final hope, it is that you won't want to think of the Victorian Age as heavy and humourless and reactionary. Someone said of Louis Napoleon's – Napoleon III's – Second Empire, 'It is like a Vaudeville entertainment: there's something for everybody' – and that certainly is true of the Victorian Age. There surely isn't one of you who won't find something there of interest.

Eton Glossary

Absence – *roll-call.*

Beak – *Eton slang for a Master. If you were taught by a beak, you said you were 'up to him'.*

Bill – *if a boy misbehaves, he may be placed 'On the Bill', which means that the Head Master or the Lower Master will see him and punish him appropriately.*

Block – *Eton is split into year groups from A (the now defunct Oxbridge half) to F (for new boys).*

Capping – *a form of salute. Boys are expected to show their respect for beaks by raising the index finger level with their brow, as if touching the brim of a top hat. The practice continued after top hats ceased to be worn after the Second World War.*

Chambers – *what other schools call break. All of the beaks gather in School Hall for coffee mid-morning and the best time to catch them is on the steps outside.*

Chronicle – *the Eton newspaper, edited by two boys who often go on to edit national newspapers in later life.*

College – *a boys' house in the old part of the school entirely populated by King's Scholars, known as 'tugs' on account of the 'togas', or academic gowns, they wore over their tails to distinguish them.*

Construe – *a form of homework designed to keep boys occupied in the evenings. We would be given chunks of Latin or Greek to translate and then hope that we were not the ones chosen in class next morning to give our versions. It was one of the building blocks of the 'classical education', but I regarded it in the same light as the hours I later spent polishing things during my recruit training in the Army.*

Corps – *abbreviation for Officer Training Corps by which the Combined Cadet Force (CCF) is known at Eton.*

Dames – *each house had a matron known as the dame. My first dame was the wonderful Miss Mary Veitch from Peebles. She had two stock remedies in large glass demijohns – camphor* *cold for internal ailments and surgical spirit for external ones – designed to ensure instant recovery. One sometimes felt that the two had been muddled up. In extremis, she would administer a Disprin gargle and during flu epidemics the corridor would echo with imitations of 'garr-gul' in her rich borders accent.*

Division, abbrev. Div – *Eton follows rigorously the practices of setting and streaming so derided by the educational establishment (one never quite knows why). One always knew where one was in the pecking order in any given subject by which div one was in, from F1 to F12. Lessons are by extension also known as divs and classrooms as division rooms.*

Dry Bob – *a boy who plays cricket in the summer half.*

Early School – *the first div used to start at 0730 hours, before breakfast. Andrew Gailey remembers me arriving for one of his History divs and going straight back to sleep again. Now abolished.*

Extra Work, abbrev. EW – *prep work set by a division master to be done out of school.*

Fags, fagging – *the practice where small boys do chores for senior boys within their houses. Prefects would shout 'Boy-Up' and the last one to get there had to run the errand. It gradually waned during Kidson's time and died out altogether by about 1980.*

Field Game – *the Eton Field Game. A mixture of soccer and rugger played only in the Lent half between teams from the different boys' houses and against Old Etonians.*

Fourth of June – *a school holiday to celebrate the birthday of King George III, who took a great interest in Eton College. It is the day when most parents and families come to visit their boys at Eton.*

Half – *terms are known as halves because there were originally only two of them in a year.*

Houses, Housemaster, House Captain – *large, often classically proportioned buildings containing the housemaster and his family (confusingly known as My Tutor and Mrs M'Tutor) in one half and about fifty boys, each with their own room, in the other. The senior boy in the house was the House Captain. He was still allowed to enforce discipline by beating when Kidson arrived at Eton, but these powers were gradually watered down.*

Keeper – *the boy officer in charge of*

an activity: Keeper of Rackets, Keeper of Squash, etc.

Leaver (abbrev. for leaving photograph) – *before leaving the school we had photographs taken of ourselves to give to our friends, including those we liked on the staff. The photographers were often budding entrepreneurs in lower years, mine were taken by Nick Wheeler, later to be a mail-order tycoon.*

Lock up – *boys' houses are locked at a given time in the evening to enforce control.*

Lower Master – *the bottom two years are treated as a separate entity and come under the Lower Master or 'Lower Man'.*

Pop – *slang for the Eton Society, Eton's prefects who wore stick-up collars, fancy waistcoats and sponge-bag trousers to denote them. They were a self-electing oligarchy until they had their wings clipped by the Head Master in the mid-1980s, when the cleaners in the Pop Room complained to the authorities that the ashtrays were insufficiently large to take all the cigarette butts. Their draconian powers were gradually diminished, although they were still allowed to fine boys for minor offences such as eating in the street.*

Praeposter – *an emissary sent by the Head Master or Lower Master to summon offenders. They were taken from 'Sixth Form Select', the academic elite of the School, and had silver buttons on their waistcoats to identify them.*

Private Business – *a generally pleasant evening session spent having one's education broadened by one's Classical or Modern Tutor.*

Provost – *similar to the chairman of the board of governors in other schools or Master of an Oxbridge College. He lives at Eton and is assisted by a Vice Provost. The saying goes that no one knows what the Provost does and the Vice Provost helps him.*

Pupil – *boys who had a beak as their tutor were said to be his pupils.*

Rip – *a poor piece of work was part ripped in two or 'torn over' by the beak and you then had to get your housemaster and tutor to sign it.*

St Andrew's Day – *30 November. Founder's Day, to commemorate King Henry VI, who founded Eton College in 1440.*

School Dress – *early-nineteenth-century garb said to have originally been worn in mourning for George III, it consists of white shirt and stiff collar, black tailcoat and waistcoat and striped trousers.*

Stick-ups – *winged collars worn with white bow ties by house captains or boys who had earned some other distinction, and by beaks.*

Tap – *the school pub in the High Street. Boys of sixteen or more in the top two years were officially allowed to buy two pints of beer each day.*

Trials – *exams at the end of the Michaelmas and Lent halves. The results were read out publicly, so that everyone knew how their peers had done. Failing trials more than once risked expulsion.*

Tutor – *often used for housemaster, but I have not done so in the book to avoid confusion. One has two tutors at Eton to assist one's academic progress, in the bottom three years he is called a Classical Tutor and is chosen by the school, thereafter one is allowed to choose a 'Modern Tutor'.*

Up to – *being taught by a beak.*

Wall Game – *traditional Eton game played against a wall on the Eton–Slough road.*

Wet Bob – *a boy who rows in the summer half.*

Index

Personal names are entered as they appear in the text.